LEARNING TO TEACH PSYCHOLOGY IN THE SECONDARY SCHOOL

Learning to Teach Psychology in the Secondary School offers a comprehensive and accessible introduction to the teaching and learning of psychology. Written for trainee teachers and those new to teaching psychology, it will help you to develop your subject knowledge and gain a deeper understanding of the purpose and potential of psychology within the secondary curriculum as well as support the practical skills needed to plan, teach and evaluate stimulating and creative lessons.

Drawing on theory and the latest research, the text demonstrates how key pedagogical issues link to classroom practice and encourages you to reflect on your own learning and practice to maximise student learning. Written by experts in the field and featuring useful resources, summaries of key points and a range of tasks enabling you to put learning into practice in the classroom, the chapters cover:

- Using psychology to teach psychology
- Teaching specific areas of psychology
- Ethics in psychology teaching
- Teaching research methods
- Teaching the skills of evaluation, analysis and application in psychology
- Assessment and feedback
- Inclusion
- Using technology
- Career progression and professional development

This exciting new addition to the market leading *Learning to Teach in the Secondary School* series is essential reading for all those who aspire to become an inspirational and engaging psychology teacher.

Deborah Gajic has over 25 years of experience in teaching Psychology and was a former Head of Psychology at an outstanding school in the Midlands. She is a Chartered Psychologist (CPsychol) and an Associate Fellow of the British Psychological Society (AFBPsS). She now works as an independent educational consultant.

Jock McGinty is Head of Psychology at Watford Grammar School for Boys. He has taught Psychology for over 20 years and is a senior A-level examiner and CPD presenter. He is a Chartered Psychologist (CPsychol) and a past Chair of the Association for the Teaching of Psychology. He is currently Vice-President of the European Federation of Psychology Teachers' Associations.

LEARNING TO TEACH SUBJECTS IN THE SECONDARY SCHOOL SERIES

Series Editors: Susan Capel and Marilyn Leask

Designed for all students learning to teach in secondary schools, including those on school-based initial teacher education programmes, the books in this series complement *Learning to Teach in the Secondary School* and its companion, *Starting to Teach in the Secondary School*. Each book in the series applies underpinning theory and evidence to address practical issues to support student teachers in school and in higher education institutions in learning how to teach a particular subject.

Learning to Teach Art and Design in the Secondary School, 3rd Edition
Edited by Nicholas Addison and Lesley Burgess

Learning to Teach Business in the Secondary School: A Companion to School Experience
Edited by Limara Pascall

Learning to Teach Citizenship in the Secondary School, 3rd Edition
Edited by Liam Gearon

Learning to Teach Design and Technology in the Secondary School, 4th Edition
Edited by Alison Hardy

Learning to Teach English in the Secondary School, 5th Edition
Edited by Jon Davison and Caroline Daly

Learning to Teach Foreign Languages in the Secondary School, 4th Edition
Norbert Pachler, Michael Evans, Ana Redondo and Linda Fisher

Learning to Teach Geography in the Secondary School, 4th Edition
Mary Biddulph, David Lambert & David Balderstone

Learning to Teach History in the Secondary School, 4th Edition
Edited by Terry Haydn, Alison Stephen, James Arthur and Martin Hunt

Learning to Teach ICT in the Secondary School, 3rd Edition
Edited by Marilyn Leask and Norbert Pachler

Learning to Teach Mathematics in the Secondary School, 4th Edition
Edited by Sue Johnston-Wilder, David Pimm and Clare Lee

Learning to Teach Music in the Secondary School, 3rd Edition
Edited by Carolyn Cooke, Keith Evans, Chris Philpott and Gary Spruce

Learning to Teach Physical Education in the Secondary School, 5th Edition
Edited by Susan Capel, Joanne Cliffe and Julia Lawrence

Learning to Teach Psychology in the Secondary School,
Edited by Deborah Gajic and Jock McGinty

Learning to Teach Religious Education in the Secondary School, 3rd Edition
Edited by L. Philip Barnes

Learning to Teach Science in the Secondary School, 4th Edition
Edited by Rob Toplis

Learning to Teach in the Secondary School, 9th Edition
Edited by Susan Capel, Marilyn Leask and Sarah Younie

Surviving and Thriving in the Secondary School: The NQT's Essential Companion
Edited by Susan Capel, Marilyn Leask and Sarah Younie with Elizabeth Hidson and Julia Lawrence

LEARNING TO TEACH PSYCHOLOGY IN THE SECONDARY SCHOOL

A Companion to School Experience

Edited by
Deborah Gajic and
Jock McGinty

LONDON AND NEW YORK

Cover image: © Dani Pasteau

First published 2023
by Routledge
4 Park Square, Milton Park, Abingdon, Oxon, OX14 4RN

and by Routledge
605 Third Avenue, New York, NY 10158

Routledge is an imprint of the Taylor & Francis Group, an informa business

© 2023 selection and editorial matter, Deborah Gajic and Jock McGinty; individual chapters, the contributors

The right of Deborah Gajic and Jock McGinty to be identified as the authors of the editorial material, and of the authors for their individual chapters, has been asserted in accordance with sections 77 and 78 of the Copyright, Designs and Patents Act 1988.

All rights reserved. No part of this book may be reprinted or reproduced or utilised in any form or by any electronic, mechanical, or other means, now known or hereafter invented, including photocopying and recording, or in any information storage or retrieval system, without permission in writing from the publishers.

Trademark notice: Product or corporate names may be trademarks or registered trademarks, and are used only for identification and explanation without intent to infringe.

British Library Cataloguing-in-Publication Data
A catalogue record for this book is available from the British Library

Library of Congress Cataloging-in-Publication Data
Names: Gajic, Deborah, 1963– editor. | McGinty, Jock, editor.
Title: Learning to teach psychology in the secondary school: a companion to school experience / edited by Deborah Gajic and Jock McGinty.
Description: First edition. | Abingdon, Oxon; New York, NY: Routledge, 2023. | Series: Learning to teach subjects in the secondary school | Includes bibliographical references and index.
Identifiers: LCCN 2022019536 (print) | LCCN 2022019537 (ebook) | ISBN 9780367753658 (paperback) | ISBN 9780367753672 (hardback) | ISBN 9781003162223 (ebook)
Subjects: LCSH: Psychology—Study and teaching (Secondary)—Great Britain. | Psychology teachers—Great Britain.
Classification: LCC BF80.7.G7 L43 2023 (print) | LCC BF80.7.G7 (ebook) | DDC 150.71/141—dc23/eng/20220729
LC record available at https://lccn.loc.gov/2022019536
LC ebook record available at https://lccn.loc.gov/2022019537

ISBN: 978-0-367-75367-2 (hbk)
ISBN: 978-0-367-75365-8 (pbk)
ISBN: 978-1-003-16222-3 (ebk)

DOI: 10.4324/9781003162223

Typeset in Interstate
by codeMantra

CONTENTS

List of Figures	xi
List of Tables	xii
List of Tasks	xiii
Acknowledgements	xv
List of Contributors	xvi
Foreword	xix

INTRODUCTION — 1

1 BECOMING A PSYCHOLOGY TEACHER — 3
DEBORAH GAJIC AND JOCK McGINTY

1.1	Characteristics and Skills of a Psychology Teacher	3
1.2	Characteristics and Requirements of Psychology as a Subject	5
1.3	The Role of Psychology in Schools	6
1.4	Why Students Choose Psychology	8
1.5	Understanding the Psychology Curriculum	8
1.6	Where to Find Support	10
1.7	Summary and Key Points	11

2 USING PSYCHOLOGY TO TEACH PSYCHOLOGY — 13
JOCK McGINTY

2.1	Threshold Concepts	14
2.2	Cognitive Load Theory	16
2.3	Spaced or Distributed Practice	18
2.4	Retrieval Practice	20
2.5	Elaboration	22

CONTENTS

2.6	Dual Coding	23
2.7	Summary and Key Points	24

3 TEACHING AREAS OF PSYCHOLOGY — 26
DEBORAH GAJIC

3.1	Cognitive Area	27
3.2	Social Area	30
3.3	Developmental Area	33
3.4	Individual Differences Area	36
3.5	Biological Area	38
3.6	Summary and Key Points	39

4 TEACHING RESEARCH METHODS — 41
DEBORAH GAJIC AND ANDY McCARTHY

4.1	Experimental Methods	42
4.2	Non-Experimental Methods	45
4.3	Inferential Statistics	51
4.4	Summary and Key Points	54

5 ETHICS IN PSYCHOLOGY TEACHING — 55
JONATHAN FIRTH

5.1	The Practice of Teaching Research Ethics in Psychology	56
5.2	BPS Guidelines	57
5.3	The Association For The Teaching of Psychology (ATP) Application of BPS Guidelines in Schools and Colleges	60
5.4	Suggested Teaching Activities	62
5.5	Summary and Key Points	67

6 TEACHING SKILLS OF EVALUATION AND ANALYSIS IN PSYCHOLOGY — 69
JOCK McGINTY

6.1	What Makes a Critical Thinker?	70
6.2	What Is Critical Thinking?	71
6.3	Barriers to Critical Thinking	72
6.4	Skills Required for Critical Thinking	75
6.5	Creating a Framework for Critical Thinking and Evaluation	76

6.6	Assessment Objectives for Evaluations	77
6.7	Providing Students with Critical Thinking and Evaluation Tasks	78
6.8	Assessing Critical Thinking and Evaluation	80
6.9	Summary and Key Points	80

7 TEACHING SKILLS OF APPLICATION　82
LIN NORTON

7.1	Problem-based Learning: An Overview	83
7.2	Text-based Vignettes	84
7.3	Constructing a TBV	85
7.4	Using TBVs for PBL	88
7.5	Summary and Key Points	90

8 DEVELOPING PSYCHOLOGICALLY LITERATE STUDENTS　93
CLARE DEAVALL

8.1	Why Is Psychological Literacy Important?	94
8.2	Students as Science Practitioners	96
8.3	Peer Mentoring and Peer-assessed Learning	100
8.4	Innovative Assessment	102
8.5	Developing Employability Skills	105
8.6	Work Volunteering	107
8.7	Summary and Key Points	107

9 LEARNING TO ASSESS PSYCHOLOGY AND GIVE STUDENTS MEANINGFUL FEEDBACK　109
MIN DUCHENSKI-JASSAL

9.1	Formative and Summative Assessment	110
9.2	Feedback	116
9.3	Student Responses to Feedback	118
9.4	Marking Better, Not More – Encouraging Self-regulating Learners	119
9.5	Summary and Key Points	123

10 INCLUSION IN TEACHING PSYCHOLOGY　125
LUCINDA POWELL

10.1	Inclusion for All – Creating an Inclusive Environment	127

CONTENTS

10.2	Supporting SEND	129
10.3	Making Psychology Accessible to All	135
10.4	Ethics	138
10.5	Summary and Key Points	139

11 USING TECHNOLOGY IN PSYCHOLOGY TEACHING 140
MATT JARVIS

11.1	Delivering Education in Changing Contexts	141
11.2	Keeping an Eye on Principles of Effective Learning and Teaching	143
11.3	Legal Constraints on Digital Education	150
11.4	Digital Platforms	153
11.5	Summary and Key Points	156

12 FUTURE DIRECTIONS AND PROFESSIONAL DEVELOPMENT 159
MIN DUCHENSKI-JASSAL AND JONATHAN FIRTH

12.1	The Scope of a Career Plan in Psychology	160
12.2	Planning	167
12.3	Summary and Key Points	171

13 REFLECTIONS AND FUTURE DIRECTIONS 173
DEBORAH GAJIC AND JOCK McGINTY

13.1	The Importance of Reflection	174
13.2	Indicators of Success	174
13.3	Maintain Vitality in Your Teaching	175
13.4	The Rewards of Being a Psychology Teacher	176
13.5	Broaden Your Horizon	176
13.6	Summary and Key Points	178

References	179
Index	189

FIGURES

3.1	Working memory model (WMM)	29
4.1	Types of correlations	49
4.2	Which statistical test and why?	54
7.1	Principles of vignette design	87
8.1	Zone of proximal development	100
10.1	Assess, plan, do, review SEND cycle	130
10.2	Example of GCSE literacy mat for students	137
10.3	Summary of Bloom's taxonomy	138
11.1	This slide encourages active engagement because the reader has decisions to make about how and when to access what information	144
11.2	The Moodle random glossary entry randomly pushes out definitions to learners	146
11.3	Increasing germane cognitive load via a hangman question	146
11.4	A Google Jamboard can be used collaboratively, either as shown here in a remote lesson or in the context of a group project	147
11.5	The adaptive interface of LearnItFast helps with distributed learning	149

TABLES

4.1	Think, pair, share	43
8.1	Top 100 concepts (Bonneau, 1990)	95
9.1	Strategies of efficient marking for pupil progress	120
11.1	Psychology dictionaries	157
11.2	Repositories of psychological articles	157
11.3	Online research methods and statistics tools	158
11.4	Descriptive and inferential statistics	158

TASKS

	1.1	Self-evaluation of prior knowledge	4
M	2.1	Threshold concepts	15
M	2.2	Creating teaching resources	18
	2.3	Creating and using interleaved quizzes	20
	2.4	Retrieve-taking not note-taking	22
	2.5	Elaboration merry-go-round	23
	2.6	Plan a lesson for storyboards	24
	3.1	Plan a lesson	30
	3.2	Design a writing frame (see Chapter 2)	33
	3.3	Egg baby	35
M	3.4	Family structures and life choices	36
	3.5	Psychometric tests	36
M	3.6	Questioning strategies	37
	3.7	Playdoh brains	38
	3.8	Core study mapping	39
	4.1	Skills and knowledge audit	42
	4.2	Ideas for practicals in the classroom	44
	4.3	Sampling	45
	4.4	Using a flipped learning technique to teach observation	47
M	4.5	Design a self-report study	48
	4.6	Design a lesson plan or series of lesson using JiTT	51
	5.1	Mind the gap	56
	5.2	Emphasis on ethics	57
M	5.3	Ethical or not?	59
	5.4	Case study 1: Ethics approval for students' research projects	60
	5.5	Ethics in practical activities	61
	5.6	Case study 2: Pitfalls and unintended consequences of experiments	62
	5.7	Ethical vignettes	66
	5.8	Variability of practice	67
M	6.1	Reflection: Knowing without understanding?	72
	6.2	Which barriers have an effect upon your teaching?	74

TASKS

M	6.3	Creating opportunities for teaching critical thinking	77
	6.4	Critical thinking question prompts	78
	6.5	Plan a critical thinking lesson	79
	6.6	Helping students write better evaluation answers	80
M	7.1	Using TBVs: Graham being cyber-bullied	85
	7.2	Learning objectives and outcomes	87
	7.3	Constructing a TBV	88
M	7.4	Strategies for teaching with vignettes	90
	8.1	Key Terminology	95
	8.2	Concept cards	99
	8.3	Focus on research methods	99
	8.4	Peer mentoring	102
M	8.5	Assessment methods	104
	8.6	Employability	106
	9.1	A memorable experience	111
M	9.2	Consider the following scenario	114
	9.3	Feedback	117
	9.4	Is there learning?	119
	9.5	An aid to learning	121
	9.6	Rank the learning	123
	10.1	An inclusive environment	127
M	10.2	Growth mindset attributes	129
	10.3	Raising awareness	134
	10.4	Case study	135
	10.5	Lesson plenaries based on Bloom's taxonomy	136
M	10.6	What to do?	138
	11.1	Online teaching challenges	143
	11.2	Introducing yourself to online teaching	145
M	11.3	Cost-benefit analysis	149
	11.4	Planning an online lesson	153
	11.5	How's my online lesson?	155
	12.1	Audit	160
	12.2	Case study 1: An example of career progression	161
	12.3	Cost-benefit analysis	163
	12.4	ABC career targets	168
	12.5	Five-year plan	169
	12.7	Nudge	170
	12.8	Growth mindset	171

ACKNOWLEDGEMENTS

We would like to thank all our contributors without whom this book would not have been possible.

We would also like to thank our families for their patience whilst we worked on this project.

CONTRIBUTORS

Clare Deavall has been a psychology teacher for over 20 years and was a former Head of Psychology in two secondary schools in Staffordshire. She was a senior assistant headteacher in charge of curriculum and has a Master's degree in Innovation and Leadership in Education. She now works as an independent educational consultant, based in France. This involves working with organisations from around the world delivering English qualifications. She also supports students through private tutoring. She was previously a member of the committee of the Association for the Teaching of Psychology (ATP).

Min Duchenski-Jassal was a psychology teacher for 14 years and Head of Psychology in an outstanding school in West London. She was subject lead for the borough's school alliance (of all psychology heads locally), a GCSE and A-level psychology examiner, and completed the National Professional Qualification for Senior Leadership (NPQSL). She is now senior lecturer (subject leader) for the PGCE Psychology in a large London university, is an external examiner for another HE establishment and a parent governor at a local primary school. She is a member of the British Psychological Society (MBPSS). Min completed a Master's (MSc) in Educational Neuroscience and is completing a PhD exploring trauma, well-being and emotion regulation.

Jonathan Firth is a teacher, researcher and author, and an active member of the psychology teaching community in Scotland. Having taught psychology at secondary school level for many years, he now works in teacher education at the University of Strathclyde, Glasgow. His research interests focus on memory and desirable difficulties, teacher metacognition and professional research engagement. He writes support books for teachers, most recently *Psychology in the Classroom* (2018, co-authored with Marc Smith) and *The Teacher's Guide to Research* (2019). He has also contributed to numerous events for psychology teachers, and is a Chartered Psychologist (CPsychol) and a member of the Association for the Teaching of Psychology (ATP).

CONTRIBUTORS

Deborah Gajic has been a psychology teacher for over 25 years and was a former Head of Psychology at an outstanding school in the Midlands. She is a Chartered Psychologist (CPsychol) and an Associate Fellow of the British Psychological Society (AFBPsS). She now works as an independent educational consultant. This involves working with major awarding bodies and publishers, writing and delivering continuing professional development (CPD) for teachers. She also likes to maintain a connection with students through private tutoring. She is an active member of the committee of the Association for the Teaching of Psychology (ATP), currently holding the position of treasurer.

Matt Jarvis is a Chartered Psychologist and Associate Fellow of the British Psychological Society, a Fellow of the Chartered College of Teachers and a Certified Learning Technologist. He taught psychology for over 20 years and is currently Learning Technology and Innovation Manager for a large Social Justice & Education Charity, an editor of Psychology Review Magazine and Visiting Tutor on the Psychology PGCE at Sussex University. Matt has authored numerous psychology text books.

Andy McCarthy has been a psychology lecturer and teacher for over 25 years. His career has included presentations at conferences around the world (Russia, America, Canada, Iceland, etc.), educational publications and various roles at universities, independent schools, state schools and further education colleges. He is a Chartered Psychologist (CPsychol), a member of the Association for the Teaching of Psychology (ATP), a member of the International Council of Psychology Educators (ICOPE) and a member of the Royal Statistical Society (RSS).

Jock McGinty is Head of Psychology and Head of Sixth Form at Watford Grammar School for Boys. He has taught Psychology for over 20 years and is a senior A-level examiner and CPD presenter. He is a Chartered Psychologist (CPsychol) and is a past Chair of the Association for the Teaching of Psychology and Vice-President of the European Federation of Psychology Teachers' Associations. Jock is interested in positive psychology, specifically the role of character strengths in student satisfaction and academic success. Away from psychology, Jock spends his time dreaming of hitting golf balls and skiing.

Lin Norton is emeritus professor at Liverpool Hope University. She is a Chartered Psychologist (CPsychol) and an Associate Fellow of the British Psychological Society (AFBPsS) combining her social science training with her practitioner approach to learning and teaching. She has been a member of the Division for Teachers and Researchers in Psychology (DTRP) since 1997, was appointed as vice chair (teachers) 2002–2004, and was Editor of the Division's journal *Psychology Teaching Review*, 2004–2008. Lin was awarded

CONTRIBUTORS

one of the first (HEA) mini grants for her work on developing vignettes known as PALS (Psychology Applied Learning Scenarios).

Lucinda Powell was a psychology teacher for 15 years in a variety of schools in London and Oxfordshire until 2017. She is a Chartered Psychologist and has an MA in Special and Inclusive education. She now works as an independent education consultant on mental health and well-being, runs a variety of teacher training courses, coaches for the School Mental Health Award (Carnegie School of Excellence for Mental Health in Schools), is a University tutor and Psychology Subject Lead for the PGCE programme at the National School of Education and Teaching, Coventry University. She continues to work with students tutoring study, revision and examination skills.

FOREWORD

This book is aimed at teacher trainees who are learning to teach Psychology and admirably meets their needs in a number of areas. It cleverly takes the subject matter of Psychology and applies relevant knowledge to the actual practice of teaching. This provides the trainee with a sound theoretical background to the complex activity of teaching advanced-level and GCSE Psychology examination students. The psychological theories laid out in the book are carefully chosen to represent the most pertinent contributions to an understanding of pedagogy, with an emphasis on learning.

The substance of the theories is always clearly outlined and then applied to classroom practice. To reinforce the trainees' own learning, the text is interspersed with appropriate activities that are clearly set out and which will further the trainees' grasp of pedagogical principles and practice. The advice given to the trainees throughout is appropriate and contemporary, reflecting the best in current classroom practice. This also has the effect of providing the trainees with many ideas for lessons, both in the planning and in their execution.

The text covers the main areas of challenge for the beginning Psychology teacher but will also be useful to experienced teachers who are teaching Psychology for the first time. While it deals with aspects of teaching that are common to all teachers, such as inclusion and the use of technology for learning – so important in the current climate – it also does not shy away from the difficulties of teaching application and evaluation skills in Psychology to the students. It also provides trainees with guidance for further reading and resourcing, with a nod to their future careers. It is therefore a text not just for the training year but for a career in teaching Psychology.

Tony Lawson
Emeritus Professor
University of Leicester

INTRODUCTION

AIMS AND OBJECTIVES OF THE BOOK

The book introduces the professional knowledge and skills required by teachers of psychology, including general principles of effective teaching. It is backed up by a further text in this series 'Learning to teach in the Secondary School: a companion to school experience. (9th edn 2022) Capel, S., Leask, M. and Younie, S with E. Hidson and J. Lawrence.' which we recommend you read for more general advice and guidance on becoming a teacher.

This book aims to supplement your training as a psychology teacher. It is designed to be dipped into where appropriate. The chapters are written by experienced teachers and educational professionals, with an emphasis on putting pedagogical theory into practice in a psychology classroom. Throughout we refer to Teacher Training as Initial Teacher Education (ITE) and it is vitally important that you cross check all the advice given by your own ITE programme with that in this book. Although this book is written primarily for trainee teachers, much of it will still be relevant throughout your time as an Early Career Teacher (ECT) and beyond.

Throughout there are practical activities you can undertake to further your understanding and suggestions for further reading. Do not feel that you have to complete all the tasks; some might not be relevant to you and what you are teaching. Some of the tasks involve you in activities that impinge on other people; for example, observing a teacher in the classroom, or asking for information. If a task requires you to do this, *you must first of all seek permission from the person concerned*. Remember that you are a guest in school(s); you cannot walk into any teacher's classroom to observe. In addition, some information may be personal or sensitive and you need to consider issues of confidentiality and professional behaviour in your enquiries and reporting. You will notice that some of the tasks are labelled <<M-level>>, these are tasks which are at a Master's level.

DOI: 10.4324/9781003162223-1

INTRODUCTION

These tasks require you to think more analytically or engage in further reading and research.

We have provided lots of further references, resources and ideas about where to get further information. Your ITE is only the beginning of your journey to becoming a psychology teacher, for all teachers professional development is an on-going process. Every day is a new learning opportunity.

This book was written with UK ITE in mind; however, effective teaching is universal. Even between the four nations of the United Kingdom, there are differences in the educational systems, so we strongly advise you to check the local requirements and regulations where you are teaching.

We strongly recommend you consider joining a professional subject association such as the Association for the Teaching of Psychology (ATP) that is very active in supporting psychology teachers with high quality professional development. When you join the ATP, you become part of a highly respected national and international community of psychology teachers with opportunities to network and collaborate. Particularly when you are training or have just qualified, it is vital that you get support and practical help, especially if you are the only psychology teacher in your institution. The ATP provides free advice on issues relating to psychology specifications and the examining process and organises regular events and conferences that are invaluable to all psychology teachers.

The British Psychological Society (BPS) promotes excellence in all aspects of psychology. Their Education and Training Board wants students, academics and practitioners to have access to the highest quality education and training resources and therefore work closely with the ATP in delivering teacher toolkits to support your teaching. For example, presentations, guides and reports focus on using pedagogical theory in psychology teaching and providing support on areas of the psychology specifications such as the mathematical requirements and statistics.

Hopefully, this book will be a useful reference as you embark on your career as a psychology teacher. The final chapter will hopefully give you some inspiration about how to further your career as a psychology teacher.

Deborah Gajic and Jock McGinty
January 2022

BECOMING A PSYCHOLOGY TEACHER

Deborah Gajic and Jock McGinty

INTRODUCTION

In this chapter, we explore what it means to be a psychology teacher and what is unique and special about the study of psychology. In England, Psychology is the second most popular A-level subject. Why is this? There is no doubt that people are interested in psychology, why people behave and think in the way they do is fascinating. As a beginning teacher of psychology, you are about to embark upon an exciting and fulfilling career and we hope this book inspires you further.

OBJECTIVES

By the end of this chapter you should:

- understand the characteristics and skills of a psychology teacher.
- understand the characteristics and requirements of psychology as a subject.
- understand the role of psychology in schools.
- understand why students choose psychology.
- understand the psychology curriculum.
- know where to find support.

Check the requirements of your initial teacher education programme to see which relate to this unit.

1.1 CHARACTERISTICS AND SKILLS OF A PSYCHOLOGY TEACHER

Teacher standards in the devolved nations are similar but do vary; please check those that apply in your context. The Department for Education teacher standards (England 2011), in the 'demonstrate good subject and curriculum knowledge section', state that teachers must:

DOI: 10.4324/9781003162223-2

- have a secure knowledge of the relevant subject(s) and curriculum areas, foster and maintain pupils' interest in the subject, and address misunderstandings.
- demonstrate a critical understanding of developments in the subject and curriculum areas, and promote the value of scholarship.
- demonstrate an understanding of and take responsibility for promoting high standards of literacy, articulacy and the correct use of standard English, whatever the teacher's specialist subject.

Therefore, a psychology teacher must have a good level of subject knowledge and the motivation to keep that knowledge up to date. There may be areas or topics that you are asked to teach which you did not cover in your undergraduate degree; however, a willingness to learn and apply the principles from your previous study of psychology will enable you to cope with this challenge. Your own enthusiasm for psychology, after all you chose to study and train as a psychology teacher, should be infectious and inspire your students. Membership of professional associations such as the BPS (British Psychological Society) and the ATP (Association for the Teaching of Psychology) will help to keep your subject knowledge up to date.

Now undertake Task 1.1.

> Task 1.1 **Self-evaluation of prior knowledge**
>
> Obtain a copy of the specification you are going to teach.
>
> RAG rate your prior knowledge (Red – No prior knowledge, need to read up, Amber – Some prior knowledge, need to revise, Green – Secure knowledge and understanding).
>
> Ask your mentor for guidance about how much you need to know and to point you in the right direction for appropriate resources to improve your level of knowledge and understanding.
>
> Do not be afraid to ask for help; no one expects you to know everything. Teaching is a journey of discovery.
>
> Gaps in your knowledge might indicate areas of research that you could incorporate into your Masters-level study or inform your choice of appropriate Master's-level courses.

Teaching your students the psychology curriculum (content of the specification you are teaching) and preparing them for assessment is only part of the role of a teacher. Being an effective teacher requires strong interpersonal skills, and the pastoral part of your role is vitally important. Knowledge of Maslow's hierarchy of needs (1954) informs us that unless students' basic (physiological and safety) and psychological (belongingness and love and esteem) needs are met, they cannot learn. Therefore, it is important that your classroom is a comfortable and safe place for students. Ensure that your classroom has a comfortable temperature for students to work in and has adequate ventilation; students should have access to water and be allowed reasonable comfort breaks. A safe classroom should have zero tolerance of bullying and discrimination of any kind. Students need to know you care about them as individuals, so take an interest in them, chat to them about things outside of the classroom, and give sincere praise when warranted. In assessments, it is important to comment on what went well, to build interpersonal relationships and esteem, as well as pointing out errors and areas for development. You will find more about using assessment productively in Chapter 9. If these physiological and psychological needs are not met, they are serious barriers to learning and must be addressed. Obviously, some barriers to learning will be outside of your control, but if you have reason to believe that a student's physiological and psychological needs are not being met outside of the classroom, you should report this to the designated child protection officer.

As psychologists you will have some insight into the possible reasons and explanations for student behaviour. You may draw upon your knowledge of behaviourism to try to shape student behaviour through positive reinforcement and being a good role model. The ability to interpret and react appropriately to challenging student behaviour will develop over time, but at the beginning of your career, it is important to seek help and advice from more experienced colleagues too.

During your study of psychology, you will have covered mental health issues and possibly some learning disabilities too; this will give you an insight into Special Educational needs and/or disabilities (SEND). Chapter 10 will give more information on this. (See also the MESHGuides research summaries for research-based advice.)

As a student of psychology, you will have developed strong study skills and critical thinking skills, which were informed by your study of cognitive psychology, for example techniques to improve memory and recall to aid revision and the ability to evaluate and analyse research. These skills are invaluable to your teaching. Students will need explicit teaching of study skills in order to fulfil their potential. These skills will be useful to them in all their subjects, not just psychology.

1.2 CHARACTERISTICS AND REQUIREMENTS OF PSYCHOLOGY AS A SUBJECT

Psychology is the scientific study of mind and behaviour. Whatever awarding body specification or qualification you are teaching, there will be common areas. These will include research methods and core areas such as Social, Developmental, Individual Differences, Cognitive and Biological Psychology. You will probably teach Behaviourism and Psychodynamic approaches to psychology too. You will find more about teaching core areas of psychology in Chapter 3.

As psychology is a scientific discipline, you will need to teach your students to approach the study of psychology in a critical manner. They need to be taught to evaluate and analyse both published studies and their own research. You will find more about this in Chapter 6. Your students will also need a firm grounding in research methods and the opportunity to carry out their own small-scale research; see Chapter 4 for more information. Finally, your students need to understand how to effectively apply their knowledge, and this is covered in Chapter 7. As psychology is all about people and in order to study people, it is necessary to have research participants, and it is vital that these participants are treated ethically to protect them and the reputation of psychology. Chapter 5 discusses the teaching of ethics. Many of your students will go on to study psychology further, and therefore, it is important that students are psychologically literate; this is covered in Chapter 8.

As a teacher of psychology, it is very common to be asked to teach a second subject to fill your timetable. If you can offer a core subject, this will make you eminently more employable. The subject matter of psychology means that you have skills in literacy from report writing and analysing research papers, which would enable you to teach English. Your study of statistics means that you have high-level numeracy skills which fit with maths. Finally, the scientific nature of psychology and your study of biological psychology would be a good fit with biology. You may not feel that you have enough expertise to teach examination groups, but you will certainly have the skills to teach younger students. Although teaching a second subject might seem like something that just adds to your workload, it is excellent career development and is useful experience if you aspire to pastoral or senior management roles in the future. Professional associations offer advice and support and they can be found through the Council for Subject Associations (https://www.subjectassociations.org.uk).

1.3 THE ROLE OF PSYCHOLOGY IN SCHOOLS

Psychology is taught in the United Kingdom, and in many parts of Europe, as a subject that students choose at examination levels rather than as part of a core curriculum. Therefore, psychology provides breadth and depth to a school curriculum, expanding the horizons of students beyond what they have been taught before. Indeed, this should be seen as beneficial to psychology, as students who opt for psychology should be motivated to learn about the mind and behaviour.

As teachers of psychology, we have a responsibility to help our students achieve grades that will allow them to move on to the next stage of their education, be that post-16, undergraduate study or employment. This proximal aim of teaching psychology needs to be balanced with more distal aims of developing transferable skills and fostering enthusiasm for the challenges that lie ahead. Developing students with intrinsic motivation to study psychology means we have to make the subject interesting and relevant to our students. After all, one of the main reasons given by students when they choose psychology is that they think it is going to be interesting – and it is! Indeed, it is very often psychological research that has obvious and real-world applications that students find most interesting as they can relate to it and understand how it has implications for their own life. That said, there is a trade-off that we need to make between the amount of time we need to devote to teaching the details of the research and the amount of time we can give to applying it to real-world examples. Perhaps, ideally, we would approach our teaching from the standpoint of teaching the minimum theoretical/research knowledge required for understanding and assessment but then giving the maximum time to application and interest.

It is clear that studying psychology at post-16 level provides opportunities to help prepare students for higher education. Exposing your students to a range of texts beyond their textbook, for example electronic resources such as PsycINFO, psychology journals and developing their critical thinking (see Chapter 6) is a good way to do this. Furthermore, the Extended Project Qualification (level 2 or 3) and the Core Maths qualification (England) provide excellent opportunities to develop independent learning and research skills.

However, studying psychology provides students with far more than simply a qualification. Psychology helps promote many of the social and emotional learning skills that are crucial to students' academic achievement and mental health. Students experience many changes as they develop, not only in terms of their own minds and emotions but also in their relationships with others; an understanding of psychology helps them manage these difficult developmental transitions. Therefore, psychology can help students apply the research they study in the class to their own lives to develop a more complex, metacognitive approach to processing their own identity, development, relationships and decisions.

Additionally, psychology as a science helps to develop scientific literacy in students by building independent research skills, and although this is not unique to psychology, it is an excellent vehicle for developing engagement in the scientific process of designing, carrying out and writing an independent research project – for example, simple memory experiments. Psychology is almost unique in its ability to combine literacy, numeracy, health and well-being. For example, psychology students need knowledge of statistics and they should be able to apply them to their research findings. They need to be able to write scientific reports that involve analysis of psychological evidence to inform arguments and discussions and be able to apply them to an issue such as stress, prejudice, mental health and well-being. Moreover, psychology is a subject that is excellent for cross-curricular learning; students of psychology can easily apply their knowledge and understanding to other subjects such as economics and business or to politics or indeed biology.

As a psychology teacher, you are a valuable resource to the school as a whole, providing an informed voice within the staff. Your ability to teach and apply a wide range of skills such as those outlined above means you will be in great demand and well equipped to engage with evidence-based approaches to teaching.

1.4 WHY STUDENTS CHOOSE PSYCHOLOGY

There has been a rapid growth in the number of students studying psychology at all levels in England. In 2020, psychology was the second most popular A-level subject with 63,490 entries (Ofqual, 2020) and it is likely that this will increase still further in the fall out of the coronavirus pandemic and the associated interest in mental health issues. In Section 1.4, we outlined some of the more global benefits for psychology in the school curriculum. However, for students themselves, we should consider the question 'what do psychology students hope to get from studying psychology?' A good place to find the answer is to look at the reasons why they choose to study psychology and the benefits it gives them.

Jarvis (2011) suggests that there are three major reasons for the popularity of psychology:

- The rigour hypothesis – that students perceive, incorrectly, that psychology is an easy subject and that they will achieve good grades with little effort.
- Sexy subject hypothesis – this follows the idea that psychology is inherently interesting and stimulating. And why not? After all psychology is about the study of the mind and our behaviour, surely something in which we all have interest.
- The therapy hypothesis – it is thought that many students study psychology as a means to find out about their own mental health problems. Actually, there is little direct evidence to support this view, though of course there are students who do derive some form of therapy benefit from studying psychology.

Benefits of studying psychology are deep rooted in students' interest in the subject and they find it enjoyable; this satisfaction only serves to increase their motivation to study psychology further. Initially from a teacher's perspective, clearly a focus on attainment grades for our students is always important. Good grades encourage social mobility and help students in terms of examination preparation; it is seen as one of the most common expectations of teaching any subject. If our students believe they are achieving well in lessons and their work is of a high standard, then they will naturally feel that studying psychology is beneficial to them.

1.5 UNDERSTANDING THE PSYCHOLOGY CURRICULUM

The core elements of the psychology qualifications are broad and open to interpretation, which means that awarding bodies are able to offer a wide range of content and approaches to the study of psychology. This diversity allows psychology teachers to choose the specification that best suits their teaching interests and their students' needs. The popularity of psychology, whilst difficult to test directly, has grown largely due to the growth in psychology-related careers such as clinical psychologists and counselling. Additionally, there are changing cultural perceptions of scientific interest where psychology is seen as having tremendously useful applications to society. Jarvis (2011) also suggests that this popularity is portrayed through exciting media representations of psychology such as Crime Scene Investigation (CSI), where forensic or clinical psychologists are given a very high profile.

The core psychology curriculum and assessment objectives in England are set out by Ofqual (2014), and in Northern Ireland, Wales and Scotland, examinations are regulated by each respective national government. In England, Ofqual stipulates that the core psychology curriculum develops students' knowledge and understanding from the cognitive, social, developmental, individual differences and biological areas of psychology. Additionally, students must develop knowledge and understanding of research in psychology, for example methods and techniques for collection of quantitative and qualitative data including experimentation, observation, self-report and correlational analysis. For example, the assessment objectives at A level in England are:

AO1: Demonstrate knowledge and understanding of scientific ideas, processes, techniques and procedures.

AO2: Apply knowledge and understanding of scientific ideas, processes, techniques and procedures: in a theoretical context, in a practical context, when handling qualitative data and when handling quantitative data.

AO3: Analyse, interpret and evaluate scientific information, ideas and evidence, including in relation to issues, to make judgements and reach conclusions and develop and refine practical design and procedures.

> The ability to use mathematical skills at a level appropriate for GCE A level Psychology must be tested across the assessment objectives with a weighting of at least 10%. Furthermore, students must show the ability to select, organise and communicate information and ideas coherently using appropriate scientific conventions and vocabulary.
>
> (Ofqual 2014 p6)

For GCSE psychology, specifications must 'inspire and engage students by providing a broad, coherent, satisfying and worthwhile course of study which develops an understanding of the ideas and values that characterise "self" and others' (Ofqual, 2015 p3). Students study the same core areas of psychology as A level, with compulsory topics such as memory and social influence and options such as perception and criminal psychology. Additionally, students have to develop knowledge, understanding and skills in relation to psychological investigation and research methods. There is also a mathematical requirement for example, arithmetic and numerical computation and handling data.

The GCSE assessment objectives for students are:

AO1: Demonstrate knowledge and understanding of psychological ideas, processes and procedures.

AO2: Apply knowledge and understanding of psychological ideas, processes and procedures.

AO3: Analyse and evaluate psychological information, ideas, processes and procedures to make judgements and draw conclusions.

If you are new to teaching psychology, it is likely that you will not be given any choice in which specification you teach. However, the choice of specification will greatly influence your daily experience of teaching psychology as the topics you teach and assessment requirements can differ markedly. If you do have the opportunity to be involved in choosing a specification, it is an important task and Jarvis (2011) offers you a set of criteria you should consider in your choice.

- How interesting do you think your students will find the content?
- The extent to which the specification lends itself to interesting teaching methods.
- Your personal perception of psychology and how this is fulfilled by each specification's focus on research studies, methodology, theory and application.
- A related question is how applied do you think the psychology course should be?
- You may wish to consider how well the specification prepares students for progression to the next level.
- Do different specifications give different opportunities to develop transferable skills in your students?
- You may also be swayed by the content load, assessment and grade distributions.

There is not a 'best' specification to teach as the criteria for choosing a specification rely on your personal perception of psychology. However, whichever specification you teach, you will be able to convey your enthusiasm and passion for psychology.

1.6 WHERE TO FIND SUPPORT

As a trainee/early career teacher, there should be many sources of support available to you. For example, if you are qualifying via a PGCE at a university, you will have the support of your lecturers and teaching mentors and also the other trainees in your psychology group. Additionally, in-school support through subject mentors or school-based teacher mentors should provide you with the assistance you require.

However, professional associations such as the ATP are very active in supporting psychology teachers with high quality professional development. When you join the ATP, you become part of a highly respected national and international community of psychology teachers with opportunities to network and collaborate. Particularly when you are training or have just qualified, it is vital that you get support and practical help, especially if you are the only psychology teacher in your institution. The ATP provides free advice on issues relating to psychology specifications and the examining process and organises regular events and conferences that are invaluable to all psychology teachers.

The BPS promotes excellence in all aspects of psychology. Their Education and Training Board wants students, academics and practitioners to have access to the highest quality education and training resources and therefore work closely with the ATP in delivering teacher toolkits to support your teaching. For example, presentations, guides and reports focus on using pedagogical theory in psychology teaching and providing support on areas of the psychology specifications such as the mathematical requirements and statistics.

1.7 SUMMARY AND KEY POINTS

You should now:

- Understand the characteristics and skills of a psychology teacher.
- Understand the characteristics and requirements of psychology as a subject.
- Understand the role of psychology in schools.
- Understand why students choose psychology.
- Understand the psychology curriculum.
- Know where to find support.

Check the requirements of your initial teacher education programme to see which have been addressed in this unit.

FURTHER RESOURCES AND WEBSITES

For general information, extending what is in this chapter, we recommend you read Section 1 'Becoming a Teacher' in the core textbook for the Learning to Teach series: Capel, S., Leask, M. and Younie, S with E. Hidson and J. Lawrence (9th edn 2022) *Learning to Teach in the Secondary School: a companion to school experience*. Abingdon Routledge Taylor Francis.

We would recommend that you join these organisations:

The Association for the /Teaching of Psychology https://www.theatp.uk/

The British Psychological Society https://www.bps.org.uk/

The **Office of Qualifications and Examinations Regulation** (Ofqual) regulates qualifications, examinations and assessments in England.

OFQUAL Information – please check for updates and equivalents in devolved nations.

https://www.gov.uk/government/publications/teachers-standards Accessed 6/1/21

Ofqual (2014) https://www.gov.uk/government/publications/gcse-psychology Accessed 27/02/21

Ofqual (2015) https://www.gov.uk/government/publications/gce-subject-level-conditions-and-requirements-for-psychology Accessed 27/02/21

For information extending what is in this chapter, we recommend you read Section 7 'The School, Curriculum and Society' in the core textbook for the Learning to Teach series: Capel, S., Leask, M. and Younie, S. with E. Hidson and J. Lawrence (9th edn 2022) *Learning to Teach in the Secondary School: A Companion to School Experience*. Abingdon Routledge: Taylor Francis.

USING PSYCHOLOGY TO TEACH PSYCHOLOGY

Jock McGinty

INTRODUCTION

Research on teacher subject knowledge has shown that teachers not only need solid knowledge and understanding of the subject they teach, but they also need to know how to teach that subject, and, more generally, how to teach (Ofsted 2019). This means psychology teachers need to be familiar with three types of essential knowledge: content knowledge, pedagogical knowledge and pedagogical content knowledge. We can view content knowledge as your knowledge of the psychology content you are teaching, pedagogical knowledge as your knowledge of effective teaching methods in general and pedagogical content knowledge as your knowledge of how to apply this to teach psychology or a particular topic in psychology.

The exact amount of knowledge necessary to teach psychology effectively will differ by age group and level at which you teach, and it is not the case that the more knowledge of psychology you have, the greater the learning of your students. Baumert *et al.* (2010) suggest that this may create a threshold effect, in that it is important for you to know a certain level of psychology to teach psychology effectively, but that beyond this a law of diminishing returns may occur. Thus, there may be a 'required level of knowledge' for psychology teachers, which is closely aligned to their knowledge of the psychology curriculum. Your knowledge of the psychology curriculum may also affect the way in which you teach psychology. Teachers with greater content knowledge have higher levels of pedagogical content knowledge, which leads to a greater attention to developing students' conceptual knowledge through strategies such as summarising and questioning (Baumert *et al.* 2010).

There is no one correct way to structure a lesson and as you become more experienced as a teacher, you will learn to vary not only the content of your lessons but also their structure. As general principles in the United Kingdom, Ofsted (2019) highlights the importance of teachers actively presenting material

JOCK McGINTY

and structuring it by providing overviews and reviews of lesson objectives, outlining the lesson content and signalling transitions between different parts of the lesson. It is also important to focus attention on the main ideas and provide opportunities for summary reviews to reinforce the learning of major points. However, for now, it is best that you follow any specific structures given to you by your teaching mentor or school. Structuring elements not only helps your students to memorise information from your lesson but also allows them to understand how each part contributes to the lesson as a whole. Using a framework such as this means the elements can occur at different points in a lesson, or over a sequence of lessons, in order to make your lessons, and therefore your students' learning, effective (Creemers & Kyriakides 2008).

The British Psychological Society defines psychology as 'the scientific study of the mind and how it dictates and influences our behaviour, from communication and memory to thought and emotion'. Learning requires thought and it is in part defined as a change in long-term memory. It is important that you use thoughtful approaches that help students to integrate new knowledge into their long-term memory and make enduring connections that foster understanding. This chapter will focus on learning sciences, a relatively new interdisciplinary field that seeks to apply principles from cognitive science to classroom practice and thus explains how we can teach psychology through the use of psychology.

OBJECTIVES

By the end of this chapter, you should be able to:

- explain how threshold concepts underpin your students understanding of psychology.
- recognise the importance of cognitive load in teaching your students.
- implement spaced practice and interleaving to maximise long-term retention of knowledge in your students.
- appreciate how to use retrieval practice to improve your students' memory of what they have been taught.
- show how the concept of elaboration can be applied to your teaching of psychology.
- understand how to use dual coding to help your teaching of psychology.

Check which requirements of your initial teacher education programme relate to this unit.

2.1 THRESHOLD CONCEPTS

The idea of threshold concepts emerged from a UK national research project into the possible characteristics of strong teaching and learning environments. As Meyer and Land (2003) put it, 'a threshold concept can be considered as

USING PSYCHOLOGY TO TEACH PSYCHOLOGY

akin to a portal, opening up a new and previously inaccessible way of thinking about something' (p.1). Threshold concepts in psychology allow your students to understand related concepts that they find difficult but when they are learned, it can lead to a breakthrough in their understanding of the subject as a whole. For example, the concepts of reliability and validity are often misunderstood and wrongly used interchangeably by many students. However, once learned, reliability and validity allow students to have a clear insight into the relative effectiveness of the methodologies used by psychologists. Importantly, these threshold concepts also provide opportunities for critical thinking and evaluation (see Chapter 6).

Hodge (2019) has suggested that these concepts can be considered a 'threshold' to fuller learning as they can pose particular problems for most students but are essential for developing a coherent understanding of psychology. Thus, if you explicitly teach threshold concepts such as reliability and validity effectively, your teaching can transform students' understanding, and interpretation of psychological research, allowing them to progress in their learning of psychology. These threshold concepts are often what you would call key concepts or terminology within psychology, but they possess the additional quality of personal challenge for students. Additionally once understood, they also have a coordinating or integrating effect on other areas of students' psychological knowledge (Hodge 2019). In this sense, threshold concepts can be seen as transformative in the understanding of psychology and you should focus on creating explicit opportunities to teach them as they provide students with a significant shift in their perception of psychology.

Now, undertake Task 2.1

Task 2.1 **Threshold concepts**

If possible, undertake this work with fellow trainee psychology teachers so you can share ideas and discuss your impact evaluations.

1. Look through the psychology specification you teach, and the lessons you are planning and identify five threshold concepts that you believe will be transformative to your students' understanding of psychology.
2. For each threshold concept, plan two ways in which you could teach it and the impact you might expect this to have on your students' learning.
3. Now, teach these concepts and evaluate the impact of your approaches through, for example an end of lesson quiz or a homework exercise with a follow-up check for understanding some lessons later.
4. Consider what went well and how you might improve your practice next time you teach these concepts. If your approach has not worked well, then you may need to reteach the concepts using a different approach.

The six-week intervention methodology employed by Richards and Rivers (2008) provides a model for this type of work.

2.2 COGNITIVE LOAD THEORY

An important contribution to learning science is made by Cognitive Load Theory (CLT). CLT is concerned with the structure of memory and the brain, and focuses on the capacity of the short-term memory to process information (Ofsted 2019). However, before entering the long-term memory, information must first be processed by the short-term memory. This short-term working memory has limited capacity to retain knowledge and the development of complex structures (schemata) that link knowledge and create meaning is hindered if the working memory is overloaded (Kirschner, Sweller & Clark 2006). For your psychology students, cognitive load is the demand placed on their working memory in order to successfully complete a thinking or learning task (Sweller, Ayres, & Kalyuga 2011). Their cognitive load depends not only on the task you set them but also on the individual cognitive characteristics of your students. This suggests you may need to prepare differentiated tasks in relation to cognitive load depending on your students and organise your teaching of psychological content into small chunks, until your students acquire the knowledge that allows them to spend less time processing content (Ofsted 2019).

So what does cognitive load look like in your classroom? What is termed *intrinsic cognitive load* is essential for learning and is caused by the complexity of the task or psychology material you give to your students relative to their expertise level for that task. Because intrinsic cognitive load is essential for comprehending instructions and completing a task, it is vital to provide students with all the necessary resources to accommodate this load without exceeding limits of their working memory capacity (Sweller *et al.* 2011). The overall learning goal of your task, for example understanding the research by Bandura (1963) into the transmission of aggression in young children, could be divided into a series of sub-goals with instructions and tasks broken down into smaller units such as outlining the research procedure, the sample and the findings. On the other hand, if some of your students have spare cognitive capacity, it may also be appropriate to increase essential cognitive processing demands, for example setting more challenging learning goals that require more complex cognitive activities such as creating a mind map of Bandura's research. This intentional increase in essential cognitive processing is referred to as an increase in *germane cognitive load*. Germane load has been associated with activities designed to extend learning and motivation such as imagining the procedures described in worked examples that you give your students or by asking students to explain their reasoning behind why psychologists used a particular experimental design. In contrast to intrinsic cognitive load, *extraneous cognitive load* is associated with a diversion of cognitive resources on activities irrelevant to learning goals because of factors related to the way in which you have designed your lesson activity. This can take the form of a poor design of presentations, inappropriate selection and sequencing of tasks, or inadequate instructional support. This means that your students need to divert some of their information processing capacity towards simply understanding what it is you want them to do, rather than focusing on using their knowledge of psychology to complete the activity successfully.

In a general sense, you should be spending much of your time trying to increase your students' knowledge of psychology so that you can help them overcome the limited capacity of their short-term memory and recall, apply and use relevant knowledge from their long-term memories. Sweller *et al.* (2011) recommend that teachers should provide as much relevant information as possible for their students and explicit teaching, at least for novices, is almost certainly preferable to asking students to discover things for themselves. In order to develop expertise, students need to increase their knowledge and in order for them to increase their knowledge effectively, they need explicit teaching.

For example, worked examples are effective for novices as they are studying the solutions to problems rather than attempting to solve them. Asking novice students to repeatedly write extended evaluation answers to questions that require critical analysis, adds to their extraneous cognitive load as they have insufficient background knowledge of psychology. Therefore, comments such as 'I don't know how to start' and 'What do I write?' are often heard in this scenario. Thus, creating worked examples for your students will be beneficial because it helps to build the background psychology knowledge in their long-term memories, information that can then be recalled and used for future questions (Sweller *et al.* 2011). These principles can be readily applied in the classroom by beginning with a model answer, then providing a writing frame with a lot of information, followed by a writing frame with less information, then finally a question that your students must complete without the use of a writing frame. See Wray and Lewis (undated) for advice on constructing writing frames.

Further strategies that use the concept of cognitive load to help your students:

- The coherence principle whereby you remove any unnecessary information from your teaching materials so students only see the essential parts and not the 'fun' pictures or animations that distract from the content or message you want to teach.
- The signalling principle that encourages you to highlight important information using bold, italics or even arrows and other graphics to direct your students to essential information.
- The redundancy principle is about avoiding simply reading what is on your presentation slides; instead have a combination of images, text and planned narration in order to reduce extraneous cognitive load.
- Use spatial contiguity by placing labels next to pictures or diagrams.
- Design your presentations with temporal contiguity which encourages labels and images to be presented at the same time, so students link these two things together in their working memory.
- Using simple-to-complex sequencing of tasks that acts as a form of fading scaffolding.

Now undertake Task 2.2.

> **Task 2.2 Creating teaching resources**
>
> 1. Using the principles to reduce cognitive load outlined above, design a presentation for a topic in psychology that you are about to teach or one for which you need to develop teaching resources.
> 2. For a psychology topic of your choice, produce a worked example task for your students. You should highlight the intrinsic, extrinsic and germane cognitive loads.
>
> As for Task 2.1, evaluate the success or otherwise of your approach and make notes about what you would do differently next time.

For an outline of how CLT can be applied to teaching areas of psychology, see Chapter 3.

We have seen that reducing extraneous cognitive load is beneficial to your students, particularly novices. However, Sweller *et al.* (2011) have shown that among expert students, enquiry-based approaches work better than the more explicit teaching that works best with novice learners. This reversal in the relative effectiveness of teaching methods has been referred to as an *expertise reversal effect* where the expert students' knowledge overlaps with teacher's external guidance, thus forcing them to waste limited resources processing the same information.

A major teaching implication of the expertise reversal effect is the need for you to tailor your guidance to current levels of students' expertise as they gradually change during their learning of psychology. At higher levels of expertise, a move away from faded worked examples to using minimally guided exploratory learning tasks such as applied learning scenarios that require problem-solving, allows for tailored, individualised learning. This adaptive approach allows different levels of students to have autonomy but does depend on your students' ability to select appropriate learning strategies. According to CLT, the level of learner expertise is a defining factor: students could have control over the content and instructional sequences when they have sufficient knowledge of psychology (Kalyuga 2007). In order to facilitate effective differentiation in your classroom, you will need to seek guidance from your mentor about prior achievement and other pertinent background information about your students.

2.3 SPACED OR DISTRIBUTED PRACTICE

As teachers, I am sure we would agree that no mental ability is more important than our capacity to learn, but the benefits of learning are lost once the material is forgotten. We perhaps are all too aware that our students forgetting what we have taught them is particularly common; much of the psychology we teach our students is lost within days or weeks of learning (Rohrer & Taylor 2006). Thus, an understanding of learning strategies that extend retention would prove beneficial not only to you but also to your students who are required to retain information throughout the duration of their course.

When your students review their lesson notes, revise using flashcards or when a topic such as memory is covered in your lessons and then later studied in a textbook, the content of your psychology course is encountered frequently by your students. Even so, when preparing for assessments, students often revise intensely immediately prior to tests and believe that this strategy is effective – the all-nighter! In the short term, although cramming is better than not studying at all, your students are better off spreading out their study of the course content (Dunlosky, Rawson, Marsh, Nathan, & Willingham 2013).

In your classroom, a distributed or spaced practice strategy requires that practice or learning of a topic or concept in psychology be divided across multiple sessions and not massed into just one session. Studies from cognitive psychology consistently demonstrate that spacing between practice sessions leads to better learning and retention than massing practice into a single session; this is called the spacing effect (Kasprowicz, Marsden, & Sephton 2019). Examples of how you can apply this to your teaching include creating four study tasks for 15 minutes each day rather than a single 1 hour task. Similarly, you can encourage your students to prepare for assessments using blocks of 20 minutes every day of the week rather than only studying right before a test or exam.

A related practice is interleaving. Traditionally, most schools and teaching departments use blocking, where practice of a particular topic or area of psychology happens in blocks (e.g. AAABBBCCC). In interleaving, we instead mix practice of A, B and C (e.g. ABCABCABC) (Ofsted, 2019). Research has shown that students score higher on tests when most practice questions are mixed with different kinds of questions – a format known as interleaved practice. Interleaving prevents students from assuming that each practice question relates to the same topic in psychology or concept as the previous question. If you use interleaved practice, you are forcing students to choose an appropriate strategy on the basis of the question itself and not thereby reducing order or practice effects (Rohrer, Dedrick, & Hartwig 2020). A simple way to do this is to assign online quizzes that interleave questions from various topics in your psychology course such as memory, attachment, mental disorders or research methods.

For an outline of how spaced practice can be applied to teaching ethics, see Chapter 5.

Now undertake Task 2.3.

> Task 2.3 **Creating and using interleaved quizzes**
>
> Implementing interleaved practice is not terribly difficult, but it does call for a bit of planning. What is needed is study and practice of different aspects of the psychology course. For example, the social area, knowledge of Milgram's (1963) research and the methodology he used.
>
> For each topic that you teach during a half-term period, create a quiz that interleaves the different aspects of the content you have taught so that students have to vary their strategies to answer the questions.
>
> For example you may include:
>
> 1. Short answer questions that focus on factual knowledge of Milgram's study on obedience.
> 2. Multiple choice questions on the methodology used by Milgram.
> 3. Questions on how Milgram's research relates to the social area of psychology.
>
> Alternatively you could create a quiz that interleaves the content of a number of areas or studies in psychology. For example, multiple choice questions that cover:
>
> 1. Types of conformity
> 2. Explanations of attachment
> 3. Types of long-term memory

2.4 RETRIEVAL PRACTICE

Another important practice for effective retention of knowledge in the long-term memory is retrieval practice. Retrieval practice involves recalling something you have learned in the past and bringing it back to mind (Barenberg, Roeder, & Dutke 2018). Retrieval practice needs to occur a reasonable time after the topic has been initially taught and therefore dovetails nicely with the concepts of distributed practice and interleaving. Ideally, it should take the form of testing knowledge, either with you as the teacher questioning students or testing them or through students self-testing using quizzes. Lots of online platforms such as Google Classroom provide the facility to create quizzes on topics in psychology that are easy to administer and allow you to provide feedback so that students can check the accuracy of their answers for themselves. A word of caution, if you use ready-made quizzes from online platforms, check them for accuracy before you assign them to students. Some are of dubious quality.

Testing is traditionally viewed as a way to measure learning, but Davidesco and Milne (2019) suggest that the act of taking a test can also significantly enhance learning. What is it about testing and retrieval that makes it more effective than restudying? There are at least two explanations for this. Firstly, Bjork and Bjork (2011) propose that the effort invested by students in retrieving information from their memories can strengthen knowledge and make it more easily accessible. More recently, it has been proposed that the process of retrieval updates the context in which information is encoded in students' memories, making it easier to recover the information in a subsequent test (Karpicke, Lehman, & Aue 2014). For example, you may have taught your students about the cognitive characteristics of phobias one week and asked them to prepare for a test the following week. Initially, students relate the cognitive characteristics of phobias to the lesson but the process of retrieval during revision for the test, updates this context (they revisit the cognitive characteristics of phobias), thereby making it easier to recall later in the test. Importantly, it should be noted that fact quizzes enhance final fact test performance and higher order quizzes enhance final higher order test performance, thereby supporting the idea that you should match your quizzes for cognitive complexity based on Bloom's taxonomy (Agarwal 2019). See also Figure 10.3 illustrating Bloom's taxonomy.

A good way to integrate quizzes into your lessons is to provide regular opportunities for retrieval practice. For example, quiz questions interspersed during a lesson produce the same benefit to long-term retention as quiz questions presented at the end of a lesson (Weinstein, Nunes, & Karpicke 2016). In addition to providing retrieval practice, this method also boosts learning by creating test expectancy throughout the lesson (Weinstein, Gilmore, Szpunar, & McDermott 2014).

Testing can be stressful for students and so testing for learning needs to be low stakes and not be used for making summative assessments. You can use ungraded quizzes (Khanna 2015) or collaborative quizzing (Wissman & Rawson 2016). For example, students can take a short quiz on biological psychology and then exchange quizzes and grade each other or have a discussion with a partner and return to their quizzes and revise their own answers. This approach reinforces learning, providing formative assessment (see Chapter 9) and saves you hours in unproductive marking. The quiz marks do not necessarily need to be collected by you as the teacher but provide you with a teaching tool to allow students to peer-assess their knowledge and understanding.

However, our students often complain that they face a barrage of testing and assessment so how can retrieval practice be implemented in a course that does not include any quizzes or tests? Instead of weekly quizzes, you could ask your students to post weekly reflections on the topic they have been taught on an online forum such as Google Classroom. This gives them the opportunity to reflect on their learning and make connections between course topics such as psychopathology and their related everyday experiences such as reading about mental health issues in adolescents. To extend this, you can encourage students to complete this task without reviewing their class notes and this work could culminate in an event at the end of the term, when students are invited to reflect on their learning of psychology as a whole.

Testing is too often used in schools as a means of summative assessment, rather than as a tool for learning and formative assessment. The use of retrieval practice suggests that not only is testing an important way of encouraging long-term retention, but feedback after testing is also important because it allows learners to correct their mistakes and memory errors (Davidesco & Milne 2019). This means that in order to encourage accurate long-term retention, you should include testing with feedback as an essential part of your teaching strategy.

Now undertake Task 2.4.

> Task 2.4 **Retrieve-taking not note-taking**
>
> How can you boost note-taking with retrieval practice?
>
> 1. Ask your students to read a section from their textbook, watch a video, or listen to your lesson presentation without taking notes (yet!).
> 2. Tell them to close the textbook, video, or pause during the lesson so students can write down what they remember.
> 3. Then ask them to re-open the textbook, continue watching the video, or with the lesson.
> 4. You are simply asking them to take notes while retrieving. This approach with retrieve-taking supports students in their existing note-taking strategies.
>
> Points to consider:
>
> Because students' retrieval may contain some inaccuracies, which is good for learning, point 3 is critical for feedback. Yes, this may take a little extra time but time spent retrieving is much more beneficial in the long-term than strategies like re-reading.
>
> Students may feel their retrieve-taking is disorganised so you can get them to do this on flash cards or on a computer. Additionally, it is recommended that you model this in your classroom before students try it at home.

2.5 ELABORATION

Humans are inquisitive by nature, seeking explanations for events in the world around us and this power of explanatory questioning can be harnessed to promote learning in your students both through elaborative interrogation and self-explanation. These concepts enhance learning by supporting the integration of new information with existing prior knowledge (Dunlosky *et al.* 2013). Therefore, it will be beneficial to ask your students questions that require them to ask 'why' as it means they have to make connections between the psychology topics they are taught with their memories and experiences (Bisra, Liu, Nesbitt, Salimi, & Winne 2018). If your students can ask and explain what factors contribute to whether one person helps another person or why some people are obedient while others are disobedient, then they are explaining the application of psychology to real-world contexts. This can be easily woven into your classroom by providing activities with example scenarios of a person in need of help and asking students to describe and explain why they think a passer-by may or may not help.

Stavnezer and Lom (2019) describe a simple student-led classroom technique, recap and retrieval practice (R&RP). As well as integrating the concept of retrieval practice, R&RP sessions require students to elaborate and explain prior course content. The benefits to your classroom are that they are short, student-led reviews of psychology course material that they have been taught or have researched themselves. Additionally, the fact that student explanations feature prominently at the start of your lessons means that your students come to the lesson ready to listen and learn. You can ask your students to do this as individuals or collaboratively and this encourages class participation, and emphasises student voices in your classroom.

Now undertake Task 2.5.

Task 2.5 **Elaboration merry-go-round**

Divide your class/students into pairs and allocate each pair a topic or concept that you have taught them.

Provide each pair with five minutes at the start of a lesson to explain their topic or concept and to elaborate on how the psychology can be applied to real-world contexts.

2.6 DUAL CODING

Dual coding theory suggests that representing information both visually and verbally enhances learning and retrieval from memory (Ofsted 2019). The principle underlying this is that visual and verbal information are processed through different channels in the brain, creating separate representations for information processed in each channel (Paivio 2006). This means that when recalling information, students can use either the word or the picture associated with it; this increases the likelihood that they will remember the psychological concept or content. This suggests that you should use visuals such as diagrams or pictures in order to support your teaching (Paivio 2006).

So how can you do this in the classroom? As pictures are more likely to be remembered than words, a phenomenon called 'the picture superiority effect' (Paivio & Csapo 1973), you should encourage your students to develop multiple representations of the same material, both pictures and words (Weinstein *et al.* 2018). For example, your students can create images or pictures that provide a visual representation of a piece of psychological research supported by a short piece of descriptive text or voice recordings. Another way you can use dual coding is to ask students to use their phones to create 'snaplogs' (snapshots and logbooks) by taking pictures of their classroom activities and adding text to explain these activities (Bramming, Hansen, Bojesen, & Olesen 2012). Comic books or storyboards are another good example of dual coding. They allow for the integration of text and images into a coherent story, engage students, motivate them to learn and boost memory (Tatalovic 2009). Additionally, you can make sure to provide video depictions of psychological research such as Milgram to go with verbal descriptions.

The explanation for the 'picture superiority effect' is that pictures are dually encoded; they use both verbal and image codes, whereas words are only coded verbally. Image and verbal codes are processed by separate brain systems, and so there are both additive and independent effects on memory retention (Weinstein, Madan, & Sumeracki 2018).

Now undertake Task 2.6.

Task 2.6 **Plan a lesson for storyboards**

A storyboard is a tool that helps writers plan out the order, or sequence, of a movie or book. You can use it to help your students plan out the story of a piece of psychological research. Points to consider:

1. Choose the psychological research to be studied such as Mary Ainsworth's Strange Situation (1970).
2. Show an example of a storyboard for another piece of research as a worked example.
3. Tell students that they need to pictorially represent the order of events in the research including the beginning, middle and end.
4. Ask students to think of some keywords that will help them remember the meaning of the pictures.
5. Once students have completed their storyboards, ask them to present them and explain each step.

2.7 SUMMARY AND KEY POINTS

Higher level thinking is critical at secondary and post-secondary level because it helps promote more effective application and transfer of course material (Richmond & Kindelberger-Hagen 2011). All of the strategies outlined in this chapter promote higher level thinking as they encourage students to actively think about psychology in new and productive ways. Active learning in psychology involves students in 'doing and thinking' about psychology, and Bernstein (2018) suggests that the key to effective learning is to produce well designed active learning tasks that make students talk about what they are learning, write reflectively about it, relate it to past experiences, and apply it to their daily lives.

You should now:

- Know how threshold concepts underpin your students understanding of psychology.
- Recognise the importance of cognitive load in teaching your students.

USING PSYCHOLOGY TO TEACH PSYCHOLOGY

- Implement spaced practice and interleaving to maximise long-term retention of knowledge in your students.
- Appreciate how to use retrieval practice to improve your students' memory of what they have been taught.
- Show how the concept of elaboration can be applied to your teaching of psychology.
- Understand how to use dual coding to help your teaching of psychology.

Check the requirements of your initial teacher education programme to see which have been addressed in this unit.

FURTHER RESOURCES AND WEBSITES

For useful teaching resources and ideas from the British Psychological Society (BPS).
https://www.bps.org.uk/member-microsites/division-academics-researchers-and-teachers-psychology/teachers-toolkit Accessed 29/11/21

Subscribe to the BPS Research Digest for weekly updates to your inbox.
https://digest.bps.org.uk/ Accessed 29/11/21

For general information, extending what is in this chapter, including observing lessons, lesson planning and teaching whole classes, we recommend you work through Section 2 "Beginning to Teach" In the core textbook for the Learning to Teach series: Capel, S., Leask, M. and Younie, S. with E. Hidson and J. Lawrence (9th edn 2022) *Learning to Teach in the Secondary School: A Companion to School Experience*. Abingdon Routledge: Taylor Francis.

3 TEACHING AREAS OF PSYCHOLOGY

Deborah Gajic

INTRODUCTION

Areas in psychology, sometimes known as approaches or themes (depending on the qualification being studied), are central to psychology; they are the paradigms used to try and explain the diversity of human behaviour. In England and Wales, OFQUAL (2014/2015) has deemed the areas we will examine in this chapter as core areas for A/AS and GCSE level. National 5 and Highers in Scotland cover Individual and Social behaviour, but within these broad areas also cover the core areas covered in this chapter. Other qualifications may vary, but all will include these core areas in some form.

It is unlikely that you will be asked to teach a whole core area during your teaching practice; you will most likely be given a topic or a series of lessons to plan and teach. However, an understanding of core areas of psychology is important in order for students to make connections between their learning and develop a synoptic level of knowledge and understanding. Therefore, it is vital that you understand where the topic or lesson you have been asked to teach fits into the broader picture. Make sure you have read the specification for the qualification you are teaching and understand the links between topics and core areas. It is important to know what students already know so that you can build on their prior knowledge. Although it is tempting, when time is short, to just focus on the minutiae of your lesson plan, it is necessary to apply a metacognition approach and consider where your lesson fits into the overall scheme of work (see Unit 2.2 on lesson planning and schemes or units of work in Capel *et al.* 2022).

The focus of this chapter will be on pedagogy – applying pedagogical theories to the core areas and suggesting practical activities to teach them effectively.

Core Areas in Psychology:

TEACHING AREAS OF PSYCHOLOGY

- Cognitive area
- Social area
- Developmental area
- Individual differences area
- Biological area

OBJECTIVES

By the end of this chapter, you should be able to:

- fully appreciate the centrality of areas of psychology to the teaching of psychology.
- have ideas for how to teach areas of psychology in an effective and inspiring way.
- understand relevant pedagogical theory and have the ability to apply it in your planning and teaching.
- have a plan to address any gaps in your own knowledge or weaknesses you have identified through self-evaluation.

Check which requirements of your initial teacher education programme relate to this unit.

3.1 COGNITIVE AREA

Teaching cognitive psychology lends itself to active learning techniques (see Unit 5.2 Active Learning in Capel *et al.* 2022) and most cognitive experiments can be repeated in the classroom with your students either taking the role of experimenter or participant. Recreating experiments will enthuse your students and expand their understanding. It does not have to be a large-scale research project; mini-practicals are the best way to accommodate research skills into a limited time frame, for example the Stroop effect (1935) is a very reliable and simple experiment to carry out; all you need are two word lists (about 10-15 colour words (can be repeated)), one where the colour of the ink and the meaning of the word are the same and the other where they conflict and a stopwatch. Simply time students with a stop watch identifying the colour of the ink the word is written in. You should find that students take longer when the colour and meaning conflict than when it is the same because reading has become an automatic process for them.

Cognitive load theory (Sweller 1988) is an apt theory to consider for teaching the cognitive area of psychology (see Chapter 2). The theory is based on the working memory model (Baddeley & Hitch 1974). As a psychology trainee teacher, you will have an advantage over trainees in other subject specialisms as you probably already have a good understanding of the limitations of human memory from your undergraduate study.

There are three main types of cognitive load – intrinsic, extraneous and germane. Your role as a teacher is to help students to manage their cognitive load to achieve effective learning.

Intrinsic cognitive load refers to the relative difficulty or complexity of what you are asking your students to learn. Teaching new concepts or ideas will always lead to a relatively high level of intrinsic cognitive load. However, it can be managed by breaking the information down into manageable chunks. Miller's Magic 7 (1956) suggests that the capacity of short-term memory is between five and nine items, but this can be extended by chunking information together. Think carefully about the amount of new information, such as key terminology, research methods or studies, you will be presenting in a lesson and try to limit it to between five and nine chunks of information. It is also useful to break any instructions down step by step, e.g. how to carry out a replication of an experiment, bullet point the procedure, to further reduce intrinsic cognitive load. Baddeley and Hitch (1974), with their working memory model, showed that the working memory has separate stores: the visuo-spatial sketchpad and the phonological loop. Their dual task experiments showed that if information is visual and auditory, it does not interfere with memory retention in the same way that two visual or two auditory tasks would. Therefore, a good way to present new information would be through an annotated diagram. Furthermore, if a diagram is used it is good practice to embed any description rather than providing a key as that adds to the cognitive load.

For example, when teaching the working memory model (see Figure 3.1):

- Get students to draw an annotated diagram from notes (words and pictures, dual processing).
- Add a third level of processing by asking them to explain the process to their partner, whilst tracing the pathway with their finger (tactile).
- For homework, ask them to explain the model to a family member.
- Test knowledge and understanding at the start of the next lesson, for example ask them to sketch the diagram from memory or give an examination question.

Extraneous cognitive load refers to factors outside of the task or information to be learnt which may provide a distraction. Sometimes, the teacher can unwittingly add to the extraneous cognitive load by including information or instructions that are overly complicated and unnecessary. When you write a lesson plan, review it and ask yourself whether everything you have included is strictly necessary, for example have you included anything not on

■ ■ ■ ■ TEACHING AREAS OF PSYCHOLOGY

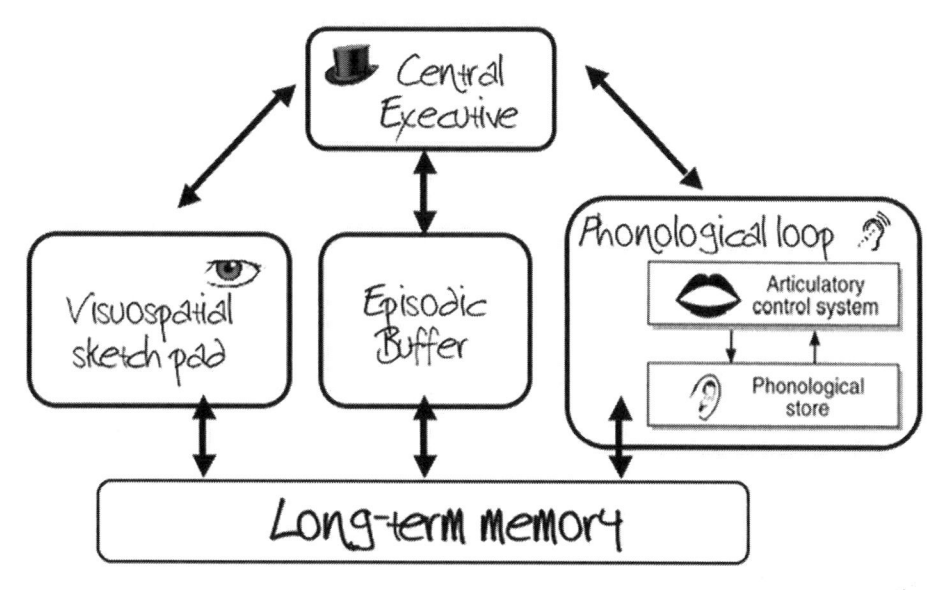

Figure 3.1 Working memory model – Use this to practice dual coding with your students when teaching memory (Baddeley & Hitch 2000, https://en.wikipedia.org/wiki/File:Baddley%27s_Model_of_Working_Memory.png)

the specification you are teaching. Her Majesty's Chief Inspector (HMCI) raised concerns about low-level disruption in English schools in his Annual Report 2012, stating that it was a serious impediment to learning and it adds to the extraneous cognitive load. Effective classroom management techniques, such as effective use of seating plans, moving around the classroom and using your voice to good effect, are central to reducing extraneous cognitive load. Consider the use of electronic devices by students too, always be guided by school/college policy, but it is reasonable to ask students to switch off and put away devices when you are presenting important, new information, to reduce extraneous cognitive load.

Germane cognitive load is the construction of schemata and this is a desirable form of cognitive load. This is when deep learning is occurring (see Chapter 2).

When you are planning your lessons, consider whether the new information, such as key terminology, research studies or theories, requires your students to assimilate knowledge into an existing schema or requires, or through the process of accommodation to radically alter or build a new schema, as in the example above. You will then be considering the germane cognitive load of your lesson.

Now undertake Task 3.1.

DEBORAH GAJIC

> ### Task 3.1 **Plan a lesson**
>
> Using the format you have been given by your training school or institution, write a 60-minute lesson plan to introduce the cognitive area of psychology. Make sure you incorporate the principles of cognitive load theory when considering how much new knowledge to include, to ensure you do not overload students with new information.
>
> Think about how you will enable rehearsal so that information is transferred to students' long-term memory. Remember to focus on what you want the students to learn from your lesson and include lots of opportunities for activities. Think about how you will demonstrate that the students have learnt what you wanted them to, so embed some type of low stake assessment such as quiz questions.
>
> You could highlight the possible intrinsic, extraneous and germane cognitive load on your lesson plan too. Think about the strategies you will employ for classroom management to minimise extraneous cognitive load.
>
> A simple questionnaire to students at the end of a lesson might be useful in assessing the success of your planning.

3.2 SOCIAL AREA

This area examines how our behaviour is influenced by other people and the situations we find ourselves in. Allport in 1924 suggested that behaviour results from social interactions between individuals, and he covered topics such as emotion, conformity and effects of an audience on others. It is this viewpoint which underpins a large proportion of current thinking. Common topics studied in psychology courses include conformity (Asch 1951), obedience (Milgram 1963) and conformity to social roles (Zimbardo 1973).

A core study that is covered in most social psychology courses is the classic Milgram (1963) study of obedience. In this section, we will consider how to effectively teach Milgram, but could be used for any study or area of psychology, using Barack Rosenshine's (2012) ten instructional principles, which he argues are used by master teachers:

- Begin each lesson with a short review.
- Present new information in steps and allow opportunity for student practice.
- Question all students.
- Provide models.
- Guide practice.
- Check understanding.
- Obtain a high success rate before continuing.
- Scaffold difficult tasks.
- Set independent work and monitor to ensure completion.
- Engage in weekly and monthly reviews.

It is important to stress that no one will be expecting you to use all ten principles in every lesson. Lessons should be seen as a series of linked learning opportunities rather than discrete entities. This section will focus on Rosenshine's principles as they apply to pedagogical theory and practice.

3.2.1 Question All Students

It is good practice not to rely on 'hands up' as the same few students will offer an answer. Try to keep a mental tally, or simply tick the names off your seating plan to ensure all students have been asked at least one question during a lesson. Use prior knowledge of student ability to ensure that you target questions to the appropriate students, but do not be afraid to challenge. For example, you could use bronze, silver and gold questions which represent increasing levels of challenge. A bronze question could test recall of facts, for example how many of Milgram's participants went up to 450 volts? A silver question could look for deeper understanding, for example why was it necessary for Milgram to deceive his participants about the true aim of his research? Finally, a gold question could present a greater challenge, for example is Milgram's research ethically defensible? Can you think of a better, more ethical way to study obedience? Another idea is to use 'phone a friend', if a student does not know the answer they are allowed to nominate three other students to answer for them. They must then choose what they think is the best answer and explain why they think it is the best.

There are numerous techniques to ensure all students answer questions, random name generators, lolly pop sticks, etc.; find ones you and your students are comfortable with. If all students realise that they can be called upon to answer a question every lesson, it will increase attention and decrease social loafing, where students simply rely on the more outgoing students to answer for them. This will ensure that students are fully engaged with your lesson as they are aware they must pay attention as they could be called upon to answer a question at any time.

3.2.2 Provide Model Examination Answers

Students really appreciate model examination answers. This is because many students lack confidence and feel like they do not know where to start and that their answers will not be good enough. Models can demonstrate that the requirements are not as complex as they thought. Many awarding bodies provide these on their websites, or you can write your own. However, some students just file them away without really reading them and understanding what makes a good answer. One possibility is to make your model answers into a cloze activity by removing key words, the students then need to fill in the missing words. You can differentiate this activity by either providing the list of missing words or not. This ensures that the students fully engage with the material to complete the activity. Another possibility is to ask students to highlight different sections of the answer, which helps to reduce the intrinsic cognitive load by breaking it down into chunks, for example all the descriptive material, all the evaluation, all the application or specialist terminology. The teacher could model this using a visualiser (or software) to project an answer onto the whiteboard and annotate, before the students do it.

Check understanding and obtain a high success rate before continuing.
How do you know students have learnt what you wanted them to learn? An ineffective teacher might ask 'Are there any questions?' at the end of the lesson and assume that if there are no questions everyone understands the content of the lesson. Students need targeted questions that check for understanding throughout the lesson. An effective teacher uses this feedback to assess the students' level of knowledge and understanding and gauge whether the new information has been successfully transferred into long-term memory. This is known as formative assessment, see Chapter 9.

Threshold concepts are an important consideration to ensure student understanding (see Chapter 2):

> A threshold concept can be considered as akin to a portal, opening up a new and previously inaccessible way of thinking about something. It represents a transformed way of understanding, or interpreting, or viewing something without which the learner cannot progress.
>
> (Meyer & Land 2003, p.1)

When teaching Milgram, there are a number of threshold concepts which students need to grasp before they can move on, some examples could include the agentic state, ethical guidelines, social support, situational and individual explanations for obedience etc. It is important to ensure that all students have mastered these concepts before moving on.

3.2.3 Guided Practice and Scaffolding Difficult Tasks

The social aspect of learning involves the teacher supporting and guiding the student until they have gained the knowledge or skills being taught. Vygotsky (1978) defined the zone of proximal development as the difference between what a learner can do without help and what he or she can do with help. Vygotsky (1978) views interaction with peers as an effective way of developing skills and strategies. He suggests that teachers use cooperative learning exercises where less competent students develop with help from more skilful peers – within the zone of proximal development.

Vygotsky (1978) believed that when a student is in the zone of proximal development for a task, providing the appropriate assistance will give the student enough of a 'boost' to achieve the task. Scaffolding is a term which describes the kind of help a teacher or more advanced peer will give to a student in the zone of proximal development.

■ ■ ■ ■ **TEACHING AREAS OF PSYCHOLOGY**

One way to scaffold is to provide writing frames for extended writing tasks. This enables the student to work within their zone of proximal development. For example, 'Discuss Milgram's research into obedience'. Students could be provided with a detailed plan which suggests content and breaks the task down for them, including the allocation of marks for the assessment objectives, for example how many marks for description, how many marks for evaluation. Advice about how to elaborate evaluation points using techniques such as PEEL technique (point, example, evaluation and link) could be included. Students could even be given the main points to include in their work. The problem that many teachers have is that they fail to remove the scaffolding and students then find it difficult to think for themselves and tackle questions in examinations. Scaffolding should be removed gradually, for example by giving a bullet point plan and eventually just a few general pointers, to build up student confidence so that early in their course of study writing plans contain a lot of detail and that level of detail is gradually reduced until students no longer need a writing frame.

Now undertake Task 3.2.

Task 3.2 **Design a writing frame (see Chapter 2)**

Read Wray and Lewis (undated) on different types of writing frames and make notes about the structuring of writing frames appropriate to the lessons you are teaching.

Choose a past examination paper's extended writing question on social psychology from the specification you are teaching.

Design a detailed writing frame to enable students to answer this; you will need to look at the mark scheme and examiners' report to enable you to do this. In particular, you should pay attention to the allocation of marks for the assessment objectives, the suggested content and any comments made about common errors made by students when answering this question. Ask your mentor to check this for you.

Now try to write other two versions, each one including slightly less detail. This activity will help you to reflect on how to successfully scaffold learning and how to gradually reduce the scaffolding to encourage independent thought.

3.3 DEVELOPMENTAL AREA

The developmental area emphasises the importance of understanding the changes in behaviour through the lifespan from birth to death. However, most psychology courses tend to focus on the changes that occur during early childhood and adolescence. This area assumes that development is an on-going process and that changes occur over a person's lifetime as a result of inherited factors and/or lifetime experiences (nature/nurture) and all individuals go through the same stages, in the same order, if not at exactly the same ages.

DEBORAH GAJIC

If you are teaching developmental psychology to adults, their life experience is a definite bonus. They will really relate to the area and be happy to share their own experiences. Younger students might find it more difficult to engage with this area. It is important to recognise when planning and teaching this area that it can be socially sensitive for many as not all families and childhoods are happy. It is important to understand socially sensitive research as a teacher, to ensure you do not inadvertently upset or offend students and leave yourself open to parental complaints. Psychology does have many areas and topics that could cause issues, so be mindful of this in your planning (see Chapter 5 on Ethics). Socially sensitive research is defined by Sieber and Stanley (1988) as research where there are potential social consequences for the participants, or the groups of people represented by the research.

Sieber and Stanley (1988) outline four groups that may be affected by psychological research:

1. Members of the social group being studied such as racial or ethnic groups. For example, Rutter's (1998) research on Romanian orphans.
2. Friends and relatives of those taking part in the study, particularly in case studies, where individuals may become famous or infamous. For example, Genie's mother (Curtiss 1977), who may have been just as much as a victim of an abusive and domineering husband.
3. The research teams. There are examples of researchers being intimidated because of the line of research they are in. For example, research that utilises animals such as Harlow's monkeys (1958).
4. The institution in which the research is conducted. For example, university departments which carry out animal research are often the target of Animal Rights activists.

If you are teaching 'attachment', you need to be very aware of these factors and ensure you refer to the critiques of the research throughout your teaching, which will also increase your students' skills of critical analysis. Before you begin planning this topic ask your mentor or the class teacher if there are any issues you need to be aware of, such as looked after children, domestic violence and deceased parents, you may also need to check with the head of year or pastoral support too. This is a topic which requires sensitive treatment and understanding from the teacher. Some students might want to confide in you about family issues; do not promise to keep secrets; it could be a safeguarding issue, which you must by law refer to the safeguarding lead in your school or college. As a trainee teacher, you are not a member of staff and you must refer issues like this to appropriate school staff. Explain this to the student.

Task 3.3 is an ethical and safe way to introduce the topic of developmental psychology. It enables students to reflect on parenthood and how parents

TEACHING AREAS OF PSYCHOLOGY

> ### Task 3.3 **Egg baby**
>
> This task enables your students to experience looking after something in an ethical way, to simulate parenthood.
>
> Ask your students to bring in a hard-boiled egg and decorate it in any way they choose. The egg is their baby; they must take it everywhere with them and keep it safe. If they need a night off, they must find a babysitter. Students could take photographs of themselves and their egg in unusual situations; you could even offer a small prize for the most inventive. At the end of the week, students can discuss their experiences and relate them to real-life parenthood.

influence development, without the need to reflect too much on their own experiences, which might be painful or uncomfortable for them.

Now undertake Task 3.3.

A popular core study is Bowlby (1946) and his theories of monotropy and maternal deprivation. This research is socially sensitive as it is very much a child of its time. It is based on the concept of a nuclear family, with mother as caregiver and father as breadwinner. Of course, the research lacks temporal validity as society has changed since the 1940s, especially family structures. Families today and the families of many of the students you teach will not fit this narrow ideal. Furthermore, the concept that childhood trauma will have lifelong effects is very deterministic and could be very concerning for some of your students. Bowlby's (1946) research is ethnocentric and is based on Western ideals of family structure and child-rearing practices.

Promote individual, social and cultural diversity in your teaching by referring to other family structures (e.g. one-parent families, extended families, matriarchal families, looked after children) and make sure you do not promote the Western nuclear family as the ideal family form. Find more recent research that looks at family diversity to extend your students' knowledge. The work of Van Ijzendoorn and Kroonenberg (1988) examines cross cultural differences in attachment styles and is useful as it demonstrates that these differences are due cultural variations in child-rearing styles and not necessarily good or bad parenting. If you are teaching Rutter's (1998) study on Romanian orphans, consider the possibility that you could have students in your class who are of Romanian descent. This means that you must be careful to ensure any critique is of the Romanian government at the time and not a critique of Romanian culture or the Romanian people. Many of the film clips you will find depicting Romanian orphanages after communism fell in 1990 are very hard hitting and upsetting, so carefully consider if they are necessary and add to the learning experience. Finally, focus on the positive, look for examples of people who have overcome difficult upbringings and been successful in life.

Now undertake Task 3.4.

DEBORAH GAJIC

> **Task 3.4 Family structures and life choices**
>
> Make a list of all the different types of family structures you would expect to find in a typical class of 30 students.
>   Reflect on your own upbringing. To what extent has it influenced your life choices and chances?
>   What family issues do you think you might encounter in your teaching practice? How will you deal with them? (This will become very important in your role as a pastoral tutor.)
>   You could undertake some research into this by interviewing pastoral staff; this would be very useful if you have ambitions to further your career into pastoral care.
>   Write up your notes and keep your findings in mind when deciding on the content of lessons.

3.4 INDIVIDUAL DIFFERENCES AREA

The individual differences approach takes an idiographic approach and focuses on the richness and diversity of individuals' experiences and lives.

The development of psychometric tests suggested that all human characteristics could be measured and quantified. The measures gained from one person are different to those gathered from another and are apparent in their behaviour. This area also allows us to understand how abnormal behaviour arises such as phobic behaviours, criminal thinking patterns, intelligence and developmental disorders such as autism (Baron-Cohen 1997).

Now undertake Task 3.5.

> **Task 3.5 Psychometric tests**
>
> Look at Beck's depression inventory as an example of a psychometric test.
>   https://www.ismanet.org/doctoryourspirit/pdfs/Beck-Depression-Inventory-BDI.pdf
>   Evaluate the test:
>
> Consider the individual questions
> The scoring system
> Reliability and validity
> Ethical issues
>
> Write your assessment of the test. Make notes about how you would introduce these aspects of psychometric tests to your students.

The way we discover things about individuals is through questioning, and questioning is a key skill for a teacher. Black and Wiliam (2003) found that on

TEACHING AREAS OF PSYCHOLOGY

average a teacher waits less than 1 second for students to answer questions before giving the answer themselves. This leads to questions and answers being rather superficial. Therefore, think about the questions you are asking, plan questions and follow up questions. Inform students that you do not expect an immediate answer, give them thinking time. Think, pair, share is a good strategy for this. For example, you could ask students to think about the issues with Beck's depression inventory, ask them to discuss it with a partner and then the whole class could share their ideas with the teacher acting as a scribe and recording all the points on the board.

Teachers often rely too much on volunteers, which means much of the class is disengaged. Instead try no hands-up techniques; students cannot shout out or put their hands up to indicate that they know the answer to the question. The teacher chooses students to answer questions; this really keeps them on their toes! Students can use phone a friend if they are really struggling. This empowers a struggling student, who does not have the answer to your question, by asking them to choose three students, who do have an answer ready, to give their answers and then the struggling student chooses the 'best' answer and explains the reasons for their choice.

Follow-up questions can be used to extend students; they can be as simple as asking them to explain their answers. For example, 'Why does that matter?', 'What are the implications of this?', 'What practical applications might this have?' Or Pose-Pause-Pounce-Bounce which is a questioning technique which elicits deeper thinking. The teacher poses a question; pauses to allow suitable thinking time; pounces on one student for an answer; and finally bounces the answer to another student who builds on the response.

Now undertake Task 3.6.

Task 3.6 **Questioning strategies**

- Choose a topic or study you are teaching in the concept area 'Individual Differences'.
- Research Black and Wiliam's (2003) work questioning further.
- Write a set of questions and questioning strategies that you will use in your lessons. Write the rationale for your choices. Refer to the learning theories in this book and in Capel *et al.* (2022).

Think and make notes about:

- How long will you wait for an answer?
- What types of questions will you ask?
- Are they meaningful?
- How will you ensure all students answer questions?
- Any follow-up questions?

DEBORAH GAJIC

3.5 BIOLOGICAL AREA

This area, as the name suggests, focuses on the biological explanation of human behaviour. Of particular importance are the influences of genes, biological structures, neurochemistry and evolution.

Students often find the biological area challenging, especially if they are studying psychology alongside humanities subjects, rather than sciences. One way to address this issue is through active learning techniques (see Section 3.2 cognitive area). As the Chinese proverb says, 'I listen and I forget, I see and I remember, I do and I understand'.

Making brain models out of Playdoh is a great way to get active. Give students a diagram of the brain and ask them to make a 3D model, using different colours of Playdoh for each brain lobe; they can make labels out of paper and cocktail sticks. If you are teaching Sperry's (1968) split brain research, students can perform brain surgery with a plastic knife and sever the corpus callosum between the two hemispheres. Another way to model the brain is by making a jelly or blancmange brain. Brain jelly moulds are generally available from shops around Halloween. A jelly brain makes a good talking point at open evenings too. (Ask your mentor if you can attend open evenings.) Having brain models helps students to visualise brain areas in three dimensions; at open evenings, it helps to reinforce the concept that psychology is a scientific discipline and dispel common myths about psychology as an 'easy' option.

Now undertake Task 3.7.

Task 3.7 **Playdoh brains**

Make your own Playdoh.
Eight tablespoons of plain flour
Two tablespoons of salt
One tablespoon vegetable oil
60 ml of warm water
Food colouring

Mix all the ingredients together in a bowl or food processor, dust your worktop with a little flour and knead until it forms a smooth ball. Store in an airtight container or plastic bag in the fridge until needed. It will keep for a couple of months.

Using Playdoh, as mentioned above, either get students to model and label brains of carryout brain surgery, for example Sperry (1968) split brain research.

If you are teaching two different classes, you could carry out some research, teach one class with Playdoh models and the other with paper diagrams, and then see which group does better in their end of topic test. You could also ask students which they prefer and why. In your evaluation, think about the strengths and limitations of using active techniques in your teaching.

TEACHING AREAS OF PSYCHOLOGY

These suggestions will increase your students' knowledge and understanding and their ability to recall information by using dual processing. Dual processing was first suggested by Allan Paivio (1971) as a way to facilitate learning by using a combination of words and images.

If you run out of inspiration about how to teach this area, it is a good idea to try and enlist the help of a friendly biologist. You could observe a practical biological lesson or ask for their ideas on how to teach a topic or study in an active way. Observing lessons in other subjects is always beneficial whilst on teaching practice; it will give you a wealth of different ideas and approaches. It is especially valuable as you will rarely get the chance to do this once qualified (see Unit 2.1 on lesson observation in Capel *et al.* 2022).

Now undertake Task 3.8.

Task 3.8 **Core study mapping**

If possible, undertake this activity with other trainee psychology teachers. Examine the specification for the qualification you are currently teaching. Map the core research studies mentioned in the specification to the five areas in psychology. For each research study, explain why it fits into the area and if there is any overlap with the other areas of psychology.

3.6 SUMMARY AND KEY POINTS

You should now:

- fully appreciate the centrality of areas of psychology to the teaching of psychology.
- have ideas for how to teach areas of psychology in an effective and inspiring way.
- understand relevant pedagogical theory and have the ability to apply it in your planning and teaching.

Check the requirements of your initial teacher education programme to see which have been addressed in this unit.

FURTHER RESOURCES AND WEBSITES

Required content for GCE A Level Psychology in England. Check for information about devolved Nations content.
https://www.gov.uk/government/publications/gce-as-and-a-level-for-science   Accessed 16/6/20

DEBORAH GAJIC

The British Psychological Society
www.bps.org.uk Accessed 16/6/20

The Association for the Teaching of Psychology
www.theatp.uk Accessed 16/6/20

Stroop effect resources
https://faculty.washington.edu/chudler/words.html Accessed 17/6/20

Article on the importance of questioning
https://impact.chartered.college/article/doherty-skilful-questioning-beating-heart-pedagogy/ Accessed 7/10/20

OFSTED report on the impact of low-level disruption
https://assets.publishing.service.gov.uk/government/uploads/system/uploads/attachment_data/file/379249/Below_20the_20radar_20-_20low-level_20disruption_20in_20the_20country_E2_80_99s_20classrooms.pdf Accessed 7/10/20

For information on Questioning and active learning which extends what is in this chapter, we recommend you read Units 5.2, 5.5 and 5.7 on active learning and communicating with students, In the core textbook for the Learning to Teach series: Capel, S., Leask, M. and Younie, S. with E. Hidson and J. Lawrence (9th edn 2022) *Learning to Teach in the Secondary School: A Companion to School Experience*. Abingdon Routledge: Taylor Francis.

4 TEACHING RESEARCH METHODS

Deborah Gajic and Andy McCarthy

INTRODUCTION

Research methods underpin the understanding of psychology theory and research at all levels (Porter, Cartwright & Snelgar 2006). However, research methods and statistics courses are challenging classes to teach because of the technical complexity of the courses and lack of student interest (Ball & Pelco 2006). Many students (and teachers!) have a negative cognitive bias towards maths. The role of the teacher is to counter this bias and make research methods and statistics interesting and even fun, through active learning techniques.

Central to research methods is the concept of the scientific method. Based on the hypothetico-deductive model, theories are suggested, which are used to generate hypotheses, which are then tested by experimentation or observation and the theory is then supported or falsified. Students should have a basic understanding of the scientific method from their previous studies of key stage 3 and 4 Science. They should have encountered terms such as variables, reliability and validity, but you will need to refresh this knowledge.

Specialised terminology is very important in the study of psychology, some of the key terms used in research methods students will be encountering for the very first time. Some, for example random sampling, will have a different meaning from how they are used in everyday life. Random tends to be used very loosely in everyday life, for example 'that's random!' students need to learn that random in psychology refers to its statistical meaning, 'every member of the population has an equal chance of being selected', like the numbers in the National Lottery. It is a good idea to encourage students to build a glossary of these key terms.

The best way to teach research methods is through active learning. Students really enjoy recreating studies and carrying out their own research. However, as a teacher you have a professional duty to ensure all research is carried out to the highest ethical standards. (See Chapter 5 Ethics in Psychology Teaching.) Consider the characteristics of your students and the context of the school/college as some research which might seem ethical could have socially sensitive implications for some participants and in some settings. If in doubt, speak to your mentor before proceeding and always err on the side of caution.

OBJECTIVES

By the end of this chapter, you should be able to:

- understand and have ideas to teach experimental methods.
- understand and have ideas to teach non-experimental methods – naturalistic observation, self-report and correlational research.
- understand and have ideas to teach inferential statistics.

Check which requirements of your initial teacher education programme relate to this unit.

Now undertake Task 4.1.

> ### Task 4.1 Skills and knowledge audit
>
> Complete a personal skills and knowledge audit for research methods. Look at the research method requirements for the qualification you will be teaching, do a RAG (red/amber/green) assessment of your own level of knowledge and skill. For example, R = Red, this is an area that you identify as a major weakness, which you will need to address, A = Amber, you have some skills and knowledge, but need to practice or revisit, and G = Green, you are confident in your skills and knowledge in this area.
>
> Revisit your skills and knowledge audit at the end of this chapter.
>
> A recommended textbook for teachers is Coolican, H. (2018) *Research Methods and Statistics in Psychology*. Abingdon. Routledge.

4.1 EXPERIMENTAL METHODS

4.1.1 Experiments

Central to the scientific method is the experiment. In an experiment, the researcher must adhere to a set criteria: It must have an aim, follow scientific methodology, have IVs (independent variables), the 'cause' and DVs (dependent variables), the 'effect', and must test an experimental hypothesis, with falsification of the null hypothesis possible. It is a test of difference and generally has two conditions: the experimental condition and the control condition.

4.1.2 Writing Hypotheses

It is clear that students have difficulty writing hypotheses. This is not surprising as writing a hypothesis is tricky.

Your students will need lots of practice, and in the beginning, it will be helpful to give them writing frames as mentioned in previous chapters (see Wray and Lewis, undated, for examples). When they are confident, you could use a think-pair-share technique (see Table 4.1) using scenarios where they have to write the hypotheses and then swap with another pair to peer-assess their answers.

Table 4.1 Think, pair, share

Think-pair-share is a collaborative learning strategy where students work together to solve a problem or answer a question.
This strategy requires students to:

- think individually about a topic or answer to a question (think)
- share ideas with a partner (pair)
- share with the rest of the class (share)

Discussing with a partner maximises participation, focuses attention and engages students in comprehending the reading material.

Students need to ask themselves the following questions:

> Is the hypothesis directional or non-directional?
> Has there been previous research?
> Alternative or null hypothesis?
> Is it looking for a difference or correlation?
> What is being measured (DV)?
> How is the DV operationalised?
> What are the two groups (IV)?
> How is the IV operationalised? (Or co-variables if it is a correlation.)

4.1.3 Practicals in the Classroom

It has been argued (Ball & Pelco 2006) that traditional chalk and talk lessons where students have been treated as passive learners, create bored and unmotivated students who have negative attitudes towards research methods. Therefore, it is important that research methods classes are as stimulating as the non-research aspects of psychology so that students understand how to apply their knowledge to practical research.

Now undertake Task 4.2.

Task 4.2 **Ideas for practicals in the classroom**

Conduct an audit of the specification or topic you are teaching in your current teaching practice. Identify opportunities to increase student motivation and learning through conducting mini-practicals. For example, if you are teaching cognitive psychology, replicate Miller's Magic 7 (1956), put students into small groups, with one student acting as the researcher and the others as participants. The student researcher will read lists of ever-increasing strings of digits (start at four digits and, finish with 12 digits) and ask their participants, individually, after each one is read out to recall the strings in the correct order and make note of the last string which was correct (should be about seven). Get students to collate their data and work out the class average of the number of digits correctly recorded. This can then be written up as a mini lab report using the writing frame below.

Mini lab report
Introduction: Review the original research and what it suggests about memory.
 Method: Describe in detail how you carried out your research. Include a step-by-step procedure that is easily replicated.
 Results: Summarise your findings, with a table of descriptive data and a suitable graph.
 Discussion: Explain your results in simple language and then compare your findings with the original research. Draw a conclusion.
 NB: If time is short, choose to simply write up the procedure or results section, or different groups can write up different sections.

4.1.4 Sampling Techniques

All experiments need participants, so it is useful to teach sampling techniques alongside the experimental method. Sampling is the process of selecting participants to study from the target population (a specified section of humankind). Since the results of the study on the sample will be generalised back to the target population (through inference), samples should be as representative (typical) of the target population as possible.

A good way to teach this is to sample the students in your class. For example, if you have 25 students in your class, you might decide you need a sample of ten:

- Opportunity sampling – select the ten students closest to you.
- Random sampling – put all the names on the register in a hat and draw out ten.
- Stratified sampling – split the names into two hats, boys and girls and draw five boys and five girls.
- Self-selected – ask for ten volunteers.
- Systematic – nth person on register.
- Snowball – select one student and then ask them to choose nine friends.

TEACHING RESEARCH METHODS

After each selection, ask your students to identify the strengths and weaknesses of each sampling technique (this works particularly well if a student who is selected by random sampling happens to be absent).

Now undertake Task 4.3.

Task 4.3 **Sampling**

Samples should be of a sufficient size to represent the variety of individuals in a target population, but not so large as to make the study uneconomical in terms of time and resources.

A fun way to demonstrate this in the classroom is by using small packets of Haribo Starmix or small boxes of Smarties. (Be aware of any allergies or religious concerns (Halal Haribo is available).)

Give each student a packet or box of sweets and ask them to draw up a table of the number of different colours or types of sweets and a total per packet. Ask them if they can draw any conclusions about the average number of sweets per packet, colours and types. They should realise that the sample (one packet) is too small to make any generalisations from. Then get them to pool their results in groups of four, working out the mean scores for types, colours and totals. They should now be more confident in drawing conclusions. Finally, get them to pool their data as a class, this will cause much confusion, especially if you have a large class, but will demonstrate the problems caused when samples become too large.

An extension activity would be to draw pie charts to represent their findings.

Can you think of any other activities that you could plan to further your students' understanding of sampling? Sharing ideas with fellow trainee teachers helps extend your repertoire of teaching approaches (pedagogical tools).

4.2 NON-EXPERIMENTAL METHODS

4.2.1 Naturalistic Observation

There are a number of common errors that students make in their study of research methods. Von Glaserfeld (1995) has argued that teachers must be concerned with what goes on in the student's head. Understanding the nature of these common errors and misconceptions is the key to effective teaching.

Students often mix up naturalistic observation as a research method and collecting data via observation in an experiment. In a naturalistic observation, the researcher does not manipulate the situation in any way; they simply observe what is happening in that situation or environment.

One way to teach observation would be to utilise a flipped classroom or learning approach. The concept of a flipped classroom is that homework becomes classwork and classwork becomes homework. It is a form of blended learning that increases differentiation and student independence. Students can learn the content at their own pace and in their own time. This frees up class time for more individualised input from the teacher for students. The teacher's role changes from sage on the stage, to guide on the side (King 1993).

There are four pillars of FLIP:

- Flexible Environment – As well as considering flexible space for learning, e.g. home and school, it is also necessary to give students different ways to learn content and achieve mastery. The teacher must be responsive to individual students and make adjustments where necessary.
- Learning Culture – Encourage students to learn independently, but scaffold where necessary. Have high expectations of your students in terms of work ethic.
- Intentional Content – Prioritise and curate relevant content for students to learn. Differentiate materials so that all students can access and learn at their own pace. Videos and narrated PowerPoints are particularly useful.
- Professional Educator – Give individual, small group and class feedback as required. Carry out formative assessment of students and give timely feedback. Develop your skills as a teacher through reflection and continuing professional development. www.flippedlearning.org

To flip the teaching of observation, you would first need to look at the specification you are teaching to determine exactly what students need to know in terms of content about observation. This is the intentional content, for example covert and overt observations, structured, unstructured and participant observations, time and event sampling, coding frames, controlled observations, increasing reliability of observations and ethical considerations.

The content you require students to learn independently could be as simple as reading the relevant chapter in the textbook, but students will be more motivated if you provide a range of tasks. A narrated PowerPoint and video content is useful as students can stop and rewind, therefore controlling the pace of their own learning. You could make use of the many live webcam streams available online; for example, Edinburgh Zoo has a choice of several different animals, which you can observe. An advantage of this is that all of your students are observing the same thing, so you can reinforce the importance of standardised procedures and how to achieve inter-rater reliability. Using webcams also demonstrates why time and event sampling are important, as a lot of time the animals will not be doing much at all. This activity also does not raise any ethical concerns. Using a range of different material and techniques to learn content and varying the context in which it is learnt, for example home or classroom addresses the flexible environment pillar of flipped learning.

To ensure students complete the work and have understood it, an online, self-checking, multiple choice quiz (MCQ) is a good tool, you simply then need to check that all students have completed the quiz (see examples in Chapter 11). Non-completion of the work should be dealt with by using the school/

TEACHING RESEARCH METHODS

college policy for non-completion of homework. It might be that you get the student to complete the non-completed work in class and then the class activity in a detention. By following up on students and ensuring they complete the work, you are establishing the learning culture that you want in your classroom and from your students. Independent learning is an important life skill which your students will need whether they go on to further education or the world of work.

The final pillar is your role as a professional educator. In class, students could now apply their knowledge of observation, with your role as a facilitator, offering advice and constructive feedback as required. You could put students into mixed ability groups and give them the task of designing an observation. This would be scaffolded by you. For example, you could give each group a scenario, for example observing how people spend their time at a gym or observing food choices in a supermarket. Students would need to decide on the type of observation and justify their choice, whether they would use time or event sampling, how they would ensure reliability, how they would collect their data, how they would ensure the research was ethical and finally when and where they would carry out the observation. The groups could then peer review each other's design before carrying out their research. The final lesson could be completing an examination style question under timed conditions. You could compare the results that students achieve on this flipped unit with traditionally taught units and evaluate the effectiveness of this approach. However, in teaching it is important to maintain variety in your approach to retain student attention and motivation, there is not a one size fits all approach, students are different, and therefore it is not recommended to flip every unit of learning.

Now undertake Task 4.4.

Task 4.4 **Using a flipped learning technique to teach observation**

Design a flipped unit of work for teaching observation. Make sure you include a narrated PowerPoint or video content. Use the information above and the four pillars of flipped learning.
  Consider:

- How do you ensure a flexible learning environment?
- What will be your intentional content?
- How will you develop independent learning and a learning culture in your students?
- What will you do about students who have not completed the work at home prior to the lesson?
- How will you check student understanding (formative assessment)?
- What classroom activities will you devise?

4.2.2 Self-reports

Self-report studies involve asking participants questions. These can be written in the form of a questionnaire or asked, orally, in an interview.

Any self-report is only ever as good as the questions asked. It is difficult to write good questions, and all surveys need a pilot study to check that the questions are unambiguous and easy for participants to understand. This increases the reliability and validity of the data collected.

Students find designing questionnaires and interview schedules challenging. One way to counter this is to provide lots of examples of good practice; however, providing a really bad questionnaire and asking students to find the errors is also an excellent teaching technique, as students find it less threatening. You can find lots of examples of really bad questionnaires online or you could write one yourself. If you decide to write one yourself, use some of the pitfalls to avoid when writing questions below as well as the more obvious errors such as asking for names, overlapping categories and overly personal questions.

A good questionnaire will include a variety of question types. Pitfalls to avoid when writing questions:

- Overuse of jargon, for example 'Do you know anyone that is protanopia?' (Colour blind in case you were wondering!)
- Emotive language, for example 'Do you approve of the oppressive uniform policy of this school?'
- Leading questions, for example 'Now that you know how bad smoking is for you, will you give up?'
- Double-barrelled questions, for example 'What is the fastest and cheapest way to get to London from here?'
- Double negatives, for example 'Would you agree that Kim Kardashian is not unattractive?'

Students also need to consider ethical issues when they design self-report studies and you have a professional duty to ensure their self-report questions are ethical before any research begins (see Chapter 5 on Ethics). A good way to increase student understanding of this is to get them to peer review each other's questionnaires before you check them.

Now undertake Task 4.5.

Task 4.5 **Design a self-report study**

During your training, you will probably be required to undertake some sort of research. Decide on a topic that interests you and is current in Education. The Times Educational Supplement (TES) is often a good place to look for inspiration or issues may arise from your teaching practice that you wish to investigate.

> Devise a schedule of questions for a questionnaire to be given to teachers. Ask your mentor to check your questionnaire and carry out a pilot study. Once you have collated your data, you may wish to carry out more in-depth interviews with a small number of teachers. Check with your tutor/mentor about the process for obtaining ethics approval. This might be from the headteacher or through the university system.

4.2.3 Correlational Research

Correlations look for a relationship between two variables. This is not to say that one variable causes another, simply that one variable varies in accordance with another. It is important to stress that correlations have two co-variables, not an independent variable and a dependent variable, because unlike experiments, correlations cannot show cause. For example, there is a relationship between the colour of grass and ice-cream sales. The more yellow the grass gets, the more ice cream is sold. However, in this case, the causal third variable is obviously temperature. Have a look at this website for further examples of spurious correlations https://tylervigen.com/page?page=1.

Students will need practice in drawing scatter graphs; as they are often asked to either draw or interpret graphs in examination questions, it also helps them understand the difference between a positive and negative correlation. It is important to emphasise that in positive correlations, both variables move in the same direction (either both increase or both decrease) and in a negative correlation, variables move in opposite directions (one increases, whilst the other decreases).

The best way to explain correlation coefficients is via a number line demonstrating that the closer the calculated value is to +1 or -1, the stronger the correlation is and the closer it is to zero, the weaker the correlation.

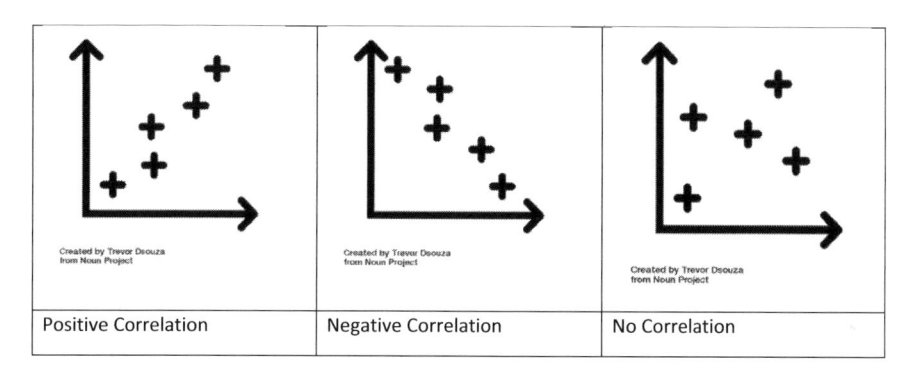

Figure 4.1 Types of correlations

Correlation coefficients are a source of confusion for students, especially when interpreting results from critical value tables. Critical value tables state that calculated values must be greater than or equal to the critical value in order to be significant (reject the null hypothesis). Students can be confused if for example the calculated value of Spearman's Rank order correlation co-efficient was −0.78 and the critical value was 0.648, they might think that −0.78 was less than the critical value, however, when a correlation co-efficient is calculated the minus sign (−) does not have a numerical value, it simply denotes the correlation is negative. In this example, the calculated result is significant and denotes a strong negative correlation.

Students also need the opportunity to practice writing correlational hypotheses. The word 'difference' should never be used in a correlational hypothesis, instead use the terminology 'relationship or correlation'. For example, there will be a relationship between length of legs (measured in centimetres) and the time taken to run 100 metres (measured in seconds) (two-tailed, non-directional) or there will be a positive correlation between length of legs (measured in centimetres) and the time taken to run 100 metres (measured in seconds) (one tailed, directional). Note that both co-variables need to be fully operationalised (stated in a measurable form).

You could use the Just in-time teaching technique (JiTT) to teach correlations. JiTT helps students achieve mastery by helping teachers engage students in their learning. Well-constructed JiTT assignments ask students to address open-end questions at a conceptual level and in writing (Novak *et al.* 1999). Students are asked to work in preparation for each class and this can be done in many ways, but one focus is provided here using the JiTT Warm-Up exercise (Novak *et al.* 1999).

For JiTT, Warm-Up exercises are delivered via online platforms and are made accessible several days before the lesson. Using this form of E-learning, the teacher identifies the objectives for the forthcoming lesson and the Warm Ups ask students to read the required resource in preparation for the lesson, for example the relevant section in a textbook. Students then answer two to four conceptual questions covered by the material in the reading; usually one question per objective (Novak *et al.* 1999); questions should take 15–30 minutes to complete. The submission of the answers is carried out electronically, for example e-mail or forum, the day before class. The teacher then reviews the answers and identifies which answers will be effective discussion points and any gaps in knowledge, and then constructs the lesson 'just-in-time'. The lesson provides for both good and confused aspects of answers to be displayed and discussed in relation to the learning objectives to ensure students have a good understanding of the material.

Now undertake Task 4.6.

> Task 4.6 **Design a lesson plan or series of lesson using JiTT**
>
> Things to consider:
>   What will you include in the Warm-Up Task?
>   What do you want students to know about correlations (use the awarding body's specification as a guide)?
>   How will you enable practice of writing correlational hypotheses, collecting data, drawing scatter graphs, calculating correlation coefficients and drawing conclusions?
>   How will you monitor student engagement?
>   How will you differentiate the activities?
>   How will students learn to apply this knowledge to assessments?
>   How will you measure student success?

4.3 INFERENTIAL STATISTICS

Motivation for learning statistics can be low because students perceive the topic as being unimportant if taught in isolation (Paxton 2006); this perception could be exacerbated if the link to research methods is not directly made (Petocz & Reid 2007). These challenges for students and their misconceptions of research methods may counteract the positive learning environment that teachers are attempting to create and further pose challenges for the teaching of research methods and statistics (Coetzee & Van der Merwe 2010). Therefore, statistics should always be taught in context and it is preferable to analyse data collected by students from their own or class research to maximise engagement.

There are two main types of statistics, descriptive and inferential. Descriptive statistics (to describe) are where a data set is summarised, for example a table of measures of central tendency and dispersion. A graph is another form of descriptive statistics. With this information, an 'eyeball test' can be carried out and an estimate made about what the data suggests and decide whether or not the data requires inferential statistical investigation. Students will have previous knowledge of descriptive statistics, but will not have used the same terminology, for example measures of central tendency (mean, median and mode) are simply known as averages at GCSE. They will also have prior experience of graphical display.

Inferential statistics are required because it is not scientific to simply claim one group to be faster than the other. Inferential means to 'infer' a conclusion from the data. This involves performing a statistical test to see if there is a significant difference between the two groups. A decision can then be made about whether to accept or reject the null hypothesis. Explaining the rationale behind inferential statistics and their importance to your students will aid their understanding.

4.3.1 Probability Testing

The probability figure (P) is the amount of data which can disagree with your hypothesis, yet still claim significance. So, for example testing a data set of 200 at 5% (P<0.05), 10 (5% of 200) pieces of data can disagree with the hypothesis, and the result can still be said to be significant. Students often struggle with this concept, turning it on its head and stating we are 95% confident that our results were due the influence of the IV, not due to chance, which makes it clearer. In your teaching, you could demonstrate some simple examples of probability to illustrate this point, for example if you toss a coin, what is the probability of it falling on heads, if you toss two coins what is the probability of them both falling on heads, what is the probability of it raining tomorrow, what is the probability of you becoming a parent in your lifetime etc.

4.3.2 Calculated Statistical Values and Critical Value Tables

When a statistical test is performed, it produces a calculated value. This value is then checked against a critical value table, for that test and shows if the findings are significant or not.

A common exam question is to be given the calculated value and be asked to comment on significance (students will need to be able to identify the level of significance, N or df value and one- or two-tailed test). Critical value tables are always supplied and the question will usually specify if the calculated value needs to be greater or equal to the critical value to be significant or less than or equal to the critical value to be significant.

Alternatively, students may receive a partially completed calculation table and be asked to complete it or substitute values into formulae. This means that students should have some practice at calculating inferential statistics in the classroom. Inferential statistics will make much more sense to students if you integrate them into your teaching when appropriate, rather than teaching as a separate stand-alone unit of work. For example, when teaching repeated measures design you could get your students to do the Stroop Effect experiment (see Chapter 3).

When the data is collated, you could demonstrate how to calculate the Wilcoxon Test on the data, as this experiment is a test of difference, with a repeated measures design and generates ordinal data. You could also analyse the data using a Sign test by converting the data to nominal and simply recording whether participants took more (+) or less (−) time to complete condition B where meaning and colour conflicted.

If you are not confident in your own mathematical ability, always ensure that you have calculated the answer in advance. Break the formula and calculation down into easy steps and walk the students through the first few examples to build up their confidence.

4.3.3 Which Test to Use and Justifications

Qualifications vary on which statistical tests you should be familiar with. Always check what you should cover in the awarding body's specifications. Students are often asked which inferential test should be used and what the justification for using that particular test is. This knowledge will also be important if students are designing their own research and if they go on to study psychology at university, where they will need to be able to make and justify these decisions.

There are two types of statistical tests: non-parametric tests and parametric tests. The strongest type of test is parametric, but data must meet certain assumptions to use these tests. The data must be normally distributed, be at an interval or ratio level and have homogeneity of variances. Most of the data you would collect in a class practical would not meet these criteria so a non-parametric test would be more appropriate.

Students need the opportunity to practice choosing appropriate inferential statistical tests. An activity that is effective is to give students outlines of studies and ask them to decide which test is appropriate. To make a decision they need to decide:

- Is it a test of difference or relationship?
- Design: Independent Measures Design, Repeated Measures Design, Matched Pairs or Correlation
- Level of Data – Nominal, Ordinal, Interval

For example:
An experiment predicting that female IQ scores on a standard IQ test will be higher than males.
Test of difference (between males and females), Independent measures design (males and females), ordinal data (IQ test scores) = Mann Whitney U Test
An analysis of the relationship between happiness and self-esteem, predicting that the higher a person rated their own self-esteem (1-10), the higher they would rate their happiness (1-10).
Relationship, correlation (happiness and self-esteem), Ordinal data (scale 1-10) = Spearman's Rho
See Figure 4.2 for a handy table to help your students learn which inferential test is appropriate to use and the reasons for those choices.

To help your students learn this table, knowledge of which is often assessed in examinations, print out Figure 4.2 and a blank grid using the same template on A4 coloured paper. Cut up the complete table and attach Velcro to the back of the titles and test names, and stick the other side of the Velcro to the blank table. The task can be differentiated by giving weaker students the table with headings on, so they just have to place the tests in the right place and more

	Test of difference		Test of relationship
	Independent Measures	Repeated Measures or Matched Pairs	Correlation
Type of Data			
Nominal	Chi-Square	Sign Test	Chi-square
At least Ordinal	Mann Whitney U	Wilcoxon	Spearman's
Interval/Ratio	Unrelated t-test	Related t-test	Pearson's

Figure 4.2 Which statistical test and why?

able students can be given a completely blank grid. This can be used as a quick starter or plenary whilst you are teaching statistics and later as a revision aid.

4.4 SUMMARY AND KEY POINTS

During teaching practice, you will be delivering a pre-determined scheme of work, but later in your career, you will have more autonomy in devising schemes of work. There are three approaches to delivering research methods: (a) a stand-alone unit of work (b) integrated into topics as appropriate or (c) a hybrid approach, with some elements delivered as stand-alone units and some integrated into topics. Which you choose will depend on personal preference and the demands of the qualification you are teaching. Choice (c) enables the design of a spiral curriculum as advocated by Bruner (1960) which enables students to deepen their understanding when a topic is revisited. When planning lessons, always try to incorporate research methods to reinforce and further your students' understanding, this can be done by recreating the studies you are teaching in the classroom.

You should now:

- have a firm understanding of how to deliver research methods in an active and interesting way and an appreciation of common misconceptions and how to address them.

Check the requirements of your initial teacher education programme to see which have been addressed in this unit.

FURTHER RESOURCES AND WEBSITES

Spurious correlations https://tylervigen.com/page?page=1 Accessed 22/7/2020
Webcams to use for observation practice https://www.edinburghzoo.org.uk/webcams/panda-cam/ Accessed 6/11/20

More information on flipped learning https://www.flippedlearning.org Accessed 16/1/21

More information on JiTT
Brame, C. (2013). Just-in-Time Teaching (JiTT). Vanderbilt University Center for Teaching. Accessed 4/12/21 from https://cft.vanderbilt.edu/guides-sub-pages/just-in-time-teaching-jitt/.

5 ETHICS IN PSYCHOLOGY TEACHING

Jonathan Firth

INTRODUCTION

This chapter focuses on teaching research ethics: debates, discussions and difficulties.

Psychology is a research-based subject. As such, students of the subject need to engage with and understand research ethics. This understanding needs to cover two main areas:

- Students need to understand on a theoretical level what is acceptable and what is not. This understanding helps them to critique research studies, and to answer examination questions on ethical issues.
- Students need to have an awareness of the guidelines that they should follow when conducting their own practical work, even if submission of written-up report is not mandatory for their course.

As well as understanding research ethics within their course, students in your psychology classes will begin to develop an awareness of issues, which will serve them later in life, too (Hulme, 2014; McGovern, 2010). Indeed, Psychology as a school/college subject is one of the best vehicles for learning about key ethical debates and principles, which are relevant throughout society. Their competence with and sensitivity to these issues will serve them well in a great many future pathways, including research careers and further study but also careers in medicine, law, politics and many other areas (BPS, 2018).

This chapter explores some of the main techniques that you can use to teach research ethics with your class. It draws heavily on principles of learning and memory from cognitive psychology, considering the issue of what makes learning meaningful, well remembered, and transferable.

After all, the learners need to be able to remember what you have taught them and need to be able to access this knowledge and apply it in future situations

(Bransford et al., 2000). If this is achieved, then research ethics in psychology could be one of the most valuable things that they learn at school or college.

OBJECTIVES

At the end of this chapter you should be able to:

- explain the role of the BPS and ATP ethical guidelines in psychology teaching.
- be aware of engaging ways of teaching ethics in the classroom.
- consider and apply techniques for making this learning stick through the use of 'desirable difficulties' based on spacing and story.

Check which requirements of your initial teacher education (ITE) programme relate to this unit.
Now undertake task 5.1.

> Task 5.1 **Mind the gap**
>
> Having checked the requirements for your ITE programme to see which of them relate to this chapter, identify gaps in your knowledge and develop a plan to further develop your knowledge.

5.1 THE PRACTICE OF TEACHING RESEARCH ETHICS IN PSYCHOLOGY

5.1.1 Why Teaching Ethics Matters

Teaching ethics is part and parcel of good psychology teaching, just as ethical practice is fundamental to good science. Students need to know that ethical behaviour is not an add-on or extra – it is a part of the subject itself, and one that psychology researchers take very seriously indeed. We cannot conduct good psychological science without observing ethical practices (Rosenthal, 1994).

While this is true for many subjects, psychology has particular pressures that make ethics even more important. Firstly, our research is largely carried out on people rather than objects or chemicals, meaning that the ethical guidelines are wider and stricter, and the potential fallout of breaking the rules would be more harmful. In addition, in psychology, we often have to fight for our subject to be respected as a legitimate science (Jarvis, 2011). It is the newcomer in terms of the natural sciences, and is frequently not treated as a science subject at all.

■ ■ ■ ■ **ETHICS IN PSYCHOLOGY TEACHING**

This is unsurprising in a way, both because the subject is relatively new in comparison to the likes of Physics and Chemistry, and because of its broad scope which overlaps greatly with social sciences such as Politics and Sociology. Nevertheless, it is important that we as psychologists can demonstrate that we understand the scientific method and are meeting the strictest standards.

For practical purposes, many of the activities that you do with your students (such as those found throughout this book) rely on a code of ethics. This is often put into place by you as the teacher; you wouldn't set up a task that required students to do something harmful and dangerous. But as time goes on, students can learn to make these ethical judgements for themselves. Building in a discussion of ethics before starting a classroom practical can be a great way to develop ethical awareness among the class – and this is a skill that can transfer well to exam situations.

A failure to abide by standard ethical guidelines in our research and practice would stand to bring the subject into disrepute. It would also reflect badly on the teaching of the subject at school level. One example of this was a 2020 headline in The Times newspaper which claimed that Scottish school teachers were running unethical experiments in psychology classes, including (according to the journalist) "Lord of the Flies" experiments.

In reality, the claims were probably greatly exaggerated and reflected at most the ill-advised choices of a tiny number of teachers, but it is a good example of how even a few cases of bad practice can reflect badly on the profession and the subject as a whole. In the long term, this could make students and their parents wary of taking the subject.

Now undertake Task 5.2.

> Task 5.2 **Emphasis on ethics**
>
> Discuss with a peer what emphasis you would place on teaching ethics, and at what point in a Psychology course you would cover it. Engage with fellow trainee psychology teachers to discuss this issue.

5.2 BPS GUIDELINES

A code of ethics is a set of general guidelines that are followed by practitioners in a field. You are probably already aware of the British Psychological Society (BPS) from your previous studies; this is the professional organisation for psychologists in Britain, and is closely affiliated with other professional organisations elsewhere in Europe around the world. The BPS provides a set of ethical standards for psychologists to follow for such activities as therapy, research, and professional practice (e.g. as an educational psychologist). As a professional psychologist yourself, it would be useful to be aware of these (alongside the professional standards and guidelines specific to your role as a teacher). The BPS also provides a set of standards, which are specific to research (BPS, 2014), and it is these that we will focus on here.

Your role as a psychology teacher includes both setting up activities in such a way that research activities in your classroom meet these standards, and ensuring that students themselves come to learn the ethical standards such that they can critique their own work and that of others.

For example, students need to be able to:

- Identify ethical flaws in classic research studies such as the work of Asch (1951) and Milgram (1963);
- Identify flaws in their own research plans if they are engaged in practical/experimental work;
- Analyse ethical issues that are presented to them in tests and examination situations, for example via scenario questions;
- Show an ethical awareness as part of their broader psychological literacy.

The BPS 'Code of Human Research Ethics' is quite long and I won't reproduce it here; see the end of the chapter for resources (and ensure that you download and read the current version as it is updated every few years). However, the key points can be summarised as follows:

- Participants must consent to take part in research activities, and this consent should be *informed* – that is, they must understand what they are consenting to. In the case of children, parental consent is usually required.
- A briefing should be given before the start of the research task, and participants should be debriefed at the end.
- Participants in research activities should not be harmed (any risk of harm should be no greater than it would be in everyday life).
- Participants have a right to withdraw, even after the data gathering has finished.
- Participant data must be stored securely, avoiding any data loss or breaches.
- Participant data and related findings and conclusions must be kept confidential and anonymised such that it is not possible to identify individuals.

Most of these principles probably seem straightforward and self-evident, especially for new teachers who already have an Honours degree in Psychology. However, there are issues that arise that may not be as simple as all that. Whether our behaviour is ethical or not can be quite subjective; sometimes, one teacher may *believe* that they are behaving ethically, but another might disagree.

Now undertake Task 5.3.

ETHICS IN PSYCHOLOGY TEACHING

M | Task 5.3 **Ethical or not?**

For the following examples, consider whether the research described is acceptable. If not, what improvements could be made?

a. A group of psychology students have been carrying out experiments into the capacity and duration of working memory as a classroom practical. The teacher inputs the findings into a spreadsheet and saves this on the desktop of her school computer.
b. One student carried out a survey on relationship preferences among the school staff. Demographic questions were asked about a participant's teaching subject, age and gender.
c. A group of senior students are concerned about homophobia, and feel that awareness should be raised among younger age groups. To gather evidence, they carry out a survey of younger students (with a mean age of 12). Questions including asking how comfortable they would be having a sleepover with a gay classmate.
d. A group of student researchers have designed a study based around an intelligence test. However, their psychology class is too small to study, and they also want naive participants. They therefore go to the classroom of the English teacher next door, and he agrees to let them carry out the test on his GCSE class of 25 students.

Using the examples above, make notes with reference to various ethical frameworks about what the ethical risks of these classroom activities are. Compare your assessment with my feedback below.
Feedback on Task 5.3

a. The task itself is relatively harmless, but the data has not been stored in a secure way. Remember that data protection and security is part of research ethics.
b. There could be concerns about investigating this topic within a school, where there are existing working relationships between students and staff. In particular, the demographic questions make it relatively easy to identify individuals, breaching their right to anonymity.
c. While the student researchers' intentions are laudable, there is considerable potential for upset and repercussions of this research. The participants are at an age where they may be feeling vulnerable or insecure about their sexuality, and may feel upset if questioned about it. A questionnaire that was not well designed could do more harm than good (e.g. by reinforcing homophobic stereotypes).
d. Teachers should not give consent on behalf of students, especially younger students; parental consent should be sought in advance. Presenting an experiment to the class without warning could make them feel pressured to take part. In addition, an intelligence test produces sensitive data that should be handled with considerable care if done at all.

Task 5.4 asks you to consider what systems for giving ethical approval to students' research projects would work in the school setting.

Now undertake Task 5.4.

> Task 5.4 **Case study 1: Ethics approval for students' research projects**
>
> In a university, there is outside scrutiny of research activities by an ethics board, rather than practitioners making the call about whether their own choices are ethical or not. However, in a school, such decisions are often made by the teachers. Freud High School recognised that there could be an issue with subjectivity when judging whether research projects carried out by a Psychology class were acceptable or not. To recreate the benefits of an ethics board, they decided to set up a panel to review ethics decisions, which included a psychology teacher, members of senior management and an invited academic.
> *Feedback on Case Study 1*

Consider the example above. Is there an issue in your school whereby you and the other teachers are responsible for both suggesting and approving student research projects? If so, would an outside voice be helpful? Perhaps you could look at setting up a formal or informal system whereby an independent colleague scrutinises these choices and provides feedback. This could be done as a partnership with another school.

5.3 THE ASSOCIATION FOR THE TEACHING OF PSYCHOLOGY (ATP) APPLICATION OF BPS GUIDELINES IN SCHOOLS AND COLLEGES

The BPS ethical guidelines discussed above are a central reference guide for psychology teachers in the United Kingdom, but because of the broad nature of Psychology as a discipline, they do not delve into all of the issues that school-based research faces. For example, they do not suggest research areas that should be avoided, and do not provide specific guidance for parental consent and data protection when gathering student data in a school setting.

Furthermore, they often assume that researchers will be adults and have at least a modicum of expertise in their area. Things are a little different when the researchers themselves are children or young people.

As a school teacher, you need to set some limits on what your students can research. Some of the specific major issues for school research studies include the following:

ETHICS IN PSYCHOLOGY TEACHING

- Could the materials included in the study be distressing to students, or distract them from their school work?
- Are students responsible enough to manage the sensitive data of their peers in a secure way?
- Could questions (e.g. in surveys) be too invasive for a school-aged group of participants?
- Is there a danger of coercion to take part, for example if an entire school class are used as participants in a study?
- How much information should be provided to parents in order for them to consent to their child's participation in an activity?
- Can teenagers who are in full-time education give informed consent for themselves?

To deal with these and other relevant issues, the Association for the Teaching of Psychology (ATP) has produced a guide which supports and extends BPS guidelines.

The ATP guidelines restrict certain things that would be acceptable for professional or degree-level psychology students. For example, school students should not carry out research on participants under the age of 16 at all, according to this code.

Now undertake Task 5.5.

Task 5.5 **Ethics in practical activities**

Consider the following question; discuss it with classmates or fellow teachers if you can, or note down your own response. The ATP guidelines rule out experimentation on under 16s, but sometimes Psychology is taught to students of age 15 or younger. Does this mean that the class cannot do practicals, which involve testing their classmates, for example administering a test of the capacity of working memory?

Feedback on Task 4

There should certainly be limits placed on what is done with under 16s, and this is a case where it is important to use your professional judgement. However, doing practicals is part of psychology as a subject as with any scientific subject. Also, there are certain things that are difficult to do by oneself – it is hard to self-administer a test of reaction time, for example. Remember that doing a classroom practical to help demonstrate a psychological phenomenon is a quite distinct thing from carrying out research where students are participants and data is gathered and published. Ethical practice is still important during practicals, but the context must be taken into account.

JONATHAN FIRTH

Now undertake Task 5.6.

> ### Task 5.6 Case study 2: Pitfalls and unintended consequences of experiments
>
> A school teacher is very interested in the psychology of sleep, and is covering this topic with a class of students aged between 13 and 14. He finds that the students are very keen to try out a practical that looks into their own consumption of caffeine and their sleep patterns. To do so, he gives each student a form to fill out on which they should fill in their consumption of caffeine and their bedtime/waking time each day for the following week. A few days later, a parent contacts the school to complain that their child was awake for most of the night as part of a school project after drinking several cups of strong coffee, and they demand an explanation.
>
> *Feedback on Case Study 2*
>
> Case study 2 helps to demonstrate some of the pitfalls of ethics in a school context. Students' enthusiasm to investigate new psychology topics can lead to unforeseen consequences. In this case, the teacher did not intend for the students to drink a lot of caffeine and stay awake late into the night. However, the students themselves interpreted the task as a chance to experiment with their own sleep cycles. This could have been anticipated and avoided. It is important for a psychology teacher to be crystal clear at the outset about what students can and can't do as part of one of their class projects. Remember that even discussing topics such as sleep could cause students to change their behaviour. For this task, it would have been better to gather the data retrospectively – that is, to ask students how many hours of sleep they got the night before. Your classroom activity can't affect something that has already happened.

5.4 SUGGESTED TEACHING ACTIVITIES

Many of the ideas discussed so far are worth raising with the students themselves. The psychological literacy that they will develop through discussing moral and ethical problems is invaluable. Here are three activities to try:

1. Set up a role play where one group of students act as an ethics board and another group provide suggested experiments for them to evaluate.

Divide the class into groups of four to five. Each student should write a short summary of what their experiment would involve, focusing on materials and procedure. The summaries of one group should then be swapped with those of another group (it doesn't matter if the groups have slightly different numbers of members). Each group then looks at the proposals and rates them, referring to BPS guidelines.

If you have time, students could write a short report as feedback on the proposals. To vary the activity, you could ask groups to write some proposals

ETHICS IN PSYCHOLOGY TEACHING

that they consider ethical and others that are clearly unethical! Alternatively, they could write proposals for studies that they actually intend to carry out. An optional follow-up would be for the students to respond to feedback by giving a short talk to the class, acknowledging the ethical weaknesses of their proposal and explaining how they would talk to it. The class could then take a vote on whether it would be accepted or not.

2. This activity involves showing students example studies in the form of a slideshow, with a one-sentence explanation of each one. In every case, there should be something unethical about the study – but it won't always be obvious. Students then have to decide for themselves what is wrong with the study (a bit like a 'spot the deliberate mistake' task).

It can be good to start with a few easy/obvious ones and then have the flaws become progressively more subtle. The task could be done in pairs or individually, and it might be better to write answers rather than having students call out. It could even be done as a form of test or quiz. If you like, real studies could be used (key studies from your course or recent examples from the BPS Research Digest), or alternatively you could devise fictional ones.

3. Presenting a range of ways to tackle a research problem, and asking pairs or groups to discuss and then pick one of the options. A good choice would be to discuss different methodologies for investigating the use of highlighting as a study strategy. This could be done in multiple ways, for example a lab experiment where one group uses highlighter pens and one does not, an interview study to find out about preferences, an observation of students at work in the school library/study area, and many others. Groups could discuss and debate the ethical pitfalls of each approach, and then make a collective decision about which option they would choose (this task could be tied together with a pre-exam lesson on effective study skills. The evidence suggests that highlighting is a popular but ineffective strategy; (Dunlosky et al., 2013).

Some other ways that you could consider presenting information about research ethics to the class include the following:

- A matching task where students have to pair up terms (e.g. informed consent, debriefing) with their definitions. A dictionary of psychology terms is a useful resource, here.
- A mini-lecture with slides that take learners through the process from a researcher's point of view, from planning a project and applying to an ethics board right through to publishing a paper. This could be supported with a short video interview of a psychology researcher.
- A presentation that makes use of 'think-pair-share' to address how a researcher would tackle a specific set of research questions or dilemmas.

5.4.1 Making Learning Stick

It is all very well to tell learners about research ethics – but will they be able to remember and use what you teach them? If they don't retain the information in long-term memory, there is little point in doing it. To achieve this, it is important that new learning is consolidated. We will now consider ways of making sure that what your class has learned about research ethics 'sticks' in the sense of becoming usable knowledge that they can draw on over the long term.

5.4.2 Timing of Practice (see also Chapter 2)

Initial learning is followed by a period of forgetting in long-term memory, as can be seen from Ebbinghaus's (1885/1964) forgetting curve. A popular assumption among educators is that consolidation should happen as soon as possible, before forgetting becomes too severe. And while that is true to an extent, there is an important caveat drawn from cognitive psychology – a period of forgetting actually makes learning better in the long run (Bjork, 2011). That is to say, it can be better to delay consolidation than to do it too soon. This phenomenon is known as the spacing effect. Essentially it means that spacing out one's practice over time is more effective – it will lead to better learning.

Researchers have been able to specify this further:

- It is important to consolidate the material well in the first study session, ideally with learners recalling it correctly at least three times in the short term (Rawson & Dunlosky, 2011).
- After that, spacing can be gradually increased (e.g. one day, followed by one week, followed by one month), but it is also effective to employ a 'fixed schedule' of spacing, such as a review activity once per month (Küpper-Tetzel *et al.*, 2014; Roediger & Karpicke, 2011).

5.4.2.1 How To Do It

The spacing effect is a natural choice to apply to the study of ethics, not least because ethical issues crop up throughout any Psychology course. It is probably best not to worry too much about the exact timing of each practice session, as long as you ensure that the original material had been studied and practised thoroughly, and that subsequent delays last for at least a few days.

If, for example, ethical principles are raised and practised within every topic that you study, then students will be returning to these and consolidating them once every few weeks. This would be a highly suitable delay to build in for practising this material.

5.4.2.2 Ensuring a Meaningful Narrative

The spacing effect is often studied via laboratory experiments with sets of unconnected facts. What difference might it make if we apply it to richly meaningful and interconnected materials? Richly meaningful information is more slowly forgotten. As such, the forgetting that occurs after initial learning will typically be less rapid, and therefore consolidation can happen a bit later and still have the same effect.

Consider how easy it is to remember a story or anecdote that a friend or colleague tells you. Even if you don't remember the words (which quickly decay from working memory), you retain the gist (stored in semantic long-term memory). And the more interesting, funny or peculiar the story, the easier it is to remember.

Stories have been described as 'psychologically privileged' information (Willingham, 2004), more likely to gain our focus and be remembered. They are easier to understand and retain than simple lists of facts for a number of reasons:

- Their richly interconnected structure makes the information easy to organise.
- Memory for the information is supported and scaffolded by our existing schema knowledge about the world.
- They prompt us to make predictions and inferences, leading to better recall. As Bartlett (1932) put it, we make an *effort after meaning*.
- Surprising and emotional information is also easier to remember than neutral information, as shown by the phenomenon of flashbulb memory.

5.4.2.3 How To Do It

It's actually quite easy to utilise stories as part of your methods of teaching ethics. Perhaps you are familiar with the vignettes used by Kohlberg (1963) to test children's level of moral development. In one example, 'the story of Heinz', participants had to consider the case of a man who stole from a pharmacy in order to get medicine for his wife who was severely ill. They were then asked to consider whether this was morally justified. A variation of Kohlberg's vignettes could be used in class, asking students to discuss and debate whether in the case of studies like Milgram's obedience experiments, the end justifies the means.

Discussion of moral ideas can help learners to take in and consolidate the new knowledge. Why? According to Mayer's (2009) select-organise-integrate (SOI) model, the processing of new information in working memory provides opportunities for learners to integrate the information with what is already in LTM. Note that this is similar to the classic Atkinson-Shiffrin 'modal model' (1968), but with a key difference – learning happens by actively and meaningfully connecting information to older learning. The SOI model is more sophisticated and up-to-date than the modal model, and better reflects what actually happens in a classroom.

Now undertake Task 5.7.

> Task 5.7 **Ethical vignettes**
>
> Find (or compose) a short set of ethical vignettes to debate with a class. In each case, the research should provide clear benefits, such as finding out something previously unknown, but should have breached ethical principles in some way.

5.4.3 Variation and Transfer

It is not enough for learners to simply retain what they have learned in their heads. They also need to be able to *transfer* what they have learned to new situations which are subtly different. For example, students may need to apply an ethical principle learned in the context of a classic psychology study when reading a newly published piece of psychology research.

This ability is what psychologists call transfer of learning. As described by Barnett and Ceci (2002), transfer is easier to do in the original learning context, and harder when out of context. But 'context' includes several elements, and there are therefore several things that can make transfer easier or harder. These include:

- The subject domain – it is harder to transfer learning to a different school subject than within the same one.
- The physical surroundings – it is harder to use what you have learned when in a different location (e.g. in the workplace).
- The framing/phrasing of the task – transfer is harder when tasks are framed in a novel way, and easier when it they are superficially similar.

It may seem to make sense to make transfer as easy as possible for students, and this can certainly be helpful during initial learning. However, presenting challenges and variations can help learning to become more flexible. Do we want students who can only use what they have learned in the classroom? Clearly not; we want them to be able to apply what they have learned at home, at work and in the examination hall!

Keeping tasks similar (low variability) is good for short-term performance, but high variability helps with long-term learning and transfer (Soderstrom & Bjork, 2015). As a teacher, we should aim to extend and vary tasks once our learners have mastered the basics. Some ways to do this could include the following:

■ ■ ■ ■ **ETHICS IN PSYCHOLOGY TEACHING**

- Practice tasks in a different physical location, such as via homework or by using 'outdoor learning'.
- Change the context by unexpectedly asking questions about research ethics in the middle of a content-based topic such as Memory or Attachment.
- Gain responses in an unpredictable way by varying the order and wording of tasks.
- Have students connect what they have learned to another school subject. For example, they could be asked to write about the psychology of obedience in the context of Physical Education.
- Have students debate a psychological principle as a role play connected to a real-world scenario. For example, they could role play a group of politicians who are considering how to use insights from the psychology of prejudice to reduce racism in society. Set up a role play, where a controversial figure from psychology such as obedience researcher Stanley Milgram (1963) is put 'on trial' to defend and justify their research. Students can take the role of defence, prosecution, judge, jury, reporters and so forth.

While these tasks are more difficult than simply going over the material in the same format as it was originally studied, they make the learning more accessible and usable over the long term, and therefore help to build practical ethical awareness among our students.

Now undertake Task 5.8.

Task 5.8 **Variability of practice**

Drawing on the above examples, write down notes outlining how you could increase the level of variability in your lessons such that students are required to practice their ethics knowledge in multiple contexts.

5.5 SUMMARY AND KEY POINTS

This chapter has explored the value of ethics in psychology, the application of the ethical codes of conduct produced by BPS and ATP, and looked at some helpful ways of teaching research to classes. It has also drawn on the cognitive psychology of spacing, narrative and transfer to show how important it is for lessons on ethics to be well remembered and for students to be able to apply them in future situations. Good teaching practices such as the ones exemplified in this chapter will help you to achieve that with your own students.

The teaching of ethics provides opportunities for discussions that can be highly stimulating to students, and can serve them well not just for the psychology studies but for their future careers as well. What's more, it helps to

establish a foundation of scientific and psychological literacy that is valuable for any young person.
You should now:

- appreciate the centrality of research ethics of psychology to the teaching of psychology;
- have ideas for how to teach research ethics in an effective and engaging way;
- understand how the principles of spacing, narrative and variation can be applied to your teaching of research ethics to boost long-term retention and application.

Check the requirements of your ITE programme to see which have been addressed in this unit.

FURTHER RESOURCES AND WEBSITES

BPS and ATP ethical guidelines can be downloaded from the societies' websites: www.bps.org.uk and www.theatp.uk

Smith and Firth (2018) 'Psychology in the classroom' includes detailed coverage of how to apply the spacing effect to teaching practice.

Perkins and Salomon (1992) provide a valuable and detailed explanation of the role of transfer in education. https://citeseerx.ist.psu.edu/viewdoc/download?doi=10.1.1.24.369&rep=rep1&type=pdf

Daniel Willingham writes a compelling short article on the benefits of story for educators: https://www.aft.org/periodical/american-educator/summer-2004/ask-cognitive-scientist

TEACHING SKILLS OF EVALUATION AND ANALYSIS IN PSYCHOLOGY

Jock McGinty

INTRODUCTION

The information age has brought a significant increase in available sources of information, and it could be argued that the variety of information sources that we have today has contributed to the spread of alternative facts (Taala, Franco Jr., & Teresa 2019). Therefore perhaps more than ever, we need to develop in our students the ability to analyse and evaluate arguments according to their credibility and to reach valid and informed conclusions.

Many students find it difficult to order their thoughts and ideas in a logical, consistent and reasoned way. This chapter starts from the premise that skills in evaluation can be developed through a better understanding of what critical thinking involves, and by practising those skills. Learning to think in evaluative ways means using critical analysis and cognitive processes such as selection and judgement (Cottrell 2017). Being able to think critically provides students with the tools to evaluate psychological research constructively so that they can effectively apply findings about behaviour to real-world situations. Critical thinking is not simply about natural traits of scepticism or personality; it is about employing a particular set of methods aimed at exploring evidence in a critical way (Cottrell 2017). Critical thinking requires psychology students to structure an argument that explores the strengths and weaknesses of research and ideas, often using scientific methodology or debates in psychology in order to do so.

Critical thinking is associated with our capacity for rational thought; how we provide reasons for our behaviour. Sometimes, the very nature of being a student in a school or college means that they are all too willing to accept the view of their teachers or what is presented to them in their textbooks or indeed in psychological research. However, for psychology students, the ability to critically evaluate their own beliefs and the beliefs of others about human behaviour is central to their understanding of the world around them. Therefore, a key battle for psychology teachers is against our students' relativism, leading to a

JOCK McGINTY

desire not to argue, debate or criticise, but simply to conform to the views that are presented to them (Dunn, Halonen, & Smith 2008). The challenge for you as a teacher is to convince your students how vital and helpful critical thinking is for learning about psychology and life.

OBJECTIVES

By the end of this chapter, you should be able to:

- recognise the personal qualities associated with critical thinking.
- understand what critical thinking is.
- recognise barriers to the development of good critical thinking skills.
- recognise the skills for create reflective and critical arguments.
- understand how to use methodology and debates for evaluation.
- create evaluation tasks for written responses.
- assess your current understanding of how students use skills of evaluation.

Check which requirements of your initial teacher education programme relate to this unit.

6.1 WHAT MAKES A CRITICAL THINKER?

Before your psychology students can think critically, they need to recognise the attitudes or dispositions of a critical thinker and that it involves acknowledging when the skill is needed and the willingness to apply it in an appropriate context. Unfortunately, it is not as easy as just telling them to 'think critically!' Indeed Van Gelder (2005) suggests that humans are not naturally critical and that we like stories that make sense and follow patterns. We prefer it when the first account seems correct and are happy not to pursue the matter further. Of course in psychology a problem arises when our students begin to ask if there really is a pattern or indeed if the story is actually true. Even this is problematic as although they may begin to question the research with which they are presented, critical thinking and evaluation requires higher order skills; it is a complex activity that is more than just the sum of its' parts, for example skills of reading and text comprehension.

Thinking in a critical way requires the conscious exertion of mental effort and your students need to understand and be prepared for the effort required. Your students need to accept that learning to think critically and evaluate research will be challenging. They are often being introduced to unfamiliar topics or researching areas in far more depth than they may have previously experienced and so it is important for them to understand what critical thinking means in relation to psychology.

It is also important at this point to separate the willingness to think critically from the ability to think critically. Some of your students may have excellent critical thinking skills and recognise when they are needed, but they may also choose not to engage in the process of using them (Halpern 1998). It is of no value to teach your students how to evaluate using critical thinking skills if they do not use them. Thus, it is important that not only do you develop your students' critical thinking skills but that you provide appropriate and frequent opportunities to practise them.

6.2 WHAT IS CRITICAL THINKING?

The content of what you teach in psychology specifications varies whether you are a teacher in the United Kingdom, Europe or worldwide. Although we may differ on which content students should learn, I would suggest we at least agree that, whatever students learn, they ought to think critically about it. Willingham (2019) suggests a commonsensical view that students are thinking critically if their thinking is novel, for example they are not simply drawing a conclusion from a memory of a previous situation and that they have autonomy over their thinking. Evaluative thought also involves following conventions such as considering both sides of an argument and offering evidence to support analysis in order to substantiate any conclusions that are made. Critical thinking is a complex process of deliberation, which involves a wide range of skills and attitudes (Cottrell 2017). It involves identifying other people's standpoints and your students need to be able to recognise a range of different viewpoints in psychology, for example that Bandura adopts a social learning approach or that Freud argues from a psychoanalytic perspective. This requires the skill of grasping an overall argument, which involves considering psychologists' reasoning.

So how can your students do this? Evaluation of research and areas of psychology requires your students to reflect on issues in a structured way. This means that they will need to adopt a detailed, analytical approach to the research they are studying, weighing up the arguments and drawing conclusions about the extent to which the arguments are valid. Your students must then create their own arguments that require making a balanced judgement of the evidence in psychological research, synthesising it to form their own position or viewpoint. Teachers and examiners need to see whether evaluative arguments presented by students are well founded, identifying any counter arguments in their reasoning and presenting analyses in a clear, well-reasoned way that will convince the reader. As teachers, we want our students to question articles they read, challenge views they listen to in class and produce effective, critical thinking that allows for the production of logical arguments.

Now undertake Task 6.1.

JOCK McGINTY

> **Task 6.1 Reflection: Knowing without understanding?**
>
> Bill believes his psychology students are unable to apply their knowledge outside the narrow domain in which it was learnt. They 'know without understanding'. After all, it is not unusual for students to rely on research that is based on a small sample of the population, or that is based on faulty reasoning without questioning it.
>
> However, Bill thinks his students should be looking for answers to questions such as 'How do we know …?' and 'Why do we believe …?'
>
> Think of your psychology students; produce a list of ten meaningful questions you could use to help them to think in a critical, evaluative manner applied to a topic in psychology that you are about to teach. Use these in the lesson and evaluate the usefulness of the questions in eliciting answers demonstrating critical thinking.
>
> If possible, ask a fellow trainee teacher or mentor to observe your lesson and help you with the evaluation of the efficacy of the questions.

6.3 BARRIERS TO CRITICAL THINKING

When you are teaching critical thinking, the aim is to have your students not only understand and successfully use the particular skill being taught but also be able to recognise where that particular skill might be appropriate in novel situations. This is often a weakness for students as they fail to transfer the external cues from the topic being taught to the thinking skills required for effective evaluation. For example research that uses a correlational design such as Monroe-Chandler, Hall and Fishburne (2008) that looks at the relationship between imagery use and self-confidence and self-efficacy in youth soccer players, ought to stimulate your students to think that the data gathered must be quantitative as the design is correlational but also that there can be no cause and effect made between the use of imagery and self-confidence and self-efficacy.

Therefore as teachers, we should be aiming to promote the learning of trans-contextual thinking skills (Halpern 2017). As thinking always occurs within a domain of knowledge, as might be expected as most psychology courses focus on content knowledge, we often fail to sufficiently develop the transferability of critical thinking skills. For this reason, teaching critical thinking poses unique problems that we need to address.

Very often students assume that evaluation or critical thinking solely means making negative comments. Therefore, when making an analysis of research methods or psychological research, they find it difficult to create a balanced argument, driven by a misunderstanding. They need to recognise that critical evaluation means identifying positive as well as negative aspects of research.

While it may not always seem to be the case, our students are, by and large, rational human beings. They have their own belief systems and have good reasons for what they do and think. However, this can often lead to lazy thinking with students either too willing to accept the views of others or good arguments are ignored. Therefore an over-estimation of their own reasoning abilities can limit the desire to evaluate research in an effective manner (Halpern 2017).

■ ■ ■ ■ TEACHING SKILLS OF EVALUATION & ANALYSIS

One of the main barriers that our students come up against and necessarily we do as their teachers is that they are unaware that strategies used for study at GCSE level and in everyday situations are not sufficiently rigorous for higher level academic thinking. Thus a lack of methods, strategies or practice will be an initial barrier that our students will face as we attempt to develop their evaluation skills. This can also lead to a lack of confidence in critically evaluating psychological research. It can seem strange for students who know little about psychology, to be asked to investigate the strengths and weaknesses of influential psychologists. However, this is where your role as the teacher is most valuable as it allows you to explore with your students the rationale for how and why research is designed and carried out in the way that it is.

Another barrier to effective critical thinking is that students often provide insufficient focus and attention to detail in their arguments. Critical thinking involves finding the specific evidence from psychological research that supports an argument, and this requires good attention to detail (Halpern 2017). If your students use weak, overly general, descriptive evidence, this will lead to poor evaluative judgements of the area of psychology or research.

Above all, critical thinking and evaluation is hard work (Van Gelder 2005). Often students approach a teacher's classes with the attitude of 'I want you to give me all the right answers', whereas as a teacher you will approach the class and students from the viewpoint of 'I want you to challenge psychologists' and use active questioning to find your own answers and this will require lots of effort'. Therefore you also need to consider ways to motivate students to become critical thinkers. Without proper motivation, students are less inclined to engage effectively in evaluation. Therefore, it is good to arouse interest immediately when the course begins and develop a commitment to improving critical thinking throughout your course. One motivational strategy is to explain why evaluation and critical thinking are important to effective assessment criteria. For example, these criteria are often worded as:

- 'The response demonstrates good relevant knowledge and understanding.
- The response demonstrates many points of analysis, interpretation and evaluation covering a range of issues.

The argument is competently organised, balanced and well developed.

- The answer is explicitly related to the context of the question.
- Effective use of examples where appropriate.
- Valid conclusions that effectively summarise issues and arguments are highly skilled and show good understanding.
- There is a well-developed line of reasoning which is clear and logically structured'.

(OCR Psychology component 3 section B Generic mark scheme part b 2019 p22-23)

JOCK McGINTY

Developing an early understanding of criteria such as these allows your students to appreciate their importance in achieving high marks for a piece of extended writing and lets them monitor the content and structure of their answers as they are writing them: a significant metacognitive skill. Additionally, it increases their likelihood of thinking successfully thereby increasing their self-efficacy in relation to evaluation and critical thinking.

Teachers can also stimulate interest by taking a class poll posing an interesting question on which students are likely to have an opinion. For example, asking students the extent to which they believe murderers with brain abnormalities are responsible for their crimes. You can use this to illustrate how psychologists draw a conclusion based on the quality and quantity of research studies as opposed to what many people commonly believe.

Now undertake Task 6.2.

Task 6.2 **Which barriers have an effect upon your teaching?**

1. On the table below, tick [√] all those barriers that you consider might affect your students' critical thinking abilities (Cottrell 2017).

Misunderstanding what is meant by criticism	
Over-estimating their own reasoning abilities	
Lack of knowledge of methods and strategies	
Lack of practice	
Reluctance to criticise those with more expertise	
Mistaking information for understanding	
Insufficient focus and attention to detail	
Unwillingness to challenge own beliefs or assumptions	
Teacher resistance to teaching evaluation	

2. Create a ten-question self-evaluation survey for your students to judge their barriers to critical thinking. Use it with your students to audit their views on critical thinking and consider how this can inform your teaching.

For example you could use instructions such as:
 For each of the following statements, rate your responses as
 4 = 'strongly agree' 3 = 'agree' 2 = 'sort of agree' 1 = 'disagree' 0 = 'strongly disagree'
 Examples of statements to use:

1. I feel comfortable highlighting potential weaknesses in the work of influential psychologists
2. I can analyse the structure of an argument.

TEACHING SKILLS OF EVALUATION & ANALYSIS

Providing opportunities for critical thinking and evaluation is straightforward in stand-alone courses. However, in a psychology course, teachers must find specific content and tasks that support critical thinking and allow students to evaluate research material. The next section examines how you can create a framework for critical thinking in your course so that you have elements in your lessons you can use daily. This will help your students build on their argument analysis, reading and writing critically, and recognising opportunities for evaluation in psychological research, for example using methodological issues and debates.

6.4 SKILLS REQUIRED FOR CRITICAL THINKING

It is important for teachers to consider the cognitive level of their students when developing critical thinking objectives. A focus on the foundation skills of evaluation before moving on to the higher level skills has been found to be beneficial as research suggests that teachers often over-estimate the evaluation skills of their students and their ability to transfer evaluation skills from one subject to another (Kerr Lawrence, Serdikoff, Zinn, & Baker 2008). We often see students too concerned about writing notes on everything they have seen on a presentation slide about the structure of the brain for example, rather than concentrating on understanding how the parts of the brain control behaviour. Asking your students to write summaries from your lessons or notes using the Cornell note system, so they transfer content into their own words, is an effective way of ensuring they reorganise and synthesise information. This is the first step to getting your students to build a foundation of good thinking skills.

Once your students have the foundations for critical thinking, you can focus on developing their higher level skills. You can do this by helping them draw connections between psychological knowledge and their everyday lives; for example keeping a journal that makes connections between course content and material outside of class, such as films, television, books and current events. Writing journals helps improve your students' understanding and application of the course material.

The more complex skills required for effective evaluation, such as analysis and interpretation, need to be specifically targeted and developed if your students are to access higher grades. Dunn *et al.* (2008) suggest one way to target these complex evaluation skills is to use Structured Peer Review Exercises (SPREs). For example, this activity can be structured so that each student (a) reads another student's answer to a question or summary of psychological research, (b) completes a review form based on the answer or summary and then (c) discusses the review with the student author. The benefits of engaging in peer review and receiving feedback from peers are that your students are exposed to a greater diversity of perspectives than just those of the researcher, textbook or indeed you as their teacher. Furthermore, this activity is especially useful for psychology where written communication is a key objective.

Additionally, students may have very limited experience of what evaluation means or indeed what is meant by 'evidence'. As a teacher you need to develop lessons and techniques to help your psychology students learn how to evaluate the strengths and weaknesses of scientific and non-scientific kinds of evidence and to help them draw sound conclusions (Bensley & Spero 2014). Learning about the quality of evidence and drawing appropriate conclusions from scientific research are central to teaching evaluation in psychology.

6.5 CREATING A FRAMEWORK FOR CRITICAL THINKING AND EVALUATION

Providing clear, initial learning objectives is important so that you determine and explain the skills that you want your students to work on during your course. Additionally, Bensley and Spero (2014) state that objectives should specify the skill that will change in a way that can be measured, for example an assignment objective might read, 'After successfully completing this assignment, you will be able to identify different kinds of evidence in a psychological discussion'.

Willingham (2019) suggests that as teachers we must:

1. First, identify what is meant by critical thinking and evaluation in psychology. Be specific. What tasks showing critical thinking should a student be able to demonstrate in psychology?
2. Second, identify the psychology content that students must know. We have seen that psychological knowledge is a crucial driver of thinking skills.
3. Selection of psychological research evidence is a critical way that students demonstrate evaluation.
4. Fourth, as teachers we must decide which skills should be revisited across years. Studies show that even if content is learned quite well over the course of half of a school year, about half will be forgotten in three years (Pawl, Barrantes, Pritchard, & Mitchell 2012).

Let's explore these points further. If students are to read and interpret psychological research in the way psychologists do, they need to learn specific skills like interpreting peer-reviewed articles, corroborating them within the conventions of scientific report formats, and putting them in context of human behaviour. You should teach these skills explicitly and your students be given the opportunity to practise it. The second point begs the question 'what knowledge is essential' to the evaluative type of thinking you want your students to be able to do? Here, your focus should be on teaching your students the course content that is most likely to lead to successful exam performance. However, this is intertwined with the third point of your students' knowledge of how to select, present and argue the evidence from psychological research. As with all skills, unless they are practised their effectiveness will diminish, therefore regular opportunities

■ ■ ■ ■ **TEACHING SKILLS OF EVALUATION & ANALYSIS**

to critique research studies from your course using methodology and debates in psychology will be vital in maintaining and improving skills of evaluation.

Now undertake Task 6.3.

M | Task 6.3 **Creating opportunities for teaching critical thinking**

Recognising the opportunities you have in your course to develop your students' skills of evaluation will be vital if they are to become critical thinkers.

Look at the psychology specification that you teach. It will identify methodological issues and debates in psychology. Your task is to map these opportunities for evaluation onto the course content.

For example, the cognitive study by Loftus and Palmer (1974) on eyewitness testimony should allow you to identify and map methodological issues such as the advantages and disadvantages of the experimental method and independent measures design. Additionally you could identify the debate of the extent to which psychology can be considered a science.

6.6 ASSESSMENT OBJECTIVES FOR EVALUATION

The assessment objectives of psychology specifications require students to demonstrate their skills of assessment across the range of content taught, from research methods to research into specific areas of psychology such as criminal psychology. This also means you should arrange to allow retrieval of evaluation skills in a way that does not depend on the content area (Halpern 2017). This allows your students to transfer their evaluation skills from one area of psychology to another. For example, if you teach your students about the strengths and weaknesses of self-report methods such as questionnaires in the research methods component of the specification, they should be able to retrieve and use this in order to critically evaluate the Eyes Task questionnaire (Baron-Cohen 1997) that was used to measure theory of mind in people with Autistic Spectrum Disorder.

Assessment objectives mean your students will need to analyse and interpret and evaluate scientific information, ideas and evidence to make judgements and reach conclusions. Additionally you need to teach so your students can develop and refine practical design and procedures of research. The previous activity should have given you the experience of critical thinking as problem recognition. The methodological issues and debates that specifications stipulate we use to evaluate research in psychology can provide your students with retrieval cues. This means your students must recognise opportunities to think critically about psychology and learn to actively focus on the problems or arguments. This provides them with a framework on which to hang supporting examples and evidence from research. Different psychology specifications and qualifications vary in the way they ask students to evaluate research and you need to be aware of these nuances. One of the best ways to do this is to read the examiner's reports that accompany each examination series: these are published on the awarding body's website. This information will inform your teaching and allow you to focus your students' evaluations directly on the questions.

Now undertake Task 6.4.

> Task 6.4 **Critical thinking question prompts**
>
> Design a series of ten question prompts to help teach one of your classes how to evaluate a research method or piece of psychological research. Your prompts should focus on analysis such as 'how convincing is the evidence presented?' and evaluation 'How does this compare to other research in this area?'

6.7 PROVIDING STUDENTS WITH CRITICAL THINKING AND EVALUATION TASKS

Because critical thinking for evaluation is a difficult skill to master, it takes a long time to become good at it. Therefore, you should not be looking for magic bullets when teaching skills of evaluation. However, providing your students with learning tasks that are rich in information that allow them to develop their judgement will facilitate their progress to becoming a critical thinker. Some information available to students may not be relevant, and part of the learning exercise involves deciding which information is important to the problem. Your learning exercises should focus on the critical aspects of the problems and arguments that utilise your students' evaluation skills.

As a teacher you can model how to think critically in psychology and the procedures for evaluating evidence and drawing conclusions. You can provide worked examples of problems, writing sample answers or writing frames, or real-world examples of good and bad thinking found in the media. Teachers can also think out loud as they evaluate arguments in class to model the process of thinking (Bensley & Spero 2014).

Halpern (2017) suggests that providing tasks and questions that require students to attend to structural aspects of a problem or argument such as the methodology used is useful in developing skills of evaluation. A range of tasks you could use are outlined here:

1. Display the argument in diagrammatic form so that information is clear and organised.
2. Ask the prompt question 'what additional information would you want before answering the question?'
3. State the problem in at least two ways in order to refine the focus of the argument.

TEACHING SKILLS OF EVALUATION & ANALYSIS

4. Which evidence is most important? Which evidence is least important? Why?
5. Categorise the findings in a meaningful way. By grouping individual pieces of evidence for example they both support a reductionist argument, a structure emerges that is not apparent when they are kept separate.
6. List two solutions for the problem thereby encouraging a more creative approach.
7. What is wrong with an assertion that was made in the question?
8. Present two reasons that support the conclusion and two reasons that do not support the conclusion. Questions of this sort highlight the importance of evaluating the extent to which an argument is supported.
9. Explain your answer. Students are required to consider the credibility of their supporting evidence.
10. What two actions would you take to improve the design of a study that was described? This highlights what better types of evidence or procedures students need to think about that might have provided different results.

Some suggestions for critical thinking writing activities include:

1. Give your students raw data and ask them to write an argument or analysis based on the data.
2. Ask your students to write about unfamiliar points of view or 'what if' situations.
3. Think of a debate or controversy in psychology, and ask your students to write a dialogue between characters with different points of view.
4. Select research articles from your course and ask your students to write summaries of them. Alternatively, you could ask students to write an abstract of what they have learned from your lesson.
5. Develop a scenario (see Chapter 7) that provides students with a realistic situation where they must reach a decision to resolve a problem.

Now undertake Task 6.5.

Task 6.5 **Plan a critical thinking lesson**

Make a plan for a lesson that you have to teach soon that evaluates either research methodology or a debate in psychology. You should consider the age of your students, their level of critical thinking and the topic content.

Other considerations should include your lesson objectives – where does this lesson fit into the scheme of work? – Your lesson starter or hook, students' prior knowledge of the research content and the methodology or debate in psychology you have chosen as a lesson focus. You also need to consider the task and how you are going to scaffold the task.

6.8 ASSESSING CRITICAL THINKING AND EVALUATION

You can use the students' responses from the activities that promote evaluation to assess whether they are, indeed, reaching your critical thinking goals. It is important to establish clear criteria for evaluating so that you can measure which skills are present, to what extent, and which skills require further development. The following are characteristics of work that may demonstrate effective critical thinking:

1. Your students accurately and thoroughly interpret the research evidence and ask relevant questions.
2. There is evidence that your students analyse and evaluate key information.
3. Students draw insightful, reasonable conclusions from the research evidence.
4. There is evidence of justification of opinions.
5. Students thoughtfully address and evaluate major alternative points of view.

It is also important to note that assessment is a tool that can be used throughout a lesson or topic, not just at the end of a unit of work. It is more useful to assess students throughout a course, so you can see if criteria require further clarification and students can practise their understanding of your criteria and receive feedback. This will help them to reflect on their own work and improve the quality of their thinking and writing. Any test questions and other assessments of performance should be similar to practice questions.

Now undertake Task 6.6.

Task 6.6 Helping students write better evaluation answers

As a method of helping students to evaluate their own answer while they were writing it, design a simple feedback checklist tool that uses the evaluation assessment objectives and criteria for your specification.

You can use this by asking your students to refer to the evaluation assessment criteria on the feedback checklist while writing their essay, and to look at it again before handing in their assignment. In doing so, you are increasing your students' familiarity with evaluation assessment criteria and providing opportunities for your students to monitor the extent to which they are developing and using their critical thinking skills.

6.9 SUMMARY AND KEY POINTS

Halpern (2017) suggests that critical thinking is a process that relies upon, and develops, a wide range of evaluation skills. For some of your students, practising evaluation skills will mean changing the way they approach their studies, such as paying attention to detail or taking a more sceptical approach to what they read.

TEACHING SKILLS OF EVALUATION & ANALYSIS

Developing good evaluative thinking skills can take patience and application. On the other hand, the rewards for your students and for you as their teacher, lie in improved abilities in making judgements about psychological research. It is important you see the relevance of spending time developing students' ability to find out where the best evidence lies for evaluating psychological research and methodology. If you provide your students with activities that explore the strength of the evidence to support different arguments, it will allow them to arrive at logical conclusions. Consistently practising how to construct a line of reasoning and selecting the best research evidence to illustrate their argument will give students the opportunity to develop a systematic approach to enhancing their evaluation skills.

You should now:

- recognise the personal qualities associated with critical thinking
- understand what critical thinking is
- recognise barriers to the development of good critical thinking skills
- recognise the skills for create reflective and critical arguments
- understand how to use methodology and debates for evaluation
- be able to create evaluation tasks for written responses
- be able to assess your current understanding of how students use skills of evaluation.

Check the requirements of your initial teacher education programme to see which have been addressed in this unit.

FURTHER RESOURCES AND WEBSITES

Further reading for promoting and assessing critical thinking https://uwaterloo.ca/centre-for-teaching-excellence/teaching-resources/teaching-tips/developing-assignments/cross-discipline-skills/promoting-assessing-critical-thinking

OCR Psychology component 3 section B Generic mark scheme part b) https://ocr.org.uk/Images/529289-mark-scheme-applied-psychology.pdf

For general information, extending what is in this chapter, we recommend you read Unit 5.7 "Developing Critical Thinking" In the core textbook for the Learning to Teach series: Capel, S., Leask, M. and Younie, S. with E. Hidson and J. Lawrence (9th edn 2022) *Learning to Teach in the Secondary School: A Companion to School Experience*. Abingdon Routledge: Taylor Francis.

7 TEACHING SKILLS OF APPLICATION
Lin Norton

INTRODUCTION

In this chapter, I present an approach to Problem Based Learning (PBL) for teachers of psychology. My emphasis is on what is practical and achievable for teachers who have little or no experience of teaching PBL. While there are many forms of PBL, I focus on using Text Based Vignettes (TBVs). I base this chapter on a resource pack I produced called Psychology Applied Learning Scenarios (PALS) (Norton, 2004), which is now available on the Advance HE website (https://www.advance-he.ac.uk/knowledge-hub/psychology-applied-learning-scenarios-pals-practical-introduction-problem-based).

PALS are mainly TBVs, which are designed to encourage your students to apply what they have learned in designated areas of psychology. Much of the approach outlined in the PALS booklet can be readily adapted to students in schools, sixth form colleges and FE colleges. TBVs are not new; in fact, they are used in many Psychology examination questions especially at GCSE and A level.

To challenge your students, the TBVs I describe here are longer and more complex than ones typically found in examination questions to try and represent some aspect of real life that psychology can explain. I argue that it is preferable to construct TBVs ourselves, rather than use ready-made examples that are available on the Internet or on the various examining boards because they can be tailored for the context in which you are teaching (see further resources: UK awarding bodies for Psychology). When I construct my own TBV, I have found that it makes me actively reflect on what I am trying to achieve with my students by focusing on the learning outcomes and designing the TBV accordingly.

OBJECTIVES

By the end of this chapter, you should be able to:

- understand PBL as a teaching approach in Psychology.

■ ■ ■ ■ **TEACHING SKILLS OF APPLICATION**

- understand the pedagogical rationale for constructing TBVs.
- have a strategy for using a TBV as a class task.

Check which requirements of your initial teacher education programme relate to this unit.

7.1 PROBLEM-BASED LEARNING: AN OVERVIEW

PBL is a mode of teaching and learning that is student-centred. It is based on constructivist theories and requires students to take an active enquiry-based approach to their learning. The origins of PBL can be traced as far back as Dewey (1916) who argued that learning occurs when students are given something to do that makes them think rather than given something to learn. PBL was pioneered in medical education by Barrows and Tamblyn (1980) as a form of teaching that encourages medical students to apply their understanding of the subject in order to tackle real-world issues. They were concerned that doctors were not being encouraged to use their knowledge but simply acquire it in traditional medical degrees. Since there are no certain answers or specific solutions, PBL stimulates students to use their critical thinking skills.

> Problem-based learning is the learning that results from the process of working toward the understanding or resolution of a problem. The problem is encountered *first* in the learning process.
> (Barrows and Tamblyn, 1980, p.1.)

It was their work that led to its wide uptake in other education contexts. There is no single definition of PBL, part of the reason is that, as Savin-Baden and Major (2004) suggest, it is more of a general educational strategy that encompasses a philosophy and leads to a teaching approach where the emphasis is on what the student learns rather than on what the teacher teaches.

PBL is different from project-based learning which confusingly has the same acronym but they have characteristics in common which is that they are part of a pedagogical approach that is student-centred (Rogers, 1969) and constructivist (Vygotsky, 1978). In short, the theories suggest that active learning by students is preferable to passive learning where the information flow is all one way (teacher-> pupil) in what is called the didactic approach to teaching. Of course, there are plenty of topics/subjects where such an approach is important but in Psychology, the application of knowledge is critical to the subject requiring that this skill is practised in different contexts; PBL is one way of facilitating the teaching of application of knowledge. Like all pedagogical approaches, there are several PBL models which may at first sight seem daunting particularly at the start of a teaching career. In my experience, when launching into any new approach to teaching, begin small, then with increasing confidence you adapt your approach to suit your own style of teaching and what it is you want your students to learn.

LIN NORTON

Problem-Based Learning in Psychology

Despite its wide take up in many disciplines (e.g. health, business, behavioural science, education), there is relatively little about PBL in Psychology according to Wiggins *et al.* (2016). They argue that as a teaching approach, Psychology is central to our understanding of how PBL works, with its emphasis on 'problem-solving, self-directed learning and group interaction' (pp.136-137). At the heart of PBL is the problem itself; Wiggins *et al.* (2016) describe PBL as

> an issue that is investigated, discussed and analysed, which could take the form of a puzzle, a scenario or a case-study (Barrett, Cashman & Moore, 2011). As there are no fixed and final solutions and numerous ways to solve these problems, students can study the same problem but learn different things from their engagement with them.
>
> (p.137)

There are many forms in which the problem can be constructed, and it can be designed to form the basis of an entire module or even the whole programme (such as happens in Maastricht university; see further resources) or PBL can be used in a much smaller way as a classroom activity, and this is the purpose that I am describing in this chapter.

7.2 TEXT-BASED VIGNETTES

Jeffries and Maeder (2005) define vignettes as 'incomplete short stories that are written to reflect, in a less complex way, real-life situations in order to encourage discussions and potential solutions to problems where multiple solutions are possible' (p.20). They list five criteria, some of which align closely with PALS; relevance; 'multiple answers to encourage independent thinking and unique responses; purposely incomplete so that multiple interpretations can be defended' (Norton, 2004, p.2). If we think about the idea of incomplete stories, we can see immediately that stories have a universal appeal; they connect directly with the reader, so they will be intrinsically engaging.

In the PALS booklet, I emphasise that the scenarios /vignettes 'are ambiguously phrased to allow students scope to develop their own thinking to the given problem' (Norton, 2004, p.2). This is one of the crucial differences between PBL where there is no single 'correct' answer and problem-solving learning where a 'solution' must be found. 'By applying different theories to a PALS case study, students realise for themselves how different approaches to the issues raised are derived from the different theoretical perspective they adopt' (Norton, 2004, p.2). In a secondary/FE context, students use vignettes primarily to apply their understanding of the subject they are learning about but we can also encourage them to see how different psychological perspectives might produce different interpretations of the same issue.

■ ■ ■ ■ **TEACHING SKILLS OF APPLICATION**

TBVs are used in Psychology examination papers but typically, they tend to be very short and be followed by quite specific questions. The TBVs I suggest you use are a little longer to help students get their teeth into an interesting and engaging scenario that will encourage group discussion and teamwork. Although much of this chapter is about the technicalities of designing and using a TBV, it is worth remembering that learning should also be enjoyable; it should enable students to feel a sense of accomplishment and a growing confidence in mastering relevant skills.

7.3 CONSTRUCTING A TBV

The first point to think about is what you want your students to achieve by using a TBV (the learning objective) and what you want your students to be able to do having engaged with a TBV the (learning outcome). These are two quite different aims, but they are important if you want to make your TBV session/s successful. The learning objective is usually expressed in a single overarching objective; whereas the learning outcomes are more detailed statements of what you expect your students to be able to do having engaged in the session/s. I suggest that you have a maximum number of three learning outcomes. I illustrate these in the example in Task 7.1.

M | Task 7.1 **Using TBVs: Graham being cyber-bullied***

Graham is a 17-year-old boy in his first year of studying computer science and mathematics at his local sixth form college. He decided to take his A levels at a college rather than at his school because he felt increasingly uncomfortable interacting with his other school friends. Over the last two years, it became apparent to everyone at school that Graham was extremely clever; he was getting top marks in all his coursework, he found exams really easy and was being constantly held up as an example of an ideal student to the rest of his class by teachers who were trying to motivate less able students. Not surprisingly, this led to a considerable amount of jealousy particularly from the other boys. Graham found himself the butt of jokes especially by Jack, one of the most popular boys in the class. Jack is all the things, Graham is not – he is strong, athletic and good looking; he also despises all things academic.

For all these reasons, Jack had a loyal following who were willing to go along with his ideas and who thought of themselves as the 'top dogs' in the school. When Jack started to jeer at Graham on the sports field and at break times, they were only too willing to fall in with Jack's behaviour. The breaking point for Graham was when this mild form of bullying moved onto social media. Graham started getting unkind tweets that slowly escalated into hostile and abusive messages on his phone, but then Jack took a photo of Graham and altered his features to make him

> look ridiculous which he then posted on SnapChat. This led to other demeaning posts on Facebook and Twitter. When Graham moved to college, he hoped that the cyberbullying would stop but to his dismay, it just went on and on.
>
> Task:
> The principal of the college has called you in as a team of social psychologists to carry out an investigation into Graham's case and to make a report.
>   In your report, use your knowledge of social psychology to:
>
> 1. Explain how Graham's situation has occurred and why it has not gone away.
> 2. Suggest some strategies to help Graham.
> 3. Make some recommendations as to what the college can do to minimise cyberbullying.
>
> * Strategies for teaching sensitive subjects:
>
> There are areas in Psychology where the topics may be upsetting to some of your students; the cyberbullying example is a case in point. However, rather than avoid difficult subjects altogether, there are many resources to suggest strategies for dealing with this in a compassionate and constructive way (see further resources: Lynagh, Gilligan, and Handley, 2010; Heath et al., 2017; Winstone and Kinchin, 2017; Hulme, 2018).

Learning objective of Graham's TBV:

1. To enable students to apply their knowledge of social psychology to explain how cyberbullying occurs.

Learning outcomes:

Having taken part in the task using Graham's TBV, students will be able to:

1. Analyse the complex situation of cyberbullying using their understanding of social psychology.
2. Demonstrate how social influence explanations (such as social group norms) maintain cyberbullying.
3. Show how resistance to social influence (such as social support) can mitigate the effects of cyberbullying.

The above are simply examples and as you can see, they could easily be adapted to the areas of social influence that you wanted your students to focus on.

When designing your own TBVs, you may find the planning framework in Figure 7.1 to be a useful tool. It has been adapted from the PALS booklet (Norton, 2004, p.6) and illustrates seven principles when constructing TBVs.

You may not wish to use all seven of these principles, but checking your TBV against each one may help when you come to refine your text.

TEACHING SKILLS OF APPLICATION

4 customer needs 1. 2. 3. 4.	4 reasons for completing market research 1. 2. 3. 4.	2 advantages of primary research 1. 2.
3 risks of starting a business 1. 2. 3.	2 reasons market research may be unreliable 1. 2.	2 advantages of secondary research 1. 2.
3 rewards of starting a business 1. 2. 3.	5 ways to segment a market customer needs 1. 2. 3. 4. 5.	1 problem with qualitative research 1. 3 disadvantages with a competitive environment 1. 2. 3.

A market map is

■ **Figure 7.1** Principles of vignette design from the literature applied to Psychology TBVs (Adapted from Norton, 2004, p.6 with permission).

Now undertake Task 7.2.

Task 7.2 **Learning objectives and outcomes**

1. Looking again at the cyberbullying TBV, make a judgement on how closely you think it meets the seven principles of vignette design (prior knowledge, relevant content, self-directed learning, elaboration through discussion, interest in the subject matter, integration of knowledge and teaching objectives).
2. Construct a learning objective and three learning outcomes for a TBV on eyewitness testimony.
3. Compare and discuss your objectives and outcomes with peers undertaking the same exercise.

7.4 USING TBVS FOR PBL

TBVs can be used in assessment as demonstrated in the A/AS-level Psychology exam papers, but in this chapter, I am focusing on using them for group teaching in class. This is one of the more traditional applications of PBL. It involves you in designing a TBV and using it to stimulate active learning within several groups in your classroom. This method of PBL uses the 'floating facilitator model (with one tutor moving between student groups) to support students working in small groups in the same classroom' (Wiggins et al., 2016, p.139).

The key to successful PBL is preparation and by this, I mean not just the usual preparation you do as a teacher but also the way in which you prepare students for a successful PBL session. For any teaching approach that is out of the ordinary, I have found that it pays dividends to explain to my students that we will be trying something new. I will also explain why I think it will benefit them – in your case, this is the importance of applying psychology knowledge and learning by doing. I try to be honest with them by saying that it may not work perfectly the first time we do it, which is why I will be looking for them to help me refine the approach when we do it again. I think it is important for students to have some ownership and input into their learning experience.

Now undertake Task 7.3.

Task 7.3 **Constructing a TBV**

1. Looking again at the cyberbullying TBV, make a judgement on how closely you think it meets the seven principles of vignette design (prior knowledge, relevant content, self-directed learning, elaboration through discussion, interest in the subject matter, integration of knowledge and teaching objectives).
2. Construct a TBV of about 250 words on eyewitness testimony.
   After you have prepared your students, it is helpful to follow a structured process. This one is adapted from stages proposed by Silva et al. (2018):

- Stage 1. Defining the problem.
- The first thing to do is to discuss the TBV with the whole class and explain how the PBL strategy will work. You will probably need to contextualise the 'problem' and set it within the relevant areas of the psychology curriculum. For example, the cyberbullying TBV should be contextualised in the area of social psychology which is about social influence, so you will need to remind your students about the salient topics in this area but without guiding them too specifically to just one approach. You might want, for instance, to ask them if there were any other areas in Psychology that might be useful in Graham's dilemma.

TEACHING SKILLS OF APPLICATION

- Stage 2. Organising your students into groups.

  Small groups of about six work best in classroom based PBL so you will need to decide whether you are going to select the groups yourself, or whether you will allow your students to form themselves into their own groups. There are advantages and disadvantages to each method. If teacher selected, then you can use your knowledge of the students to work out which students will work best together, however you might think this goes against the student-centred philosophy of PBL. If the students select groups themselves, there may be the risk of some of them feeling left out, or the brighter more motivated students might club together to form a strong, successful team which might leave other groups in weaker positions, which could be demotivating. Neither method is perfect so you might have to make adjustments if the groups are not working out too well. There are some useful suggestions about both methods in further resources at the end of this chapter.

- Stage 3. Diagnosing the problem.

  This involves getting your groups to share what they know and encouraging them to work out together what they need to find out to address the problem. You can help them here by posing questions to get them to reflect on what they already know. Pooling knowledge in this way is underpinned by the theory of social constructivism (Vygotsky, 1978). It also resonates with Mercer's (1995, 2000) work on the role of talk in the classroom in developing children's thinking.

- Stage 4. Doing the research.

  It is usual, but not essential, for students to do their research outside the classroom. Inside or outside, your students need to look at academic sources such as books and journals to help them to understand the problem better. You may need to guide them in how to analyse the problem in more detail and make suggestions about how they might connect their psychological knowledge to the situation. Research tasks could be allocated by the group to either individuals or pairs (the latter works well). Each group should then be advised to organise the information they have gained under three main headings in their report:

  1. describe the problem;
  2. suggest hypotheses about the cause of the problem;
  3. decide on the proposed solutions.

- Stage 5. Sharing understandings.

  Each group presents their report to the class. You can ask the group about their different solutions, what they had learned about the topic and what they learned from the task.

  I have always been an advocate of active reflection since being inspired by Schön's (1983) book *'The Reflective Practitioner'*. Following your first experience of designing and using a TBV, it is inevitable that some things will have gone well, others less so. Reflecting on the various stages as described enables you to build on this first attempt and to improve. I very much hope that you find the PBL process in using TBVs to be valuable and one that you increasingly develop and refine for your own approach to teaching psychology.

Now undertake Task 7.4.

> Task 7.4 **Strategies for teaching with vignettes**
>
> Looking again at the cyberbullying TBV, make a judgement on how closely you think it meets the seven principles of vignette design (prior knowledge, relevant content, self-directed learning, elaboration through discussion, interest in the subject matter, integration of knowledge and teaching objectives).
>
> List strategies you would use for a TBV with sensitive material.
>
> Suggest ways in which you can encourage non-motivated groups to work on a TBV.

7.5 SUMMARY AND KEY POINTS

In this chapter, I have made a case for a particular form of PBL as an effective way of helping your students to understand the psychology topics they are introduced to by encouraging them to apply their knowledge to representations of 'real-life' issues in the form of a TBV.

PBL is a broad approach to constructivist teaching and learning where the emphasis is on what the students learn rather than what the teachers teach. While it has not yet been widely adopted in the secondary school and FE sector, the literature would suggest there are many benefits to psychology students. There are many forms of PBL but I have argued that designing and using a TBV is an approach that works well.

You should now:

- understand PBL as a teaching approach in Psychology.
- understand the pedagogical rationale for constructing TBVs.
- have a strategy for using a TBV as a class task.

Check the requirements of your initial teacher education programme to see which have been addressed in this unit.

FURTHER RESOURCES AND WEBSITES

For information, extending what is in this chapter, we recommend you read Section 14 'Helping pupils learn' in the core textbook for the Learning to Teach series: Capel, S., Leask, M. and Younie, S. with E. Hidson and J. Lawrence (9th edn 2022) *Learning to Teach in the Secondary School: A Companion to School Experience*. Abingdon Routledge: Taylor Francis.

The Maastricht Seven Jump Approach to PBL

University webpage with details of how the PBL process works https://www.maastricht university.nl/education/why-um/problem-based-learning [Accessed 3.11.20].

Teaching Sensitive Topics

Hulme, J.A. (2018). "Touching a nerve": Studying sensitive topics in psychology. *Psychology Review*, 23(3). https://eprints.keele.ac.uk/4266/ [Accessed 2.11.20].

Heath, M., Due, C., Hamood, W., Hutchinson, A., Leiman, T., Maxfield, K. and Warland, J., 2017. Teaching sensitive material: A multi-disciplinary perspective. *ergo*, 4(1). https://ojs.unisa.edu.au/index.php/ergo/article/view/1450 [Accessed 2.11.20].

Lynagh, M., Gilligan, C. and Handley, T. (2010). Teaching about, and dealing with, sensitive issues in schools: How confident are pre-service teachers? *Asia-Pacific Journal of Health, Sport and Physical Education*, 1(3–4), 5–11.

Selecting Groups

The TeachHUB Team (2019) 30 ways to arrange students for group work https://www.teachhub.com/classroom-management/2019/09/30-ways-to-arrange-students-for-group-work/ [Accessed 2.11.20].

Theories of Constructivism

McLeod (2019) Constructivism as a theory for teaching and learning.
An accessible web page that explains simply and clearly the principles of constructivism and the main constructivist theories. https://www.simplypsychology.org/constructivism.html#:~:text=The%20constructivist%20theory%20posits%20that,their%20perceptions%20of%20that%20world. [Accessed 2.11.20].

UK Examining Boards for Psychology

England

Assessment and Qualifications Alliance (AQA)

AQA (2019) AS AND A-LEVEL PSYCHOLOGY AS (7181) A-level (7182) Specifications For teaching from September 2015 onwards For AS exams in May/June 2016 onwards For A-level exams in May/June 2017 onwards Version 1.1 24 June 2019.
https://www.aqa.org.uk/subjects/psychology/as-and-a-level/psychology-7181-7182 Accessed 2.11.20

EdExcel/BTEC-Pearson Qualifications
https://qualifications.pearson.com/content/dam/pdf/A%20Level/Psychology/2015/support/AS-and-A-level-Psychology-guide.pdf Accessed 2.11.20

OCR (Oxford, Cambridge and RSA Examination)
https://www.ocr.org.uk/Images/171732-specification-accredited-a-level-gce-psychology-h567.pdf Accessed 2.11.20

Wales

Wales Joint Education Committee (WJEC)
https://www.wjec.co.uk/media/veplsnrk/wjec-gce-psychology-spec-from-2015-e-14-05-20.pdf Accessed 2.11.20

Scotland

Scottish Qualifications Authority (SQA)
https://www.sqa.org.uk/files/hn/DD9P804.pdf Accessed 2.11.20

Northern Ireland

Council for the curriculum, examinations and assessment (CCEA)
Awarding bodies for Psychology: AQA, Pearson, WJEC and OCR https://ccea.org.uk/regulation/qualifications-regulation/qualsni/alevels-accredited-first-teaching-2015 Accessed 2.11.20

8 DEVELOPING PSYCHOLOGICALLY LITERATE STUDENTS

Clare Deavall

INTRODUCTION

If you have ever read a piece of psychological research and immediately applied it to your own life, then you are probably aware of the concept of psychological literacy. Indeed, it could be argued that with the growing numbers of psychology graduates in society, and increasingly easy access to psychological knowledge online, we are all 'armchair psychologists'. However, being able to utilise relevant and valid psychology research effectively in the classroom requires a little more skill than the lifestyle magazines might have us believe.

McGovern et al. (2010, p11) define psychological literacy as 'being insightful and reflective about one's own and others' behaviour and mental processes' and having the ability to apply 'psychological principles to personal, social, and organisational issues in work, relationships and the broader community'. The definition given on the website www.psychliteracy.com (a website initiated by Jacqueline Cranney, Associate Professor of Psychology at the University of New South Wales (UNSW Australia) and a major contributor to this area) is that 'it is the intentional application of psychological science to meet personal, professional, and societal goals'; in other words, using our psychological knowledge to improve the outcomes in our own and others' lives. It follows, then, that we can help our students achieve more because we have knowledge of the theories of learning, for example and how to study and retain course content more effectively.

This chapter gives you an idea of how psychological theory can be applied to both different aspects of pedagogy as well as helping you think about the development of students as psychological thinkers outside of the content of the examination board specification. The focus, then, is to suggest practical activities that encourage students to 'think psychologically' and develop their skills beyond the course content that they can use in later life.

DOI: 10.4324/9781003162223-9

CLARE DEAVALL

OBJECTIVES

By the end of this chapter you should be able to:

- understand why is psychological literacy important.
- see students as science practitioners.
- understand the role of peer mentoring and peer-assisted learning.
- be able to develop innovative assessment.
- recognise the importance of developing employability skills.
- understand the contribution of work volunteering.

Check which requirements of your initial teacher education programme relate to this unit.

8.1 WHY IS PSYCHOLOGICAL LITERACY IMPORTANT?

In England, while there is no specific mention of psychological literacy in the GCE subject-level conditions and requirements for psychology, possibly because it is placed alongside biology, chemistry and physics, there is reference to a minimum requirement of 'specialist vocabulary and terminology' (https://www.gov.uk/government/publications/gce-subject-level-conditions-and-requirements-for-psychology (OFQUAL, 2014, p28). On the other hand, in the English Department for Education's guidance for psychology GCSE, psychological literacy is prominent in the aims and objectives of the course:

> Students will be equipped with a psychological literacy that enables them to apply their knowledge and skills in their everyday lives, including making informed decisions about further study and career choices.
>
> (DFE-00213-2015, p3)

Psychological literacy is central to the study of psychology at undergraduate level:

> the skills acquired "represent a coherent set of knowledge, skills and values that underpin students' psychological literacy and which enable them to apply psychology to real life contexts."
>
> (BPS, 2019, p19)

It makes sense, then, given the numbers of students choosing to study psychology that as teachers we give our students an understanding of the term and, more importantly, use our own psychological literacy within our pedagogy.

The term was originally used by Boneau (1990), to describe the core knowledge and skill set acquired through the study of psychology. While this has now widened out to become more applied as seen above, it is a useful starting point when thinking about initial planning for schemes of work and lessons (Chapter 2). Boneau (1990) focused on the 'terms and concepts ... judged to be of sufficient importance that they should be general knowledge within the psychological community' (p.891). Using questionnaires given to authors of textbooks in ten psychological subfields, he identified 'Psychology's Top 100' concepts and ranked lists of the top 100 terms in each of the subfields. While these would undoubtedly have changed over the last 30 years, the terms identified are still in very common usage today. Within the classroom, the idea of a common language of the subject is a powerful way to create an ethos of 'thinking like a psychologist'. Indeed, the use of specialist terminology is a way for subjects to be unique and identifiable. Actively planning the language that you use in lessons is a deliberate and intention application of the knowledge you have. Going further and deciding how your students will record and retain this knowledge is even better for them. You could, for example use concept maps, vocabulary lists, or definitions charts.

Now undertake Task 8.1.

Task 8.1 **Key terminology**

In Chapter 3, threshold concepts were discussed. Look back at these explanations.

Using Table 5 'The Top 100 concepts' from Boneau (1990) available at (see Table 8.1): https://web.archive.org/web/20150227074717/http:/people.auc.ca/brodbeck/4007/article12.pdf discuss with your peers or mentor which of these are threshold concepts for students. This could be extended to each topic by looking at the concepts identified in Boneau's Table 6 for the relevant subfield.

Look at the topic you are going to plan next. Identify from the specification what key terms are stated. Decide if there are others that you would also include. On your next lesson plan, highlight the key terms to be used and identify how students are going to record and retain this knowledge.

Table 8.1 Top 100 Concepts (Bonneau, 1990)

Absolute threshold	Hypothesis testing
Action potential	Id
Aggression	Independent variable
Anxiety	Infant-mother attachment
Anxiety disorder	Information-processing approach
Artificial intelligence (AI)	Instrumental behaviour
Associationism	Intelligence
Attachment	Intelligence quotient
Attitude change, factors influencing	Introversion-extraversion
Attitudes and behaviour	Just noticeable difference

(Continued)

Attribution theory	Law of effect
Avoidance learning	Long-term memory
Binocular depth cues	Longitudinal research
Central nervous system	Meaning
Cerebellum	Mental illness
Cerebral cortex	Mental imagery
Cerebral hemispheres	Milgram's obedience experiment
Childhood, characteristics of	Nature-nurture controversy
Classical conditioning	Neocortex
Cognitive development	Neurotransmitter
Cognitive dissonance theory	Normal distribution
Conditioned stimulus	Operant conditioning
Conditioned reflex	Origin of Species
Conformity	Personality
Consciousness	Phobia
Contrast	Placebo effect
Control group	Positive reinforcement
Correlation coefficient	Prejudice
Correlational method	Prosocial behaviour
Dendrite	Psychoanalytic theory
Deoxyribonucleic acid	Psychosis
Dependent variable	Psychosomatic disorders
Depression	Psychotherapy
Depth perception	Rehearsal
Determinism	Reinforcement
Developmental stages, theories of	Right hemisphere
Distance cues	Sample
Ego	Semantic memory
Electroencephalograph	Serial position function
Empiricism	Short-term memory
Aetiology	Significance level
Evolution and functionalism	Significant difference
Experimental group	Social influence
Extinction	Socialisation
Forgetting curve	Socioeconomic status
Free association	Traits
Free recall	Unconscious
Frequency (audition)	Unconscious motivation
Gestalt principles of organisation	Visual angle
Gestalt psychology	Visual depth perception

8.2 STUDENTS AS SCIENCE PRACTITIONERS

Psychology qualifications place considerable emphasis on psychology as a scientific discipline. While this is still up for debate in the wider academic world, there is no escaping from the fact that research methods are directly and indirectly assessed in all areas of the examinations. Students, then, need to view themselves as science practitioners from the outset of the course. It seems impossible to discuss any piece of research without understanding what method was used to find the results and what impact this has on evaluation. The setting, the way participants were selected, the control of variables and many other factors can be used to assess the reliability and validity of the research.

8.2.1 Teaching the Science Content

This leads to a dilemma when starting planning for teaching classes at the start of term – how do we teach research methods? I have tried it numerous ways and all have advantages and disadvantages. Teaching it as the first topic gives an excellent foundation and helps with developing vital skills to understand the later topics but can be a less engaging way of starting the course. Teaching it as a discrete topic once some basic psychological knowledge is established can be very useful when getting students to design studies but can halt the flow of understanding of the different areas within the subject. Teaching the relevant aspect of research methods embedded within the rest of the curriculum (see Chapter 3) makes the content relevant and memorable but can be confusing when revising the topic. This dilemma would make an excellent discussion point within a mentor meeting or peer meeting while training especially if coupled with trying to come up with ways to minimise the disadvantages.

Whichever way you teach it, one thing is clear, there must be a focus on the role of science in every lesson and every opportunity taken for students to undertake practical studies as much as possible. In my experience, this can be a challenge: some students take psychology even though they do not have strength in science and others take it as a further science subject alongside biology or chemistry. This inevitably leads to a large variation in the skill set they bring with them. This is where the effective use of cognitive science can be most helpful to ensure your teaching is effective.

8.2.2 Knowledge, Understanding and Application

Students need to know, understand and be able to apply their scientific knowledge. Let us use validity as an example of an important threshold concept for psychological literacy.

The first step in being able to know, understand and apply validity is that they need them to *know* what *validity* is and the various forms they will come across. The concept of validity was defined by Kelly (1927, p14) who stated that a test is valid if it measures what it claims to measure. According to Atkinson and Shiffrin (1968), just by repeating the definition enough times, it will be transferred to long-term memory and be available for recall should it be needed. This is often described as rote learning. However, there are issues with this. Craik and Watkins (1973) criticised the multi-store model (Atkinson & Shiffrin, 1968) by showing that it was not just a case of how many times something was repeated but the type of rehearsal that led to learning. The more effective type is elaborative rehearsal (a memory technique that involves thinking about the meaning of the term to be remembered, as opposed to simply repeating the word to yourself over and over), which is where we make associations with pre-existing knowledge in LTM or think about the meaning of a new memory. A simple demonstration can be given to help students use elaborative rehearsal to learn the definition. For example, we could measure the circumference of students' heads in the class with no explanation of what we are doing. Then we could tell them that we now know who is the most intelligent in the class. This is virtually guaranteed to lead to a discussion around the fact that head size does not indicate intelligence – and then we introduce the definition of validity and in this way it has meaning and is more likely to be able to be recalled in the future. (This simple task can also introduce reliability, ethics, confounding variables and several other concepts in research methods!)

The second step in being able to know, understand and apply validity is *understanding* – means that material can be interpreted and described in a different way. Once a term has been learnt (the knowledge is there), we need as teachers to see that this has been understood. If our students are science practitioners, then they need to be able to see where the abstract scientific concepts they have learnt are relevant to studies in the course content. Take one of the many laboratory experiments used in the memory topic such as Peterson and Peterson (1959). Students will often regurgitate that lab experiments are high/low in validity (depending on whether they are talking about internal or external validity). This is correct but only demonstrates knowledge and not understanding so does not gain high marks in exams. A simple way to check understanding when using questioning would be to say 'because…' if a student states the simple knowledge. By having to complete the sentence in their own words they are demonstrating that they have understood how the concept relates to the research.

The final step in being able to know, understand and apply validity is *application*. This gives excellent opportunities for modelling by both the teacher and peers. Bandura (1977) stated that:

> Learning would be exceedingly laborious, not to mention hazardous, if people had to rely solely on the effects of their own actions to inform them what to do. Fortunately, most human behavior is learned observationally through modelling: from observing others one forms an idea of how new behaviours are performed, and on later occasions this coded information serves as a guide for action.
>
> (pg. 22)

Much research has been done to show the effectiveness of modelling in the classroom. Rosenshine's must-read work 'Principles of Instruction' (2012) lists modelling as one of the ten research-based principles to use. He advocates using teacher thinking aloud as well as worked examples to provide cognitive support. One way to structure this is through the 'I do, We do, You Do' method as this can introduce difficult concepts without increasing cognitive load.

DEVELOPING LITERATE STUDENTS

For example, an extended writing question:

Discuss Ainsworth's Strange Situation (1970) as a way of assessing types of attachment.

This requires the student to describe Ainsworth's (1970) study and evaluate/discuss it. When teaching this study, and only after students have learnt what validity is, the following tasks could be used:

1. I Do: Teacher models by thinking out loud how Ainsworth's (1970) study could be argued to be valid if other research suggests that there is a consistency between early attachment type and later attachment type, whereas it could also be argued that because it only includes the mother, it is in fact measuring the mother-child relationship specifically and not the attachment type the child has in general.
2. We Do: In pairs, students could discuss the teacher's points, finding research support to justify or challenge the line of argument. Then they write a summary paragraph in answer to the extended writing question.
3. You Do: Students could design a new study to test attachment type that addresses the issues with validity which have been discussed.

In this way, students are learning what the scientific concept is, and can use it effectively in practice.

Now undertake Task 8.2.

Task 8.2 **Concept cards**

Create a bank of research methods concept cards based on the specification and laminate them to keep on your desk/have them in an electronic format. Examples might be 'What method is the researcher using?' or 'What measure of central tendency was used?'

When you are teaching a new piece of research, randomly pick a question and a student to answer.

If they cannot answer the question, then you could pick another student at random until you get the correct answer. Then get the original student to explain why that answer is correct.

NB If they cannot answer the question because the information was not available (as is sometimes the case for research summaries in the textbooks), then you could model searching for the answer on the Internet from the original research.

Now undertake Task 8.3.

Task 8.3 **Focus on research methods**

Give students a method and results section from a study relevant to the topic that you are teaching. Use one that is relatively simple if this is the first time you have used original research with them.

> Students read through the study and highlight anything that is related to the research methods used. They could have their research methods glossary or a copy of the specification to help them.
>
> Use whole-class questioning to check understanding of the concepts highlighted.
>
> Reflect on what you have learned from this activity and how you might improve your method of teaching it another time.

8.3 PEER MENTORING AND PEER-ASSISTED LEARNING

There has been for some time a confusion over whether peer mentoring and peer-assisted learning are the same thing. Traditional mentoring usually has a hierarchical nature which Clutterbuck (1991) argues is perceived to be an older, more experienced individual passing down knowledge of how a task is done to a younger less experienced colleague. Peer mentoring though, which is less well researched, 'is typically conducted between people of equal status' (Topping, 2005, p321). This allows for the supportive role to be two-way and beneficial to both.

8.3.1 Zone of Proximal Development

A knowledge of Vygotsky's theory on 'The zone of proximal development' is useful to understand the pedagogical value of peer learning. ZPD is defined by Vygotsky (1978) as 'the distance between the actual developmental level as determined by independent problem-solving and the level of potential development as determined through problem-solving under adult guidance or in collaboration with more capable peers' (p. 86) (Figure 8.1).

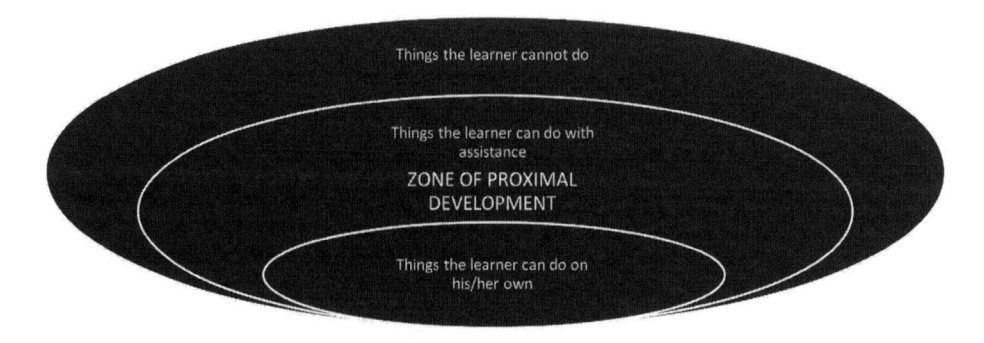

Figure 8.1 Zone of proximal development

8.3.2 Peer-Assisted Learning

Peer learning, then, could be argued to be when students have equal status but different skills. In the British Higher Education system in the 1990s, many institutions adopted a 'peer-assisted learning' (PAL) approach. This involved identifying students with good communication skills and academic brilliance to be PAL leaders and training them through an induction course to work with students in their cohort under the supervision of a coordinator (usually a member of staff). This approach has been widened to include many forms of peer support, coaching and mentoring but as Andrews and Clark (2011) state in their comprehensive review of the research 'Peer Mentoring Works!' They do, however, also point out that the form peer learning should take depends on the purpose for which it is being used. It is important to consider whether the point is to improve academic outcomes, to help with socio-emotional development of students identified as vulnerable during transition, to create an ethos of excellence shared by all students or encourage a sense of belonging to the subject or class. I would argue that effective peer learning can do all these things.

8.3.3 Peer Mentoring – Study Buddies

Often students embark on psychology courses with little knowledge of what the subject involves. In other words, their psychological literacy is low. A possible technique to rapidly increase this is pairing up students from different year groups to be 'Study Buddies'. This takes advantage of the 'superior' skills and knowledge of the older students, for example who have a greater knowledge of the key terminology, the areas of the course, the structure of essays such as examination technique, homework, which can be shared with younger students. The benefit for the older students and the teacher is the constant review of the younger students' course content and a sense of pride in their contribution enhancing the ethos of the subject. This works particularly well online via online platforms, I found with my students, and to be most effective needs to be really focused. For example, prior to younger students handing in a piece of homework, their buddy could pre-assess for accuracy of terminology, balance between description and evaluation or any other skills/content focus that the teacher has identified as an area of need. Younger students could then amend any work prior to hand-in and indicate their amendments as part of developing their metacognition.

8.3.4 Using Peer Learning in Lessons

PAL can be seen as advancing pair work and can be very effective during lessons as well. Rather than creating pairs due to location (e.g. table pairs), consider pairing students of equal ability or due to identified areas of strength/weakness. Discuss methods of pairing in a mentor meeting or as part of a study group to see how peer-assisted learning can be more effectively utilised within lessons.

Now undertake Task 8.4.

> Task 8.4 **Peer mentoring**
>
> Following assessment of a significant piece of work, for example extended writing/ essay, rank order students according to their grade. If you have students with the same grade identify them as +/=/- against the banding level criteria.
>
> Divide the class into pairs according to the focus you have for the feedback. For example, if you want to improve the level of detail in their description, you could pair students of similar ability and each takes a section to improve and then teaches each other. If you want to improve the line of argument in discussion, you could pair a stronger student with one who needs to improve on this area and get them to compare essays.
>
> Reflect on the outcomes for both students and for you as a teacher. What level of instruction do you need to give students to enable them to understand the purpose of the activity in terms of psychological literacy?

8.4 INNOVATIVE ASSESSMENT

The Education Endowment Foundation in their Teaching and Learning Toolkit (https://educationendowmentfoundation.org.uk/evidence-summaries/teaching-learning-toolkit/) rated high-quality assessment as the strand of teaching that had the most impact on pupil progress. Their summary of international research indicated that effective feedback and pupil monitoring could add eight months of progress. Rosenshine (2012) also refers to feedback, assessment and pupil monitoring in several of his principles. While it would be entirely relevant here to discuss the psychology and research that underpins this (see, for example, Dunlosky, 2013; Hattie, 2009), I have decided to focus on five practical ideas that engage students and reduce teacher workload while at the same time encouraging psychological literacy.

8.4.1 Creative Use of Multiple Choice Questions (MCQs)

MCQs are a great way of quickly assessing what individual students know and can be used as a simple method of retrieval practise. Many textbooks have a section of MCQs at the end of each topic. The most important thing though is what happens after the students have answered. Rather than stopping after each student has revealed how many answers they have correct, consider using selected questions as learning opportunities. Instead of asking students what the right answer is, why not ask them for a wrong answer and get them to explain WHY it is wrong. This not only will help other students to understand why they are wrong if they selected that answer but will also allow the student answering to reflect on their own learning. It will also identify misconceptions and misunderstandings. All with very little effort from you.

8.4.2 Concept Mapping

A form of visual representation of the relationships between concepts in a topic, these are a great tool and can be used in a variety of ways. There are several ways that they can be set out: mindmaps, hierarchy charts and spider diagrams are some examples. They can be used at the start of a topic to assess current knowledge, as a midpoint assessment to identify gaps or at the end of the topic as an assessment of progress. They can also be used as a form of spaced learning or as a whole-class activity where you get students to help you create a giant one for display! There are some excellent free online tools such as Lucidchart and Mindomo that can be used either to construct a map that you want them to fill in (using the awarding body specification as the nodules), or that students can use together and share their ideas.

8.4.3 Online Study Tools

A powerful device I use regularly is online gaming through websites such as Quizlet or Kahoot. If you are short of time, there are often resources that have been prepared by other teachers on topics that follow the specification (but I would always advise you to carefully check all the answers). Quizlet works based on questions/definitions and answers – like interactive flashcards which is great for assessing psychological terminology. These can be used as a recap activity at the start of a lesson, a test at the end of a lesson or as a game. This has lots of uses to make your assessment more efficient. Kahoot uses mobile technology to allow students to log in and play as individuals or as a team to answer questions you have pre-set. These can be projected onto a white board so that there is no hiding and always creates lots of discussion and competition – very useful to engage and motivate.

8.4.4 Keynote Speaker

This requires some preparation beforehand but is a creative way of assessing learning, as well as giving students the opportunities to develop other skills. Within a topic, allocate each student a keynote question (e.g. Was Zimbardo right to stop the Stanford Prison Experiment after six days?). This could be teacher-led or student-led. At the start of the lesson following this section being taught, the student who is the keynote speaker delivers a five-minute speech answering the question with their opinion. They can then be questioned by the audience to develop their line of argument. This can also be used to draw synoptic links with other topics as well as encouraging evaluation.

8.4.5 Whole-Class Feedback

Dylan Wiliam (2017) in *Embedded Formative Assessment* says that effective feedback should not just be pointing out errors but showing students how to

CLARE DEAVALL

take action to improve. Traditionally, students have written their work to be assessed and then teachers have spent many hours writing comments on it.

There are two issues with individual written feedback:

- It is not always useful as the comments are often taken from the assessment criteria on mark schemes, which are descriptive rather than analytical. This means that they are often vague and meaningless to the student.
- It takes a very long time.

Of course, there is a need for individual written feedback and students do need a personalised approach, but there are many times that whole-class feedback would be a far more effective way of delivering the messages that need to be heard.

So how do we move from commenting to a recipe for action? Imagine you have read your class's essays about behaviourism and half of them have failed to describe the difference between reinforcement and punishment correctly. If you were writing a comment it would likely be 'describe key terms correctly' – but if they knew the correct term, they would not have got it wrong. In whole-class feedback, you could put the statement 'Reinforcement *increases* the likelihood of a behaviour being repeated, punishment *decreases* the likelihood of a behaviour being repeated'. Ask students to give examples or explain why to check their understanding. Then ask students to read through their essay and highlight if they got this correct or underline if they got it wrong. Those who got it wrong then write the correct version out. Those who were correct could look if they had gone on to explain the difference between positive and negative reinforcement for example.

There are many ways of assessing students' progress and each school will have an assessment policy that guides you as well. You could discuss with your mentor what effective assessment techniques they use that you could also try.

Now undertake Task 8.5.

Task 8.5 **Assessment methods**

Look at this A–Z list of assessment methods https://www.reading.ac.uk/web/files/eia/A-Z_of_Assessment_Methods_FINAL_table.pdf

These include: – Abstract, articles, book review, case studies, concept maps, designing learning materials, essays, examinations, essay plans, learning logs, make or design something, mini-practicals, MCQs, observations, online discussion boards, oral presentations, posters, role play, short answer questions, wiki/blogs, viva voce.

With your mentor, pick one method that you will trial in a lesson. Think about what the PURPOSE of this assessment method is. Consider what might be the benefits for you as a teacher as well as the benefits for your students. After the

> lesson, reflect on what happened. Did the assessment fulfil its purpose, what went well, what did not work and what would you do differently next time? You could ask students for feedback on the method and also what innovative methods of assessment they have seen in other lessons.

8.5 DEVELOPING EMPLOYABILITY SKILLS

Yorke and Knight (2006) define employability skills as 'a set of achievements, understandings and personal attributes that make individuals more likely to gain employment and to be successful in their chosen occupations'. They include the soft skills that allow you to work well with others, apply knowledge to solve problems, and to fit into any work environment. In the Youth Employment UK Employability Review (2017) of the frameworks and research about employability in the United Kingdom, five skills were seen as the most important: teamwork, communication, problem-solving, self-belief and self-management.

Success at School which is a national careers website for students aged 13-19 (https://successatschool.org/) identify those and several others:

- Communication
- Teamwork
- Initiative
- Problem-solving
- Computer/IT skills
- Organisation
- Leadership
- Hard work and dedication
- Creativity
- Numeracy
- Reliability

In England, 63,490 students were entered for Psychology A-level in 2020 according to Ofqual, and according to UCAS, of the over 75,000 students who studied psychology at university in 2014-5, 72% went directly into employment following graduation. The top graduate destinations were:

1. Human health and social work
2. Education
3. Retail/administrative and support
4. Legal, social and welfare professions
5. Business, HR and finance
6. Marketing, PR and sales

CLARE DEAVALL

Most psychology students, then, do not go onto become psychologists so it is important that as teachers, we encourage them to recognise and develop those skills that they will need to become more employable.

Suggestions to improve employability

- Peer Mentoring. As identified previously this can aid academic achievement but it also helps with the soft skills of experience of responsibility, time management and developing communication (Clark & Andrews, 2012).
- Designing Research. This supports several of the skills, including initiative, problem-solving, organisation and numeracy as well as potentially teamwork and communication – a useful way to develop skills in project management.
- Presentations. These can be in class to start with and work particularly well if there is a reflective activity at the end, which could focus on the skills involved. If your school runs events to support mental health awareness, for example students can act as information hubs on some of the common mental health conditions, providing they are supported by a member of staff or professional to signpost to additional support if needed.
- Extended Project Qualifications. Many schools offer this to provide evidence for employability skills as well as a deep interest in a topic.

Now undertake Task 8.6.

Task 8.6 **Employability**

Using a scheme of learning or curriculum plan for a unit that has not yet been taught:

Identify the tasks that could be used to develop the skills outlined below.

At the end of these tasks, show students this list of employability skills and ask them to identify which they feel they have developed as well as self-belief and self-management.

- Communication
- Teamwork
- Initiative
- Problem-solving
- Computer/IT skills
- Organisation
- Leadership
- Hard work and dedication
- Creativity
- Numeracy
- Reliability

Encourage your students to keep a record of examples of these skills that they can use to write college or UCAS applications or to include in their CVs.

8.6 WORK VOLUNTEERING

For those students who want to embark on a career in psychology or are interested in finding out whether it would be a good choice for them, work volunteering is an excellent way of getting experience to include on applications for university or future careers. However, there is a problem for students in that there are very few opportunities for volunteering (or indeed, work experience placements), especially in clinical psychology. Due to patient confidentiality, data protection and other issues, there are limited roles. Some NHS trusts do have schemes where volunteers can work within other related areas and encourage this as any experience in a care or clinical setting is well-regarded. It is worth checking the local trusts' websites to see if there is an application system in place.

Students, then, who want to gain experience need to be creative. Volunteering in old people's centres can be a valuable way of seeing how the social care system works and how specific conditions such as dementia are treated. Volunteering to teach reading in schools or at a play scheme can be an excellent way of building knowledge of theories of education and child development. Any volunteering can lead to other opportunities and is an excellent way of developing and demonstrating the soft skills discussed above. Discussions in class about the role of psychology in society can often lead to great ideas or connections that can be utilised as well as encouraging students to see psychology in its wider context.

As a psychology undergraduate there are more opportunities as students are then considered as adults. Many helplines and crisis centres have volunteers who work with vulnerable people or act as advocates for them. Many universities also have helplines or buddying schemes to support other students. For those students applying to university with the aim of a career in psychology in mind, researching the potential for volunteering can be another factor to consider when selecting the best university for them.

8.7 SUMMARY AND KEY POINTS

It is clear that an understanding of psychological literacy is important as it provides students with the key psychological terminology that allows them to demonstrate their knowledge of psychology. Furthermore, developing students' ability to help each other through peer assessment and peer mentoring schemes allows them to develop a critical eye on psychology. Through the development of employability skills and work volunteering students are able to see how their knowledge of psychology applies to the real world to the benefit of their future careers.

You should now:

- understand why psychological literacy is important.
- see students as science practitioners.

- understand the role of peer mentoring and peer-assisted learning.
- be able to develop innovative assessment.
- recognise the importance of developing employability skills.
- understand the contribution of work volunteering.

Check the requirements of your initial teacher education programme to see which have been addressed in this unit.

FURTHER RESOURCES AND WEBSITES

The Youth Employment UK Employability Review (2017) (online) available at: https://www.youthemployment.org.uk/dev/wp-content/uploads/2017/07/Youth-Employment-UK-Employability-Review-June-2017.pdf (Accessed 27th September 2020)

Education Endowment Foundation (2011) Teaching and Learning Toolkit (online) available at: https://educationendowmentfoundation.org.uk/evidence-summaries/teaching-learning-toolkit/ (Accessed 26th September 2020)

Success at School (2020) What are Key Skills (online) available at: https://successatschool.org/advicedetails/523/What-are-key-skills%3F-Employability-skills-to-help-you-get-a-job%C2%A0-%C2%A0%C2%A0 (Accessed 27th September 2020)

Office of Qualifications and Exam Regulation (Ofqual) (2014) GCE subject level conditions and requirements for psychology (online) available at: https://www.gov.uk/government/publications/gce-subject-level-conditions-and-requirements-for-psychology (Accessed 24th September 2020)

Department for Education (DfE) (2015) GCSE subject content for Psychology (online) available at: https://www.gov.uk/government/publications/gcse-psychology (Accessed 24th September 2020)

University of Reading (2020) An A-Z of Assessment Methods (online) available at: https://www.reading.ac.uk/web/files/eia/A-Z_of_Assessment_Methods_FINAL_table.pdf (Accessed 26th September 2020)

Government statistics and useful resources about psychological literacy
Data showing the relative number of psychology students against other subjects. Ofqual (2019) Entries for GCSE, AS and A-level available at: https://www.gov.uk/government/statistics/provisional-entries-for-gcse-as-and-a-level-summer-2019-exam-series

The UCAS guide to psychology at university including available courses and information about post-graduate pathways available at: https://www.ucas.com/explore/subjects/psychology

A website that discusses psychological literacy, its applications and research summaries available at: http://www.psychliteracy.com/

9 LEARNING TO ASSESS PSYCHOLOGY AND GIVE STUDENTS MEANINGFUL FEEDBACK

Min Duchenski-Jassal

INTRODUCTION

According to the English Department for Education, affective assessment systems help drive improvement for students and teachers in several ways: they should be linked to improving the quality of teaching; they should ensure feedback to students helps to improve learning, focussing on specific and tangible objectives and they should produce recordable measures in order to make comparisons against expected standards and reflect progress over time (Department for Education, 2014).

There is a wealth of research into assessment and feedback, and this chapter explores some of this research, to allow you to make informed decisions on effective methods of assessment and feedback in the classroom. No one method is best, but rather the context of your school and your students must be considered when making decisions about what is appropriate for you and your students to aid learning and progression.

As you already have relevant knowledge of psychological theories related to thinking, development and learning, you are already at an advantage in understanding how young people learn. For instance, this chapter discusses the social constructivist theory of teaching and learning, drawing on the work of the famous developmental psychologist, Vygotsky.

This chapter outlines what formative and summative assessments are and a variety of teaching and learning strategies are discussed. It also explores research into meaningful and effective feedback and gives you some tips on how you can implement these in the Psychology classroom.

OBJECTIVES

By the end of this chapter, you should be able to:

- understand the purposes of formative and summative assessment and the value of using them to support pupil learning.

DOI: 10.4324/9781003162223-10

- plan effective Assessment for Learning (AfL) strategies that you can use in the Psychology classroom.
- begin to understand what effective meaningful feedback looks like in the Psychology classroom.

Check which requirements of your initial teacher education programme relate to this unit.

9.1 FORMATIVE AND SUMMATIVE ASSESSMENT

9.1.1 The Purposes of Formative and Summative Assessments

The Teachers' Standards for England state that teachers should 'make use of formative and summative assessment to secure pupils' progress' (Department for Education, 2011, p.12), therefore it is important to understand the purpose and value of each. Formative assessment is the process by which teachers evaluate their pupil's work, providing feedback to be used to modify and improve their responses. It is during this 'modification' process that students can reflect on their work and learn from their mistakes, to make progress. For teachers, formative assessment allows them to inform their teaching and decide the next steps for their students. For example, whether there has been misunderstanding and so re-teaching needs to take place, or whether students have grasped the concepts well and so teaching (and learning) can move forward. Types of formative feedback include written feedback, oral feedback, self-assessment and peer-assessment.

Summative assessment, on the other hand, is used as a form of assessment that forms a judgement of the pupil's achievement at a certain point of time. It usually takes place at the end of a unit of work or topic and is assessed with a grade or mark to indicate the pupil's level of attainment. It is for this reason that it is often referred to as assessment *of* learning (Stobart and Gipps, 1997). External assessments and examinations are considered examples of summative assessments. Whilst many schools have certain points in the year where formal summative assessments are carried out (e.g. to coincide with report writing or publication of attainment and predicted grades to parents), the reality of assessments within schools is that they form part of everyday conversations in lessons in order for teachers to monitor the progression of their students and move learning forward.

9.1.2 The Importance of Formative Assessment

In 1998, Paul Black and Dylan Wiliam conducted a large review of research evidence into formative assessment, concluding that formative assessment does indeed improve learning, with considerable gains in achievement (Black and Wiliam, 1998a). They specifically suggested that 'the effective use of formative assessment would increase achievement by between 0.4 and 0.7 standard deviations, which would be equivalent to a 50-70% increase in the rate of student learning' (Wiliam, 2017, p.38). Following up with their influential booklet for policy makers and practitioners, 'Inside the Black Box', Black and Wiliam (1998b) argued that the only way to raise standards was to make changes to the way teachers and students operated within the classroom. Indeed, many would agree that 'teachers must constantly change themselves based on the interactions they have with their learners in order to produce intellectual and behavioural success' (Rodriguez, 2012, p.177).

In their current use, the terms 'formative' and 'summative' do not apply to the assessments, but rather to the functions that they serve (Black and Wiliam, 2003). So, it is not the instrument that is formative, but rather the information gathered from it – which informs a teacher on how to modify the teaching and learning process to improve learning – that is 'formative' (Chappuis, 2015). For instance, a graded end of unit exam paper would appear to be a form of summative assessment. With marking and feedback, to which the students are expected to respond and improve their answers as part of the learning process, this assessment now functions in a formative manner, what Black, Harrison and Lee *et al.* (2003) have referred to as 'formative use of summative tests' (p.53). Thus, 'an assessment functions formatively to the extent that evidence about student achievement is elicited, interpreted, and used by teachers, learners, or their peers to make decisions about the next steps in instruction that are likely to be better, or better founded, than the decisions they would have made in the absence of that evidence' (Wiliam, 2017, p.48).

The importance in England of formative assessment is evident with the recent return to linear A Levels instead of modular assessments. In line with the re-introduction of linear qualifications, there has been a steady decline in the awarding of A*-C grades In A-Level Psychology from 2017 to 2019 (Schools Week, 2019). For a content-heavy subject like Psychology, students need to understand and retain a considerable amount of information. Therefore, the use of formative assessment, as well as summative assessments used in a formative way, is important for students to make progress over the course of two years.

Now undertake Task 9.1.

Task 9.1 **A memorable experience**

Think back to your own experiences of learning in the classroom. Write about one experience that is particularly memorable, in which you were able to learn and retain the information well. In doing so, consider the following questions:

- Did this learning result from formative or summative assessment (or both)?
- Why do you think you were able to learn and retain the information?
- Could you adapt something similar in your Psychology classroom?

9.1.3 Assessment for Learning (AfL)

Assessment for Learning (AfL) is a teaching and learning approach that creates opportunities for teachers and students to receive and act on feedback, to guide students forward in their learning. Many researchers use the terms formative assessment and assessment for learning (AfL) synonymously (e.g. Wiliam, 2017), whilst others draw distinctions between the two (e.g. Swaffield, 2011). This chapter considers both as going hand in hand with one another, with AfL being the approach and purpose of the assessment (*for* rather than *of* learning) and formative assessments (or AfL strategies) being the tools by which the approach can be achieved.

Hawe and Parr (2014) argue that AfL strategies are only effective when students are given ownership over their own learning. By engaging with the learning process, formative feedback can enhance self-regulated learning (SRL) strategies (Clark, 2012). SRL strategies lead to improved academic performance and motivation through the development of autonomous learning strategies as well as to improved employability (see Chapter 8). This approach stems from theorists such as John Dewey and Lev Vygotsky who believed learning was achieved through social and experiential means. So, for learning to take place, it is important for teaching to be pupil-centred (within the context of the school and classroom), which requires students to be active and responsible learners.

Thus, the traditional view of teachers being the 'experts' with students receiving content as passive recipients or 'empty vessels', is not conducive to effective learning (Rodriguez, 2012). In contrast, the social constructivist approach of more active participation in the learning process, with students at the centre of their own learning, places teachers as facilitators of this context-dependent learning process. For example, consider the teaching of the different approaches to Psychology. Rather than adopting a lecture-style approach of delivering the content, students could be given the responsibility of researching, planning and presenting (thus becoming experts in their topic area) the content to their peers. They can also be responsible for peer assessing each other's presentations and so encouraging a collaborative approach to assessment (see more on this in Section 3.4). Thus, the students are active, self-regulated learners, whilst teachers are more supportive than directive and as such, this approach is closely associated with AfL.

Pollard (1987, 1990) drew on the work of Vygotsky, Bruner and Walkerdine, Edwards and Mercer, as contributing to a social constructivist approach to teaching and learning and argued that 'since understanding can only be constructed in the mind of the learner, it is essential that learners exercise a significant degree of control of the process' (Pollard, 1990, p.247). Pollard (1990) stressed the importance of the teacher as a 'reflective agent', one who provides "meaningful and appropriate guidance and extension to the cognitive structuring and skill development arising from the child's initial experiences...(thus) supports the child's attempts to 'make sense' and enables them to cross the Zone of Proximal Development (ZPD)" (Pollard, 1990, p.251). The Zone of Proximal Development, first introduced by Vygotsky (1978), is the difference between what students can achieve on their own and what they can potentially achieve, with support from others. The teacher therefore can be the 'more knowledgeable other' (MKO; Vygotsky, 1978) who can help students in crossing this zone in learning and help the pupil make progress, with appropriate scaffolding and modelling. For example, when introducing students to Psychology exam questions for the first time, a Psychology teacher can aid students in developing their examination skills by providing an essay writing frame.

Of course, the teacher may not be the only person who is the MKO. For instance, a child's more capable peer may have superior knowledge and skill in a certain topic area and thus collaborative learning activities, such as group work or carousel tasks may be appropriate strategies to implement (see also Chapter 8 on the role of peers in supporting learning).

With regards to the MKO, teacher educators working in higher education (HE) often find that trainee teachers worry about their subject knowledge, with the fear that their students will 'catch them out' and they will be exposed as a failing MKO, if they do not know the answers to their students' questions. These trainee teachers find that part of their own learning (and refreshing of subject knowledge) takes place during the lesson planning process and creation of resources for their students. What should be noted is that most studies that have attempted to increase teacher subject knowledge, have found little or no subsequent effects in pupil achievement (Wiliam, 2017). Thus, suggesting that there is more to good teaching than just knowing your subject.

Nevertheless, it is often observed that the less confident teachers are with subject knowledge, the more *over*-planning takes place. Teachers can spend many hours creating wonderfully creative resources and PowerPoint presentations, full of images and 'interactive' animations. However, if their students had created those informative resources themselves, could they have learnt more and been at the centre of their own learning (and saved hours of teacher planning!), rather than being the passive recipients of that information through lecture-style 'teacher talk'? Like the approaches example above, rather than preparing resources and PowerPoint slides to introduce a new topic (e.g. issues in Psychology), students could be given the task of researching the different issues in small groups and be responsible for the planning and delivery of presentations of each issue to the rest of their peers. The teacher in this case is a facilitator who guides the students in search for the correct research and ensures that any misunderstandings are addressed. The approach to learning therefore is one of collaboration between teacher and pupil (Hooks, 1994), rather than one that is analogous to the banking system where the educator makes 'deposits' into the educatee (Freire, 1996).

Now undertake Task 9.2.

> **Task 9.2 Consider the following scenario**
>
> A trainee teacher is planning a 50-minute introductory lesson on research methods in Psychology.
>
> How could the trainee teacher incorporate a social constructivist approach to learning in this lesson? Use the lesson plan template used by your school or institution to help you plan this lesson.
>
> Some things to consider:
>
> - What will your lesson objectives be? What do you hope students will have learnt by the end of this first lesson?
> - What will your learning outcomes be? *How* will students achieve the lesson objectives?
> - What starter task could be used to engage students from the start of the lesson to encourage active participation and get them thinking about the importance of research methods?
> - Think about how students will be organised throughout the lesson and activities, for example will they work independently or in small groups or in a carousel?
> - How many main activities will students be able to take part in, considering the length of time you have?
> - What plenary task could be used to check what students have learnt in this lesson and to check that they have made progress since the starter task?

9.1.4 Assessment for Learning (AfL) Strategies

There are many strategies that can be used to assess and enhance learning. Table 2.4 lists some of these, although the list is not exhaustive! Furthermore, AfL strategies are not independent of one another, rather they are interdependent, 'each feeding into and from the others in an iterative manner' (Hawe and Parr, 2014, p.212).

How many of these strategies have you seen in the classroom and how effective in enhancing learning (specifically self-regulated learning) were they? - whether it was your own teacher when you were a pupil, a teacher you have observed, or yourself on teaching placement.

9.1.5 Some AFL Strategies

Becoming the 'expert' (peer instruction) - students can be assigned a small piece of information that they must become an expert in and 'teach' to their peers, for example different ethical considerations or the strengths and weaknesses of different research methods. This can be done in several ways, such as a carousel task or a prepare and present task.

Debates - students can be split into small groups to argue the case for or against topics or statements posed by the teacher, for example with any research study, students could debate whether the ends justified the means with regards to ethical considerations. Or with any of the classic debates in Psychology (e.g. free will vs determinism), students could argue opposite cases using theory and research to support their claims.

Exam questions – To check learning in the lesson students can complete short answer exam questions that can immediately be peer or self-assessed if the success criteria (mark scheme) is clear. The focus here is less on the grade and more on checking of understanding.

Exit/Entrance cards – students can indicate on arrival how much they already know about a topic and can do the same on exiting a lesson, so the teacher can inform their planning of subsequent lessons to fill in any gaps in knowledge.

Four corners – students move to one corner of the room to indicate their response to questions or statements posed by the teacher, for example 'Psychology is a science' and corner choices might be 'strongly agree', 'strongly disagree', 'not sure' or 'somewhat agree'. This can lead to further discussions and debates.

Hand signals – students can indicate their understanding by thumbs up, middle or down.

Questioning – see Chapter 3 on good-quality questions.

Quizzes – quizzes are a quick and easy way of checking knowledge. students can use response cards (below) or with a little more preparation these can be done interactively using tablets/mobile phones, for example Kahoot. Note: this is only effective as an AfL strategy if incorrect responses are addressed, students understand where they made mistakes, and know how to improve.

Reflection time – students can be given time to respond to teacher oral or written feedback to improve their work. Some schools encourage students to write their responses in another colour (e.g. green pen marking) so that students and teachers can easily see what improvements the students have made. This is useful for students when it comes to revision and useful for teachers when it comes to marking and future planning.

Response cards – students can write their answers to questions or statements (individually or in pairs/groups) and hold responses up for the teacher to quickly scan the whole room to check understanding, for example using mini-whiteboards.

Think-Pair-Share – students can initially think about their personal responses to a question or statement posed by the teacher, then share their thoughts with a partner. Finally, this can be shared with the class to allow for class discussion.

Using analogies – some psychological concepts are abstract and difficult to understand. The use of analogies may help students grasp the concepts better, for example in teaching Freud's concepts of the id, ego and superego the different components of personality are often compared to an angel (superego) and devil (id) sitting on either shoulder, with conflicting thoughts.

Using props – to help illustrate novel concepts, students can be encouraged to use props, for example in understanding sampling methods students can use different colour sweets (e.g. Skittles or Jelly Beans) to demonstrate how the sampling method is carried out, as well as practising the mathematical requirement of calculating percentages. Some schools also use animal brains bought from local butcher's shops (or plastic/rubber brains for the more squeamish!) that students can dissect to label and understand the different parts of the brain.

3-2-1 – a variation of the exit card, students can reflect and write three things they have learned from the lesson, two things they want to know more about and one question they have about the topic. Responses from students can inform future planning.

9.2 FEEDBACK

9.2.1 Effective Feedback – What Does This Look Like In Practice?

Feedback is one of several elements of formative assessment that are dependent on the existence of each other to be effective. Hattie and Timperlay (2007) argue that feedback is among the most powerful and critical influences on pupil learning and raising achievement. The Teacher Standards for England state that teachers should 'give pupils regular feedback, both orally and through accurate marking, and encourage pupils to respond to the feedback' (Department for Education, 2011, p.12). Whilst this does not mean that students must respond immediately in written response (as they may respond in subsequent work), feedback needs to be meaningful to the students. It also highlights that marking is not the only way to assess students, although it is part of the assessment process.

To be effective in enhancing learning, Hatziapostolou and Paraskakis (2010) suggest that high quality feedback should be 'timely, motivating, personalised, manageable and in direct relation to assessment criteria' (p. 121) (see Hatziapostolou and Paraskakis, 2010, for full explanations). The reference to assessment criteria is particularly important, as students need to know what it takes to be successful in a task. After all, if your students do not understand how or why they are adapting their responses to your feedback, then it is like their part in the journey of formative assessment between teacher and pupil is being completed blind-folded.

In addition, according to the Education Endowment Foundation (2018), effective feedback that takes a research-based approach, such as Bloom's 'mastery learning' tends to have the most positive impact on learning. Such an approach involves the pupil focussing on mastering the content, whilst demonstrating a willingness to engage in the learning process. Thus, good feedback should be individualised and should cause students to think (Black and Wiliam, 2003), as well as motivate students to learn.

Now undertake Task 9.3.

Task 9.3 **Feedback**

Look at the two examples of written feedback below. Which of the two approaches do you think is most effective and impactful on learning? Why?

Question: Outline and evaluate the multi-store model of memory (six marks)

Candidate 1 response:
　　The multi-store model of memory consists of three stores, the sensory store, the short-term memory store and the long-term memory store. ✓ The sensory store receives information from the environment and holds information for a very short time. ✓ If it is paid attention to, the information moves to the short-term memory (STM), where it will last only 30 seconds, but if the information is rehearsed it will move into long-term memory (LTM) where it can last forever. ✓ The good thing about the model is that there is a lot of evidence to support it. The bad thing is that it only considers STM to be one store, but other research has found that STM consists of multiple stores. ✓

Teacher feedback:
Mark: 4/6
Overall comment: Well done on your answer. The outline is very good, but you need to work on your evaluation, it needs further elaboration.

Candidate 2 response:
　　The multi-store model of memory is a model of memory that tells us how information moves from one store to the next. It is made up of the sensory memory, short-term memory and long-term memory. Information stays in the sensory memory for a matter of milliseconds unless it is paid attention to, so will move into the STM. It will only stay in the STM for a short time, approximately 15–30 seconds and can only hold seven plus or minus two items. If the information is rehearsed it will move into the LTM which can hold infinite amounts of information for up to a lifetime. The strengths of the theory are that it is an influential theory that is supported by a lot of evidence. For example, research into those who have amnesia proves that there are separate stores of memory. Like HM who had a damaged LTM but his STM was ok. The weaknesses of the model are that research has shown that the STM is made up of more than one store.

Teacher feedback:
　　WWW (What went well): The outline of the model is good as you have given the capacity and duration of each store as well as explaining how information is processed from one store to the next in a linear fashion.
　　EBI (Even better if): Your evaluation has begun to discuss relevant research which could be further explained. For example, consider explaining the research that shows STM is made up of more than one store by bringing in the alternative model of memory.

The first method of marking involves the ticking of correct points made by the pupil, an award of a grade and some praise alongside an overall comment. Feedback such as this, which is judgemental in nature, is classified as evaluative and performance goal orientated (Tunstall and Gipps, 1996). Whilst the teacher can gauge how well the pupil has understood the material, how effective is this feedback for the pupil? For instance, does the pupil know what 'further elaboration' means, or what it should look like? Unless the pupil engages with the feedback in a meaningful way, then chances are they are not going to improve their understanding (or mark) any further. What is important is that the feedback is effective. For instance, feedback at the personal level (e.g. praise) is not effective in enhancing learning as it is evaluative. This is because feedback that draws attention to the self, leads to the avoidance of risk in completing difficult assignments. This type of feedback (e.g. saying 'well done') also contains very little information about learning.

Take the second example. By providing comments on what has gone well and what could be improved, students can begin to understand how they can make progress. To go a step further, what if the pupil were to provide their own suggestions for improvement, by responding to some carefully framed questions? For example, in an essay that has only mentioned supporting evidence when evaluating the learning theory of attachment, a teacher may provide a question such as, 'What would Bowlby's monotropic theory argue as an alternative?' or 'can you offer an alternative argument?'. Feedback that is task-related, such as this, is classified as descriptive and mastery goal orientated, as teachers using this type of feedback appear to 'shift the emphasis more to the child's own role in learning' (Tunstall and Gipps, 1996, p.399). Thus, feedback that is task-related (and therefore descriptive) is of most value, and when combined with effective instruction, that allows students to reflect and critically evaluate their work, can enhance learning (Hattie and Timperlay, 2007).

Furthermore, if you find that the same formative feedback applies to several students, try to consider time-efficient ways to feed this back to your students without having to write the same comment out again and again.

9.3 STUDENT RESPONSES TO FEEDBACK

How do you know your students have understood your feedback? Teachers are under immense pressure to teach to the examination specification in a timely manner and assess students' work through written feedback, but there is little point in moving onto the next topic if students have not understood the material, or have not understood your feedback (including whether they have been able to read your handwriting!). Assessment can support learning if the learner actively engages in actions to improve their learning, 'after all, the best designed feedback is useless if it is not acted upon' (Wiliam, 2011, p.12).

Many schools adopt some in-class directed time for improving work (e.g. dedicated improvement and reflection time, or DIRT). This directed time could

■ ■ ■ ■ **ASSESSING PSYCHOLOGY**

allow a teacher to monitor and facilitate students' responses to feedback, to ensure the time spent on written feedback is addressed by students. This allows students to reflect on their progress, improve their work and consolidate their learning.

Of course, this is not always possible, given time constraints in teaching the whole specification and in some cases oral feedback may be more effective than written. Addressing the whole class when giving feedback (perhaps using students' work as examples on a visualiser or interactive white board), could be an effective – and more time-efficient – way for students to learn from their mistakes and misunderstandings.

Feedback can take many forms including written feedback, oral feedback, class discussion, peer- and self-assessment. Whatever form it takes, feedback that allows learners to learn from their mistakes is key to pupil progress. Simply put, if it is not making an impact on student progress, then it is an unnecessary time-consuming task.

Now undertake Task 9.4.

Task 9.4 **Is there learning?**

In the planning of a lesson consider where/when the learning will be taking place. Consider the following questions for each task covered (whether it involves teacher talk, group work or individual work):

■ How do you know your students are learning something in this task?
■ How are you assessing the learning that is taking place?
■ How do you know they are making progress?

9.4 MARKING BETTER, NOT MORE – ENCOURAGING SELF-REGULATED LEARNERS

The report from the Independent Teacher Workload Review Group (2016) recommends that marking should be 'meaningful, manageable and motivating' (p. 5), with trust in the professional judgements of teachers on what is best for their students and contexts.

There is little evidence that providing extensive written comments on pupil's work, leads to long-term improvements in pupil outcomes (Independent Teacher Workload Review Group, 2016). Rather, too much feedback can make students less responsible for their own work, reduce resilience building and reduce retention in the long term (Independent Teacher Workload Review Group, 2016). In contrast, empirical evidence suggests that self-regulated learners are more effective in their learning, more persistent, confident and achieve higher (Zimmerman and Schunk, 2001). Therefore, the unnecessary burden of written marking should be replaced by more efficient strategies (Elliot, Baird, Hopfenbeck et al., 2016) for there to be a more positive impact on pupil progress. In a review of the evidence on written marking, Elliot, Baird, Hopfenbeck et al. (2016) concluded with several findings outlined in Table 9.1.

Table 9.1 Strategies of efficient marking for pupil progress. Adapted from Elliot, Baird, Hopfenbeck et al. (2016). A Marked Improvement? A review of the evidence on written marking

Errors in students' work due to misunderstanding should not be marked the same as careless mistakes	Spending time writing 'you must use a capital letter' is less beneficial than just marking the mistake as incorrect, without giving the correction. When marking misunderstandings, rather than giving the correct answer, giving hints or questions allows students to be more engaged in their own (self-regulated) learning. For example, where a pupil has used a study to support the multi-store model of memory in their essay, but not clearly indicated *why* it is supportive evidence, rather than marking with 'This supports the model as it shows the model has multiple stores of memory' a teacher could mark with 'Why is this a supporting study?' or 'consider why it is called the *multi-store* model of memory?'
Do not grade every piece of work	The impact of marking may be reduced by awarding grades for every piece of work. students can become preoccupied with grades, rather than considering formative comments that could allow them to make improvements to their work.
Use specific and actionable targets	Marking using specific and actionable targets ensures students can respond appropriately and is likely to increase pupil progress. For example, 'explain *why* this study supports the working memory model, with regards to capacity', rather than just saying 'elaborate' or 'not enough detail', which students may not understand due to lack of specificity.
Allow some response time	Similar to DIRT time mentioned previously, students are most likely to benefit from marking if they are given time to think about and respond to marking. If students are not given time to act on formative feedback, then is there any point in giving it?
Some marking will not enhance student progress	Some marking, for example acknowledgement marking, is unlikely to aid pupil progress. There is limited evidence relating to the impact of speed and frequency of marking, so it is not possible to give definitive guidance on how quickly or how often work should be marked. Schools should consider that teachers need to mark better, not mark more.

■ ■ ■ ■ **ASSESSING PSYCHOLOGY**

9.4.1 Peer- and self-assessment

The full potential of AfL is when students take a meaningful role in their own learning through self-assessment and peer evaluation and thus there is a joint construction of feedback (Hawe and Parr, 2014). The purpose of peer- and self-assessment is to make appropriate judgements on the work of a peer, or own work, to correct any misunderstandings and to reiterate what went well, so that this is repeated in the future.

Peer instruction gives students the opportunity to work in pairs or small groups to critically evaluate each other's work and decide what constitutes successful work against the assessment criteria. Not only can this help improve the work of others, but in the process of assessing peer work, students can also clarify their own understandings and misunderstandings of the material (Hawe and Parr, 2014). See Chapter 8 for further information on peer learning.

For accurate and effective self-assessment to take place, students must fully understand the task at hand, including being clear on the success criteria. In fact, more accurate self-assessment takes place with the use of concrete, specific, well-understood criteria (Panadero and Romero, 2014). Students should be encouraged to be honest and reflective when assessing strengths and weaknesses in their work. Self-reflection can also be improved by receiving feedback from the teacher on the accuracy of their comments. Then, once students become more confident in being self-reflective and better understand the assessment process, they can become more autonomous (Swaffield, 2011), with less dependency on the teacher.

Now undertake Task 9.5.

Task 9.5 **An aid to learning**

Consider how the following scenarios could incorporate formative assessment to aid learning:

1. Students complete a mini quiz on attachment, which the classroom teacher collects in. She returns the answers back to the students the following lesson with no marks made to the answers. How can the students be encouraged to self-assess?
2. Students complete an exam question on conformity for homework and bring it into school ready to hand in to the classroom teacher. The classroom teacher does not collect in the answers but instead encourages a peer-assessment task. How can the students peer assess each other's work? What will they need for this task to be successful?

9.4.2 What Are Good-Quality Questions?

Teachers ask many questions throughout the day, mostly low order questions that require the recall of facts. Engaging the class and encouraging a love of learning and enquiry requires teachers to ask good-quality, high-order questions to indicate if students are making effective progress. Simply asking 'did you understand that?' or 'is anyone unsure?' will not allow you to check if students have really understood the information. Questions need to be carefully articulated and differentiated, so that the right questions are asked to the appropriate students. Whilst 'hand signals', as listed above, may be an AfL strategy to quickly check pupil understanding, this is not necessarily the best (or only) way to check pupil progress in your lesson.

There are many resources and sources of information available that give advice to teachers on effective questioning (see further reading and resources). One example of varying your questions to suit the needs of your students and a technique often used to differentiate, is by using Blooms Taxonomy, which provides teachers with a hierarchical framework of cognitive skills, to focus on higher order thinking. For example, Level 1 (Knowledge) questions can include 'How would you describe…?' or 'how would you define…?' Level 3 (Application) questions may include 'How would you show your understanding of…?' or 'what would happen if…' and Level 6 (Evaluation), 'Can you assess the value or importance of…?' or 'what is your opinion of…?' Such variation in questioning also allows the classroom teacher to encourage students to consider the different assessment objectives (AOs) that the final external examination will cover (AO1, AO2 and AO3, respectively, for example in England).

As much as you try to construct your questions carefully, you may frustratingly get little or no response from students. There may be several reasons why (and this could vary by pupil), for example they may not have understood the question, they may be too shy or embarrassed to speak in front of the class, they may not be listening, or they may not know the answer. There are ways to aid students in answering questions (presuming they have understood what you are asking). For example, give students some 'thinking time'. You may do this without telling them you are giving them time to think, and simply wait a few seconds, or explicitly tell students they have 20 seconds to think about a response. You could also do a 'Think, Pair, Share' task in response to a posed question, that begins with thinking time that they then discuss with a partner and finally share with the class. Asking closed questions that require one-word answers may not elicit a response, as students can be led to believe that there is only one way to answer the question, and so may be embarrassed if they get that wrong. So, asking open questions that invite more of an opinion, may elicit more response from students, for example 'what do you think the researcher was trying to find out..?' or 'what is your opinion of that…?' rather than 'was the researcher right?'

Now undertake Task 9.6.

Task 9.6 **Rank the learning**

Look at the five examples of feedback below:

- Rank those in order of most to least learning that you think would take place.
- Give a cost/benefit analysis outlining the strengths and weaknesses of each.

1. Written feedback that is full of praise, for example 'this is a very good point' and 'well done, you have understood this well'.
2. Written feedback that students have to respond to using hints/questions – for example 'explain *why* this is a strength of the biological approach' or 'what would the learning theory argue in contrast?', 'consider the nature/nurture debate in Psychology'.
3. Verbal feedback using a model answer on the interactive white board. The teacher highlights what is good about the pupil's work and indicates how it can be improved in relation to the success criteria in the mark scheme.
4. Peer evaluation and instruction – students in groups of four are asked to look at their four exam answers and select the parts of each answer that most closely answer the examination question. They must co-construct a new answer together as a group.
5. Self-assessment – using the mark scheme and success criteria on the board, students must give their own work a comment for what they have done well and a comment for what could be improved. They are then given an additional 10 minutes to make those improvements.

9.5 SUMMARY AND KEY POINTS

You should now understand that:

- Formative assessment (Assessment *for* Learning) involves an interaction between pupil and teacher, whereby the teacher provides feedback to the pupil (who responds appropriately) for progression of learning to take place.
- Summative assessment (Assessment *of* Learning) provides a summary of learning that has taken place.
- Effective AfL takes place with students in the context of the school and class.
- Effective feedback requires students to understand what they need to do, in order to improve their work.
- Oral feedback is just as important as written feedback (by way of marking). As long as students respond appropriately to this feedback, then learning and progression can take place.
- Joint construction of feedback through self- and peer-assessment, allows students to become better self-regulated learners.

MIN DUCHENSKI-JASSAL

- Good-quality questions allow teachers to assess if pupil progress is taking place. They also allow teachers to differentiate to suit the needs of their students.

Check the requirements of your initial teacher education programme to see which have been addressed in this unit.

FURTHER RESOURCES AND WEBSITES

For general information, extending what is in this chapter, we recommend you read Section 6 "Assessment" In the core textbook for the Learning to Teach series: Capel, S., Leask, M. and Younie, S with E. Hidson and J. Lawrence (9th edn 2022) *Learning to Teach in the Secondary School: A Companion to School Experience.* Abingdon Routledge: Taylor Francis.

Anderson, L.W., and Krathwohl, D.R. (2001). A taxonomy for learning, teaching, and assessing: A revision of Bloom's taxonomy of educational objectives. New York: Longman.

Free resources for teachers (including 'Assessment for Learning Toolkit') – https://mikegershon.com/resources/

Education Endowment Foundation toolkit – https://educationendowmentfoundation.org.uk/school-themes/

Kahoot – https://kahoot.com/

Psychology Review – https://www.hoddereducation.co.uk/psychologyreview

10 INCLUSION IN TEACHING PSYCHOLOGY

Lucinda Powell

INTRODUCTION

It is often believed that one of the reasons young people choose to study psychology is the 'Therapy Hypothesis' (Jarvis, 2011) and that psychology teachers feel that they have a disproportionate number of students with Special Educational Needs and Disabilities (SEND) and mental health problems who want to gain some understanding of their condition. However, there is little direct evidence of this in research (Banyard, 2003; Walker, 2010) though of course it remains important that as a psychology teacher, you are aware of the range of learner diversity within your classroom in order to have a clear understanding of inclusion in your classroom.

What Is Inclusion and Why Is It Important?

The introduction of compulsory state education in 1870 highlighted the difficulties of a one-system-for-all approach and thus the creation of special schools enabled the smooth running of 'normal' schools: the socially constructed notion of special needs had been created (Tomlinson, 1982). Since then, categorisation of what we now call Special Educational Needs and Disability (SEND) has varied, from terms such as 'idiot' and 'severely sub-normal' to Special Educational Needs in an attempt to move away from stigma, to a more inclusive educational system. We now have the SEND Code of Practice (DfE, 2015), which outlines four broad areas of SEND:

- Communication and Interaction
- Cognition and Learning
- Social, Emotional and Mental Health difficulties
- Sensory and/or Physical Needs

Inclusion, however, does not focus only on those with Special Educational Needs but is equally about social inclusion. The English DfE's (2011) first requirement in the teachers' standards is to 'set *high expectations which inspire, motivate and challenge pupils... set goals that stretch and challenge pupils of all backgrounds, abilities and dispositions*' (p.10). As a teacher, you need to be aware of social issues and stereotypes and be able to challenge these both personally and in the school context in order to create an inclusive classroom. The suggestion here is that inclusion is not simply about being *in* the mainstream educational system but something more fundamental. It is the feeling of being part of the community, being able to contribute to society in a positive way.

In addition, labelling students' academic potential can unintentionally exclude students from the learning environment. Ability is a word banded around every staffroom, but it is a concept that is difficult to measure, is not static and is largely subjective. It is, however, a concept that can make or break a child's educational career: being labelled as 'high ability' or 'less able' may have a devastating impact on teachers' perceptions, peers' perceptions and a student's self-perception of what they are capable of achieving in a school context (Rosenthal & Jacobson, 1964). It is a concept that is used to justify many of the teaching practices in schools in the United Kingdom today, for example, in systems of setting and streaming (Boaler *et al.*, 2000).

Research has shown that the move towards inclusion depends greatly on the attitude of teachers (Avramidis & Norwich, 2002). Training that equips teachers with the knowledge and skills to enable inclusion may result in a positive attitude towards inclusion, as the teachers see the beneficial effects it can have (*ibid.*). From the anecdotal accounts in Van Der Post *et al.* (2009), the teachers who are remembered as particularly good are those who have listened to both professional advice, to the parents *and* been prepared to adapt. Therefore, to create an inclusive classroom, training and understanding of the issues is an important part of your teaching journey.

OBJECTIVES

By the end of this chapter, you should understand:

- practical strategies, underpinned by theory, that will encourage inclusivity in your classroom and help you to overcome some of these barriers.
- inclusion for all – creating an inclusive environment.
- supporting SEND.
- making Psychology Accessible to all.
- ethical code of conduct – your competencies.

Check which requirements of your initial teacher education programme relate to this unit.

■ ■ ■ ■ **INCLUSION IN TEACHING PSYCHOLOGY**

10.1 INCLUSION FOR ALL – CREATING AN INCLUSIVE ENVIRONMENT

There are many barriers to creating an inclusive classroom:

- The tension between what is required in terms of the 'standards in education' agenda and the realities of students' lives
- The requirement to teach to the test
- The time given to teach content may be insufficient to also teach higher skills
- Access to the funding and resources needed to differentiate effectively
- Large classes
- Lack of teacher knowledge and understanding of the issues
- Poor support services
- Negative attitudes of other students
- Environments that are poorly designed or no longer fit for purpose.

Classrooms are complex places – there are *'complex interactions between learners' and teachers' histories and "learning biographies", institutional ethos and culture, group dynamics and expectations and between the curriculum and student/teacher relationships'* (Ecclestone & Brown, 2002, p.4). But there is a body of contemporary research that suggests that a focus on the social relations in the classroom including creating a sense of belonging, feeling safe and valued, can be beneficial (Watkins, 2005). Students do not leave their feelings and emotions outside the classroom, so if they do not like a teacher their learning will be affected. Having said that, students often see teachers as having a unique place in their lives, being able to offer an adult viewpoint that is important for them in making the transition from childhood to adulthood (Bernstein-Yamashiro & Noam, 2013). Teachers are important for reassurance and building confidence and thus need to intentionally create a classroom atmosphere that is non-judgemental, a safe place to learn and to deliberately build positive relationships with their students.

Now undertake Task 10.1.

Task 10.1 **An inclusive environment**

What does 'an inclusive environment' mean and how can you ensure that all your classroom is truly inclusive? Make a list using the table below creating a respectful environment that promotes diversity and fairness.

Physical classroom?	Your behaviour?	Your teaching?
Desks laid out to allow discussion.	Greet the students as they enter the classroom.	Role model that making mistakes is ok.

LUCINDA POWELL

A student's approach to learning is driven by many things including the teacher's mindset, the way they feel they are perceived as a learner and how learning is discussed within the school or college. Awareness of these orientations may help teachers to create supportive environments which encourage a learning orientation and to move away from the more traditional performance orientation seen in more traditional teaching, resulting in more inclusive practice.

Carol Dweck's Growth Mindset (Dweck, 2006) is one educational theory or philosophy that encourages teachers to develop inclusive practices, through building confidence, resilience and a sense of self-worth in students. Growth Mindset is the idea that intelligence is something that is constantly changing and growing as we experience life and learning – from a neuropsychological point of view, this makes sense as we constantly grow new neural connections – moving away from the idea of labelling children's ability. With this in mind, how well students do academically has only a small part to do with their innate ability and a lot to do with how hard they work and the effort they put into learning. Their attitude to learning though is influenced by those around them – teachers, parents, peers and school values. With so much focus on exam grades, as teachers, it is easy to overlook the process of learning and the skills and attitudes we can foster in the young people in front of us.

Dweck (1986) discusses motivation behind learning and how this affects outcomes. She identifies *'Learning goals'* as

> ...goals in which individuals seek to increase their competence, to understand or master something new.
>
> (Dweck, 1986, p.1040)

And *'performance goals'* which are:

> ...goals in which individuals seek to gain favourable judgments of their competence or avoid negative judgments of their competence.
>
> (Dweck, 1986, p.1040)

If students are oriented towards learning goals, they are more likely to have a growth mindset and this can have a wide range of benefits. However a fixed mindset will persist if the teacher and/or students are oriented towards performance goals.

It is helpful to think of the features of growth vs. fixed mindset more as a spectrum than categories; equally we can be at different places on the spectrum for different aspects of our lives – for me, I have a very fixed mindset around my ability to play tennis but an incredibly growth mindset about my ability to learn how to use technology more effectively. What do you have a fixed mindset about and what do you have a growth mindset about?

Now undertake Task 10.2.

■ ■ ■ ■ **INCLUSION IN TEACHING PSYCHOLOGY**

> **M** | Task 10.2 **Growth mindset attributes**
>
> Consider the following growth mindset attributes:
>
> - View failures or challenges as opportunities to grow.
> - Acknowledge and embrace weaknesses.
> - Learn to give and receive constructive criticism.
> - Intelligence and talent are dynamic and ever improving.
> - Prioritising learning over seeking approval.
> - Persists in the face of setbacks.

For each point, consider the impact on your students and how it might affect their attitude to learning, your relationship with them, how safe they feel to try new ways of learning and the effort they put into learning.

From my own MA research, students say they feel most included in the classroom when they are able to take risks with their learning, are not judged by grades but on their willingness to have a go and are encouraged to reflect upon their own learning, all aspects of a growth mindset.

10.2 SUPPORTING SEND

The SEND Code of Practice for England was updated in 2015. The Code aims to ensure that the child and parents/carers are involved in decisions made about the child's education, not just the professionals, so they have greater choice and control over what happens to them. It is important that identification of needs is made early so that interventions and support are timely, any provision is high quality and removes barriers to learning. The result is that children and young people are prepared for adulthood (DfE, 2015, pp.19-20). In England, students who are identified as having SEND but stay within a mainstream school may be supported by an Education and Health Care Plan (EHCP), which gives access to additional funding and support. In order to qualify for an EHCP, there is a complex process where the need for this additional support has to be demonstrated. When the need is less severe, students will be added to the SEND register. These students will benefit from any additional support the school or college can provide but do not receive additional funding. This support will therefore be in the form of things such as use of a laptop, additional time to complete tests, adapted resources and group interventions. Regardless, the first step is to always provide *'high quality teaching, differentiated for different pupils'* (DfE, 2015).

Identifying children who may need additional support in secondary school will be done by teachers and the SENDCo (Special Educational Needs and Disabilities coordinator) or equivalent where a young person is identified as not making expected progress in comparison to their peers or previous progress. If

LUCINDA POWELL

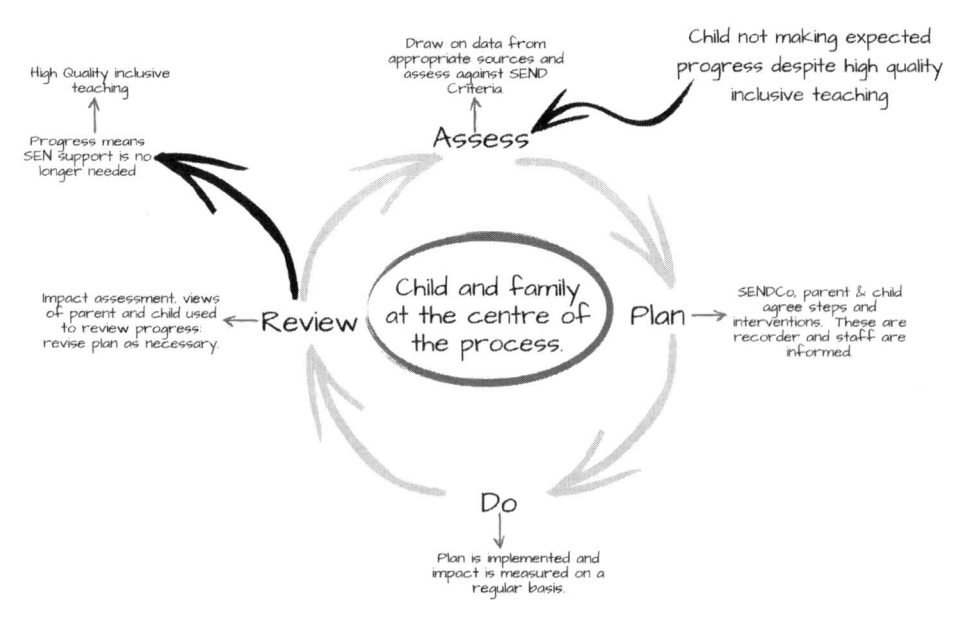

Figure 10.1 Assess, plan, do, review SEND cycle

a SEND child is identified, the SENDCo will normally, in England, put into action an Assess, Plan, Do, Review Cycle (see Figure 10.1).

Whilst it is beyond the scope of this chapter to detail the wide variety of Special Educational Needs that you may come across in your teaching career, it is worth considering the most common under the four categories in the English Code of Practice or the regulations applying to your context, and how you might support these students. However, the examples below are very broad and all pupil profiles and needs will be different regardless of labels and their needs will change over time. Labels offer a general guide of what to expect but specifics vary from child to child – for example Autism Spectrum Condition may mean that the young person cannot express themselves verbally or that they cannot read body language or both. It is essential that you read the Individual Educational Plan (IEP) for every child to fully understand the adaptations that are required to remove the barriers to learning. If you are unsure of exactly what support is required, then speak to your SENDCo or equivalent or if appropriate, the Teaching Assistants that work with the student.

10.2.1 Communication and Interaction Difficulties

These can encompass a wide range of challenges but refer to young people with speech, language and communication needs (SLCN). Essentially these difficulties will impact how young people communicate with others. In the context of education, this may mean they struggle to articulate their thoughts and ideas, they may have difficulty understanding or following instructions or they may struggle to understand non-verbal communication. In the classroom, this can not only create a barrier to learning and achievement but also in the interactions they have with peers.

10.2.2 Autism Spectrum Conditions/Disorders (ASC/D)

There are several well-known theories of Autism and related conditions such as Baron-Cohen's lack of 'Theory of Mind' (e.g. Baron-Cohen *et al.*, 1985) and Wing's (1988) 'Triad of Impairments'. Those with an ASC diagnosis can vary enormously in the severity and type of impairments. The most relevant challenges in the classroom are the inability to understand non-verbal communication (including sarcasm, jokes and facial expressions) and the need to give clear instructions – they like rules to be unambiguous and adhered to. ASC children often have sensory processing difficulties so can be overly sensitive to noise, visual stimuli (e.g. a flickering light), and discomfort of clothing.

Ten ways to support Autism Spectrum Conditions/Disorders (ASC/D) in your classroom:

1. Check understanding if you use colloquialisms such as 'it's raining cats and dogs'.
2. Make instructions unambiguous.
3. Use their name when talking to them.
4. Make it clear when you are joking and do not use sarcasm.
5. During group work, ensure they work with students who will support them.
6. Ensure group tasks are well structured.
7. Ensure you are clear about classroom rules and that you stick to them.
8. Ensure that the environment is as calm and uncluttered as possible.
9. Try to incorporate the student's special interests into your lesson where you can.
10. Have clearly established routines, try to give advanced warning if these are going to change, and be flexible if your student cannot be.

10.2.3 Cognition and Learning

This covers a multitude of issues from Moderate Learning Difficulties (MLD) through to Profound and Multiple Learning Difficulties (PMLD). In a mainstream classroom, you are most likely to come across Specific Learning Difficulties (SpLD), which, as the name suggests, create a specific barrier to learning and encompass conditions such as dyslexia, dyscalculia, and dyspraxia, as well as issues with working memory.

10.2.4 Dyslexia

Predominantly dyslexia is thought of as problems with reading, writing and spelling and usually it is picked up because the written work or reading speed of the young person does not match their verbal contribution.

10.2.5 Dyspraxia

People with dyspraxia struggle to perform actions that require novel or non-habitual motor skills. Often, this is most seen as poor handwriting in the classroom, but affects organisation and planning.

10.2.6 Dyscalculia

This is best seen as a difficulty with processing and manipulating numbers, which can lead to a wide range of difficulties for the young persons.

It is really important to note that there are many symptoms that appear in all of these such as poor organisational skills, lack of concentration (remember they are working doubly hard just to keep up with the lesson), issues with working memory such as holding long sequences of instructions in their head and muddling left and right. Assessment profiles of children with these types of conditions usually show very disparate scores on the cognitive assessments so for example a child may score in the 90th centile for spatial rotation but score well below average for word recognition or sequencing tasks.

10.2.7 Working Memory

Many young people struggle with working memory – the ability to take incoming information, combine it with already existing knowledge and manipulate this to solve problems, follow instructions, respond to tasks, etc. As a teacher and a psychologist you should be aware of the working memory model (e.g. Baddeley and Hitch, 1974).

Ten ways to support in your classroom:

1. Use a different colour background on your smart board (set to beige or blue) rather than white.
2. Break down tasks and worksheets in to smaller parts so students do not feel overwhelmed or get distracted.
3. Provide students with cloze exercises to stick in their book rather than copying from the board.
4. Provide students with literacy mats of key words on their desks (see Figure 10.2) or charts of key mathematical facts.
5. Give students 'thinking time' to process information or when you ask them questions.
6. Where appropriate use assistive technologies such as speech recognition software.

7. Use easy to read fonts and stick to one font on PowerPoints and worksheets.
8. Seat students carefully so they can see the board, ask questions easily and away from distractions.
9. Provide tick lists of tasks that need to be completed or revision lists of learning.
10. Have clearly established routines in your classroom.

10.2.8 Social, Emotional and Mental Health Difficulties (SEMHD)

10.2.8.1 Mental Health

There is strong evidence that there has been an increase in young people coming forward with long-standing mental health conditions (Pitchforth *et al.* 2019), and the COVID-19 pandemic has only exacerbated this problem. This can have a huge impact on learning and progress and these problems often develop in adolescence (75% of mental health disorders appear before the age of 14 (Kesler *et al.* 2005)). Teachers are in the prime position to identify and support young people struggling with their mental health. Social and emotional difficulties can present in many ways, and it is important that you are adequately trained to spot the signs that a student may be struggling and that you are aware of the referral pathways within your school or college should you have concerns.

What should you be looking out for? This is a really tricky question to answer but the simplest answer is a change in behaviour that cannot be explained by normal adolescent development – this includes weight loss or gain, change in class contributions (e.g. was outgoing and is no longer contributing), isolating during breaks where once they were with friends, changes in clothing or personal hygiene, unexplained cuts or bruises, drop in academic performance. Of course some people are really good at hiding behind a mask of positivity, so checking in with students on a regular basis can be really vital.

Ten ways to support:

1. Be prepared to listen.
2. Spend time getting to know your students and build positive relationships.
3. Ensure you have appropriate training on mental health issues.
4. Ensure you know the referral routes and safeguarding pathways in your school.
5. Praise small achievements and brave attempts.
6. Find compromise with work but do not allow avoidance.
7. Have empathy.
8. Create an atmosphere where it is safe to take small risks and students do not feel judged if they get it wrong.
9. Encourage students to reflect on the positive things in your classroom.
10. Always think 'what if I'm right' not 'what if I'm wrong' if you are concerned about a student.

Now undertake Task 10.3.

> Task 10.3 **Raising awareness**
>
> Common mental health conditions are depression, anxiety, obsessive compulsive disorder, eating disorders (e.g. anorexia nervosa and bulimia nervosa). Choose one and research the signs and symptoms, and your school/college's referral pathway.
>
> Make a poster or infographic of the signs and symptoms of that disorder and the information about what to do if you are worried about someone; the poster should be suitable for a staff or classroom display.

10.2.9 Neurodevelopmental Disorders

Under Social, Emotional & Mental Health Difficulties (SEMHD) also come a number of Neurodevelopmental conditions such as ADHD, ADD and attachment disorder.

10.2.9.1 Attention Deficit (Hyperactivity) Disorder (ADD/ADHD)

Young people with ADHD/ADD struggle to concentrate in lessons and often appear inattentive. In class this can also manifest as an inattention to detail, careless errors, and a failure to notice mistakes and very easily distracted. It also is reflected in a lack of organisation, losing things and forgetfulness. The hyperactivity symptoms in ADHD will be seen as restlessness and fidgeting, impulsive and risky behaviour, calling out and interrupting others.

Ten things you can do to support:

1. Ensure students sits away from distractions.
2. Seat students near you so you can prompt them to return to the task.
3. Give them tasks in small steps.
4. Use their name to bring them back on task.
5. Allow rest and movement breaks where possible.
6. Give them fidget toys or allow doodling if it helps them to listen.
7. Give them extra time in tests.
8. If they tend to shout out in lessons ask them to write their ideas on a post-it note for you to look at later.
9. Create outlines for written work to help organise thoughts.
10. Give time to organise their materials and work at the beginning and end of the lesson.

10.2.10 Sensory and/or Physical Needs

For young people with a physical disability appropriate support and resources should be put in place by the school or college but you should be aware of the needs of the student.

■ ■ ■ ■ **INCLUSION IN TEACHING PSYCHOLOGY**

Ten things you can do to support:

1. Ensure you know how to use any assistive technologies appropriately.
2. Check in with the student to ensure they have everything they need.
3. Ensure resources planned and ready, for example enlarged worksheets.
4. Organise your seating plan to ensure the students can see/hear/move around as well as possible.
5. Encourage independence where possible.
6. Ensure students have extra time where appropriate to complete tasks.
7. Make your classroom as inclusive as possible so students feel part of the community.
8. Do not be afraid to experiment, working with the student to agree what works for them and what does not.
9. Be aware that not all assessment formats may work so be prepared to be flexible.
10. Educate yourself on the specific need and get creative in how you can work round it.

10.2.11 Comorbidity

Many young people with SEN often have more than one label or diagnosis that are not clear cut, increasing the challenges that the young person faces in school or college. For example, many young people with Attention Deficit (Hyperactivity) Disorder may have Autism Spectrum Conditions/Disorders. Or someone with dyslexia may also have issues with their working memory. Often, these challenges are misinterpreted as laziness and can undermine a young person's self-esteem and we often see young people with learning needs with mental health issues such as anxiety and depression as well.

Now undertake Task 10.4.

Task 10.4 **Case study**

Identify at least one student in your school or college that has Special Educational Needs and familiarise yourself with the school's support plan for them – in England, their IEP or ECHP. Use a 'learning walk' to follow them for a day and note

■ How different teachers adapt their lessons and planning for that student.
■ Talk to the student about their experiences of lessons.
■ What they feel teachers do well and what could be improved.
■ How will this inform your teaching?

10.3 MAKING PSYCHOLOGY ACCESSIBLE TO ALL

The great thing about psychology is that it is everywhere, and students can link their learning to all areas of their life. It is already taught in schools under topics such as addiction, relationships and peer pressure in Personal, Social, Health and Economic education (PSHE). When students are taught study skills should it not rely heavily on sound psychological principles of memory and learning? From this viewpoint, it seems that psychology is a subject that everyone could relate to and in fact, many do, with psychology being one of the most popular A-level choices.

As a teacher, your role will be to ensure your teaching is adaptive responding to the differentiated needs of individuals within the class.

10.3.1 Support Materials

One of the things students find hardest to master is the wide range of new terms that they have to use accurately in their writing. You can support this with wall displays or a literacy mat that is placed on all desks or for those who need extra support (see Figure 10.2). You could create a similar one for the mathematical skills required for psychology – including how to work out measures of central tendency, the different statistical tests, flow charts and different graphs.

10.3.2 Catering for Different Levels

The psychology specifications in the United Kingdom have a variety of assessment objectives – students are required to demonstrate knowledge and understanding, application and evaluation. These skills are based on Bloom's taxonomy (Bloom et al., 1956) where knowledge is seen as easiest to master and evaluation, the most difficult. These are skills that can be learned (see growth mindset above) but some will find them easier to master than others. To create tasks that allow students to access the lesson content at all levels, think about how you can use Bloom's taxonomy (see Figure 10.3) to help create a wide range of activities.

Now undertake Task 10.5.

Task 10.5 **Lesson plenaries based on Bloom's taxonomy**

Plan a variety of lesson plenaries using the following points from Bloom's taxonomy. An example is given to start you off – can you think of two more for each level that would help you to make your lessons more inclusive?

- Remembering (Knowledge), for example three key points from the lesson.
- Understanding, for example write a 50-word summary for a key point.
- Application, for example how might today's learning be useful in the real world?
- Analysis, for example create a table of strengths and weaknesses on a topic.
- Evaluation, for example turn today's learning into an infographic.

Additionally by giving students choice, they have power over their learning and are more likely to engage with the task and to strengthen the skills they need. You could use the plenary tasks you have created as options for extension work, homework or setting them as tasks to check progress.

INCLUSION IN TEACHING PSYCHOLOGY

GCSE Psychology - Key terms

Literacy

Connectives to justify ideas with evidence
For example, as evidenced by, this suggests, this infers, this implies, alluding to

Connectives to sequence ideas
Firstly, secondly, next, then, finally, meanwhile, after, previously

Connectives to compare and contrast
Similarly, likewise, but, on the other hand also, both in the same way, equally, correspondingly, mutually, however, alternatively, in opposition, in contrast

Research Methods

Reliability, Validity, Independent or Dependent Variable, Control, Hypothesis, Questionnaire, Experiment, Observation, Case Study, Independent Groups or Repeated Measures Design, Subjective, Objective, Participant, Generalisable, Ethics, Quantitative and Qualitative Data, Sampling, Social Desirability, Response Bias, Standardised instructions

Key Skills

Create
Synthesise
Evaluate
Interpret
Analyse
Explain
Describe

CRITICAL THINKING

Topic A

Optic Chiasma, Visual Cortex, Depth Cues, Size Constancy, Texture Gradients, Relative Size, Height in a Plane, Superimposition, Stereopsis, Gestalt Laws, Visual Illusions, Schema, Ambiguous Figures, Motions and colour after-effects, Proximity.

Topic B

Freud, Manifest Content, Displacement, Latent Content, Condensation, Dreamwork, Secondary Elaboration, Hobson & McCarley, Random Activation, Movement Inhibition, Sensory Blockade, Biological, Neuron, Axon, Synapse, Neurotransmitter, Impulse.

Topic C

Limbic System, Amygdala, Hormones, Social Learning Theory, Role Model, Vicarious reinforcement, Modelling, Observational Learning, Identification, Aggression, Natural Experiment, Nature vs. Nurture, Adrenal glands, Testes.

Topic D

Phobia, Classical Conditioning, Association, Extinction, Preparedness, Flooding, Anxiety, Relaxation Techniques, Hierarchy of Fears, Hypnotherapy, Cognitive Behavioural Therapy (CBT), Psychometric Testing, Nature vs. Nurture

Topic E

Genetics, XYY, Chromosome, Twin Studies, Family Patterns, Childrearing Strategies, Self-fulfilling Prophecy, Offender Profiling, Forensic Psychologist, Defendant Characteristics, Testimony, Stereotype, Mandatory, Psychopath.

Figure 10.2 Example of GCSE literacy mat for students

LUCINDA POWELL

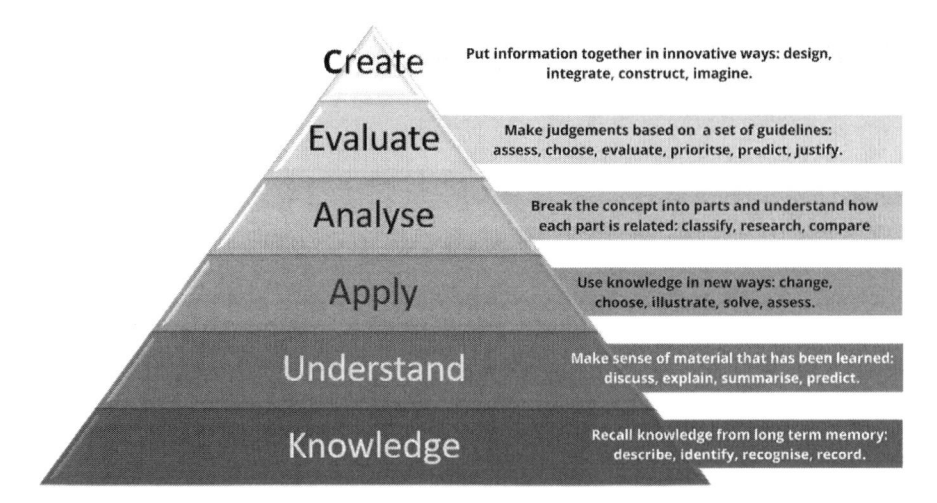

Create — Put information together in innovative ways: design, integrate, construct, imagine.

Evaluate — Make judgements based on a set of guidelines: assess, choose, evaluate, prioritse, predict, justify.

Analyse — Break the concept into parts and understand how each part is related: classify, research, compare

Apply — Use knowledge in new ways: change, choose, illustrate, solve, assess.

Understand — Make sense of material that has been learned: discuss, explain, summarise, predict.

Knowledge — Recall knowledge from long term memory: describe, identify, recognise, record.

Figure 10.3 Summary of Bloom's taxonomy

10.4 ETHICS

There is a lot of misunderstanding about psychology in teaching and also the general population. Having a background in psychology (such as a degree) is not the same as being a trained clinical psychologist. However, many people do not understand the difference and therefore you must be clear about your professional boundaries. You should also read the British Psychological Society's Code of Ethics and Conduct (2018) available online (see further resources) and apply the ethical code in your professional practice.

Red Lines

Unless you have had specific training and hold the appropriate qualifications to make diagnoses or to offer therapy you should never offer to do so. Always make it clear what your competencies are and know how to explain these to others. It is possible that members of your school or college community (staff, students and parents) will seek your advice as they see you as an 'expert' and you need to know, in advance, how you will deal with these sorts of scenarios.

If you are concerned, ask your school or college for the appropriate training - for example doing a mental health first aid course, a counselling qualification, or training in specific areas of special needs. Finally ensure you are really clear on the safeguarding procedures and referral pathways for your school or college.

Now undertake Task 10.6.

> **Task 10.6 What to do?**
>
> In the following scenario, what would be the appropriate course of action?
> Mike is a student who struggles to tell whether or not you are joking or being serious, often getting it wrong and becoming upset. In his written work, he interprets

INCLUSION IN TEACHING PSYCHOLOGY

> instructions very literally and though you feel he is capable of doing well, his writing is often too brief. To encourage him you have suggested some additional reading but because it is not homework, he will not do it.
>
> From your understanding of psychology and from your knowledge of Mike, you think he may be on the Autism Spectrum. Outline the actions you should take in order to improve his learning experience.

10.5 SUMMARY AND KEY POINTS

Inclusive classrooms are influenced by a range of variables of which you need to be aware. As a teacher you are able to create an *inclusive environment for all* students through awareness of your own biases, building positive relationships with your students and encouraging a growth mindset. Through understanding how to adapt and differentiate your teaching effectively, you will *support students with SEND* and improve your inclusive practice. This good practice will then enable you to create effective lessons that remove barriers to learning and help students build skills and confidence making *Psychology accessible to all*. However, it is important to know the limits of your own competencies and the boundaries of these in light of the psychological *ethical code of conduct*. If you are ever unsure, never be afraid to ask for support, get more training or consult the wealth of psychology teacher networks for advice.

You should now:

- have practical strategies, underpinned by theory, that will encourage inclusivity in your classroom and help you to overcome some of these barriers.
- be more confident supporting SEND in your classroom.
- be aware of the ethical code of conduct.

Check the requirements of your initial teacher education programme to see which have been addressed in this unit.

FURTHER RESOURCES AND WEBSITES

British Psychological Society's Teacher Toolkit for further resources https://www.bps.org.uk/who-we-are/education-and-training-board/teachers-toolkit

British Psychological Society's Ethical Guidelines https://www.bps.org.uk/news-and-policy/bps-code-ethics-and-conduct

MESHGuides research summaries for teachers on autism, deaf education and classroom acoustics http://meshguides.org/guides/

National Association for Special Educational Needs
National Association for Special Educational Needs (NASEN) https://nasen.org.uk

Psychology in the Classroom Podcast – Season 3 SEND: www.changingstatesofmind.com/season-3

USING TECHNOLOGY IN PSYCHOLOGY TEACHING

Matt Jarvis

INTRODUCTION

The coronavirus pandemic brought an intense period of change in educational practice, and the world has begun at last to appreciate the potential of digital education. Change can be rapid and some of the applications and examples I talk about in this chapter will look dated in a couple of years. However, the core principles around which I have based this chapter – thoughtful balancing of synchronous and asynchronous technology, legal compliance, principles of effective learning, catering for students with diverse needs in a range of circumstances and the balance between generic and subject-specific technology – should remain relevant for the foreseeable future.

Time pressure means that inevitably we often end up planning for the immediate future and frame planning in mechanical terms of 'how do I make x resource available to y group tomorrow?' This is not a 'how-to' chapter, although it contains practical tips. The idea is to equip you to plan some sustainable, future-proof strategies for digital psychology education in a world of continued rapid change.

OBJECTIVES

By the end of this chapter, you should be able to:

- understand the current context and the changing role of technology in teaching, and appreciate the role of asynchronous and synchronous digital education.
- apply some principles of effective learning to planning digital psychology education and use educational technology in ways that enable effective learning.

■ ■ ■ ■ USING TECHNOLOGY IN PSYCHOLOGY TEACHING

- be familiar with legal constraints around the use of educational technology, including GDPR, the EU Accessibility Directive and Copyright Law.
- be able to evaluate the strengths and limitations of alternative digital platforms and make informed choices/work around their constraints.
- use psychology-specific as well as generic technology and apply some generic technology to create bespoke psychology-specific tools.

Check which requirements of your initial teacher education programme relate to this unit.

11.1 DELIVERING EDUCATION IN CHANGING CONTEXTS

The 2020 Coronavirus Lockdown brought the importance and potential of digital education into sharp focus, in particular the wide-scale adoption of communication tools like *Zoom, Microsoft Teams* and *Google Meet*. The existence of these apps means that 'Snow Days' will never look the same again, and there will undoubtedly be vastly improved access to education for students whose access to the physical classroom is limited by disability or simple geography. However, while mastery of these tools allowed education to continue and teachers to feel they were responding effectively to the sense that Kim and Asbury (2020) describe as 'like having a rug pulled from under you' (2020: 1062), this is a far cry from saying that psychology education has continued unaffected or that as a profession we have mastered digital practice.

Predicting what technology will be used in the future by the typical psychology teacher and student is far from straightforward (Nickerson, 2020). If the rise, fall and rise again of Covid-19 has taught us one thing it is that digital education practice needs to be flexible enough to cope with the following scenarios and agile enough to switch rapidly between them:

- Technology-enhanced conventional classroom teaching, probably using digital resources for flipped learning
- Blended learning involving reduced face-to-face contact supplemented by a substantial level of independent digital learning
- Remote digital teaching, in which all or most contact between teacher and learner is mediated by technology

11.1.1 Synchronous and Asynchronous Delivery and Technology

The key to understanding how to best use technology across conventional, blended and remote modes of teaching lies in the distinction between synchronous and asynchronous use of technology. Amiti (2020) describes synchronous technology thus: 'an environment where the teacher and the students meet online on a specific online platform for teaching and communicate about a lesson' (2020: 62). *Zoom*, *MS Teams* and *Google Meet* are all examples of synchronous technology. Synchronous teaching has some advantages – it is an exciting dynamic experience in which teachers are aware of student engagement and can respond to emerging needs in real time. It also provides a relatively friendly environment for introverts, who may prefer remote teaching to the conventional classroom (Stephen & Pritchard, 2021). On the other hand, synchronous delivery requires that students structure their time in an inflexible way and can be an unsustainably tiring experience for teachers and students (Wicks, 2021).

In the flurry of excitement around mastering the shiny new tools of synchronous technology in 2020, schools and teachers may have deprecated the role of asynchronous technology to their cost. Asynchronous environments do not revolve around live interaction but rather the posting of resources and tasks for students to work through at their own pace. Traditional virtual learning environment technology (lots more about this later!) provides a classic asynchronous environment, but so do tools like *Google Classroom* and the *Office365* tools available through *MS Teams*. Asynchronous delivery allows students to learn actively and independently at their own pace, and asynchronous technology affords a range of opportunities to reflect, interact and think deeply through a wide range of tasks and tools.

11.1.2 The Wider Social Context

We should be very wary of the whole idea of planning with the 'typical' or 'notional' student in mind in the context of the existence of digital divides, most obviously between those who can and cannot afford the necessary hardware and connectivity (Andrew *et al.*, 2020). With the best will in the world, education discriminates, and it may be that without keeping a careful eye on the implications of changing practices our new reliance on digital education will exacerbate this. Think for example of students working in poverty or unsupportive family contexts who may now have reduced opportunities to work in a better equipped and more supportive school environment and victims of abuse, who may have fewer of the kinds of interactions that allow teachers to spot warning signs. The UK government largely failed to provide the hardware (e.g. laptops) and connectivity (e.g. 4G dongles) they promised at the start of the first 2020 lockdown, and the impact of that delivery where it did take place remains unclear.

2020 has also seen unprecedented collaboration between schools and colleges on one hand and the multinational technology providers like *Google* and *Microsoft*. With their vast resources, these companies have been quick to offer tools like *Teams* and *Classroom* and have been rewarded with a huge growth in their importance and influence in education. To what extent they continue to develop the kind of tools that serve our needs as psychology teachers and to offer them at affordable prices is an open question.

Now undertake Task 11.1.

■ ■ ■ ■ **USING TECHNOLOGY IN PSYCHOLOGY TEACHING**

> Task 11.1 **Online teaching challenges**
>
> What aspect of online teaching feels most challenging for you? What is the most worrying or what is most difficult? Rank the following points with the most challenging first:
>
> 1. Supporting students pastorally
> 2. The quality of materials to use
> 3. Keeping students interested and engaged
> 4. The limits of technology knowledge
> 5. Accessibility and access for all learners
> 6. Timing and scheduling
>
> Write a sentence for each, justifying your choice. Talk to colleagues about their concerns and solutions.

11.2 KEEPING AN EYE ON PRINCIPLES OF EFFECTIVE LEARNING AND TEACHING

If good use of technology can improve your teaching then *bad* use of technology will definitely make it worse (Jarvis, 2012). Digital learning is after all just learning mediated by technology, and all the same principles that underlie effective conventional learning and teaching will apply. There are naturally a range of views around what exactly these principles are and how important each is, but I have found the following to be useful:

- Learning should (usually) be an active process
- Learning should (usually) be an interactive process
- Learning should be *salient*, that is, have clear relevance to the learner
- Learning should be memorable
- Learning should be personalised to the needs of the individual.

11.2.1 Active Learning

Generally, learning should be an active process rather than passive. BUT there are a couple of provisos to this that go some way towards explaining why the teaching styles we traditionally think of as 'active' don't always work better than alternatives.

1. The 'active' in active learning refers to cognitive processes *not* to the superficial appearance of activity. Think of it as roughly equivalent to Craik and Lockhart's (1972) 'depth of processing'. So listening is not necessarily passive, though it is likely to become so over time without a supplementary task. Nor is participating in a project necessarily active (Ofsted, 2018). The

degree of cognitive engagement in a task is much more important than the task *per se*.
2. There are now alternative learning strategies that are not particularly active in a behavioural or cognitive sense, but nonetheless have some supporting evidence. Thus micro-learning (at least micro-learning in its simplest form) involves pushing out small chunks of material that can be taken in with very little cognitive activity because their cognitive demands remain within the capacity limits working memory can easily cope with (Major & Calandrino, 2018). See below for examples.

Technology can help both with making tasks active and with facilitating simple micro-learning. Giving students presentations to read independently rather than going through them in a classroom or synchronous online lesson *may* increase cognitive activity but putting tasks into the presentation *definitely* will, unless learners choose to actively subvert the process. This is best done by bespoke technology where you have access to it (see, for example, H5P, p000), but if this is not the case then you can largely recreate this in generic tools like *Google Slides*. Take the slide shown in Figure 11.1. A slide like this can be made on any presentation tool or website builder.

■ **Figure 11.1** This slide encourages active engagement because the reader has decisions to make about how and when to access what information

The rationale for this style of slide is that the reader cannot simply cast their eye over a few text bullet-points. They are forced to make cognitively effortful decisions about what they want to read/watch/listen to and this requires the kind of deep, effortful processing associated with successful learning. Note that a slide like this can either be viewed and the button-decisions made

■ ■ ■ ■ **USING TECHNOLOGY IN PSYCHOLOGY TEACHING**

independently and asynchronously or synchronously in the context of an interactive class discussion. Ofsted (2018) have emphasised that whole-class interactive teaching has a supportive evidence base, and is not the same as lecturing, which is not recommended because of the passive role of the learner.

Now undertake Task 11.2.

> Task 11.2 **Introducing yourself to online teaching**
>
> Record an introductory video or audio about yourself. Show or describe your personal work space and the view out your window, talk about your hobbies, passions or pets – it shows you're human! Ask your students to do the same (only using video if they are comfortable with this); it helps to understand their situation and will give you ideas for learning activities that draw on their interests.

11.2.2 Micro-Learning and Cognitive Load

The idea of micro-learning offers both an alternative to active learning and a way to make learning active. Our understanding of micro-learning owes a lot to John Sweller's work on cognitive load (see Chapter 2). Cognitive load theory applies our understanding of working memory to optimising learning. Sweller (2011) has identified that once we eliminate extraneous cognitive load (mental processes that take up working memory resources without contributing to learning, e.g. listening to music), we are left with the intrinsic cognitive load of the information itself and germane cognitive load – the working memory demands of mental tasks that help learning. Effective learning tends to involve tasks that minimise extraneous cognitive load and increase germane cognitive load.

Micro-learning involves pushing out bite-sized chunks of information to learners. This can be simply in the form of simple facts with modest intrinsic cognitive load that require so little working memory resources that they pass to long-term memory without much effortful processing. This is an alternative to the active/deep learning approach. However, micro-learning can also be used to increase cognitive activity and incorporate germane cognitive load by including tasks like a question that promotes deeper processing of the information.

On a technical level, there are various ways to push out micro-learning to learners. A definition or short-answer question can be sent via SMS or mobile app. If you have a virtual learning environment (VLE) like Moodle, you can automate this process using the random glossary entry block – see Figure 11.2.

You can also push out tasks that increase germane cognitive load, for example a short quiz or game task. An example is hangman, available on VLEs like Moodle via gamification plug-ins (Figure 11.3).

Random glossary entry

obedience

Following orders from an authority figure. See also destructive obedience.

Add a new entry
View all entries

■ **Figure 11.2** The Moodle random glossary entry randomly pushes out definitions to learners.

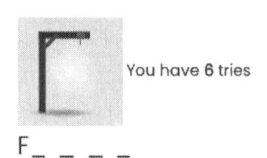

You have 6 tries

F _ _ _ _

Letters: A B C D E F G H I J K L M N O P Q R S T U V W X Y Z

Grade : 20 %

Grade in whole game : 7 %

■ **Figure 11.3** Increasing germane cognitive load via a hangman question

11.2.3 The Expertise Reversal Effect

Classic examples of active learning involve the setting of independent tasks. So for example we might think of having learners write an extended-prose plan independently as active, while talking through a worked example with a whole group as less so. However, experience tells us that the latter can be at least as effective as the former. It appears that the clue to understanding this apparent paradox is the expertise reversal effect (Renkl & Atkinson, 2003). More expert learners do better with more independent tasks, while novices to a topic or skill do better with direct instruction, for example a whole-class worked example. You might respond to the expertise reversal effect by planning indirect instruction tasks like presentations and worked example questions during synchronous sessions and following them up later with independent tasks after some expertise has been achieved (see Chapter 2).

11.2.4 Interactive Learning

The social constructivist tradition emphasises the role of interaction in learning. In the conventional classroom interaction takes place between peers, for example via group work, peer tutoring and peer marking, and between teacher and learner, for example through tutorials, feedback and whole-class interactive discussions. All of these interactions can be replicated in digital education, and

USING TECHNOLOGY IN PSYCHOLOGY TEACHING

working digitally also introduces the possibility of interaction with software and even artificial intelligence.

Synchronous interaction takes place in the form of remote class teaching and tutorials. This is where video conferencing tools like Google Meet and MS Teams come in. Asynchronous interaction can be through assignment feedback and peer marking, and through collaborative project work. Well-designed and set up VLEs include a range of collaboration tools including peer marking, blogs and wikis. Most of these can be simulated to some extent in generic systems like *Google Suite* and *MS Office*. *Google Classroom*, *Moodle* and *MS Teams* all include good assignment submission and marking systems.

11.2.5 Salient Learning

Learning is a motivated process, and learners tend to be more motivated when the material or activity has clear relevance. This can be personal salience, that is the relevance of material to learners' own lives – and here psychology has a clear head start over most subjects – or goal-related salience, that is, activities with a clear link to attainment. We don't have much discretion with the core curriculum, but personal salience probably plays a role in subject option decisions. Goal-related salience of activities may encourage participation. Thus, a group essay-planning exercise on a Google *Jamboard* or *GoogleDoc* may attract more active engagement than, say, a collaborative poster task (Figure 11.4).

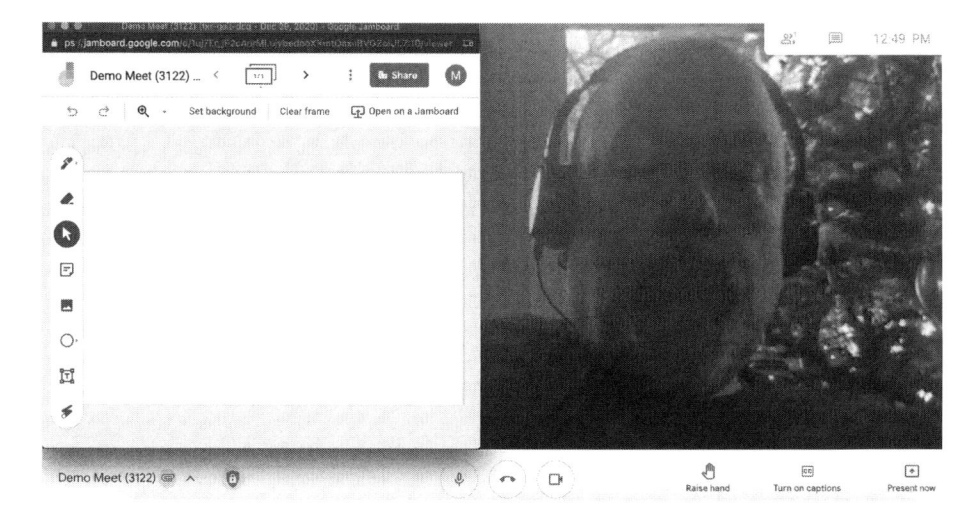

Figure 11.4 A Google Jamboard can be used collaboratively, either as shown here in a remote lesson or in the context of a group project

11.2.6 Memorable Learning

Clearly active and interactive learning of salient material is likely to lead to good retention. However, when it comes to learning in the sense of preparing for exam-based assessment there are additional principles that can be applied (after Dunlosky, 2013; Higham, 2018).

- Practice testing: practicing recall of material is perhaps the single most important factor in exam preparation. This does not require the use of technology; however, you can make sure that you make available ample digital resources such as self-marking quizzes and – if you have access to the technology – self-marking short-answer prose questions. There are a plethora of applications that can provide quizzes, from Google and MS *Forms* to *H5P*, *Kahoot*, *Quizlet* and others. Some of these are particularly well-suited to synchronous learning (*Kahoot* being the obvious example), while others like H5P quizzes come into their own when used for independent learning. Note that *Kahoot* integrates neatly with MS *Teams*, so if you are using *Teams* for remote teaching *Kahoot* is particularly convenient.
- Test-potentiated learning: A side benefit of practice testing is that recalling prior learning appears to increase the efficacy of subsequent learning. So by starting synchronous digital sessions with a recap quiz and encouraging learners to begin independent study sessions with a quiz you can not only practice recall but also improve the effectiveness of the rest of the session.
- Distributed or spaced learning: Learning is most effective when it is distributed across time (see Chapter 2); so for example three 1-hour sessions are more effective than a single 3-hour session. Planning for distributed learning does not require a particular technology but the use of micro-learning strategies can help distribute learning and timeline tools such as that in *H5P* or *TimeGraphics* (https://time.graphics/editor) can be used to plan distributed activities.
- Successive re-learning: A particularly effective adjunct to distributed learning is *successive re-learning* (Rawson et al., 2018). This involves revisiting the same material on different occasions, for example using flashcards. There are numerous digital tools for creating flashcards, for example *H5P* and *Quizlet*. Some like *Cram* (https://cram.com/flashcards) have a large searchable bank of existing psychology flashcards. Planning using a timeline tool with scheduled links to flashcard sets may be particularly effective.

Tools like *LearnItFast* (https://learnitfast.io) allow you to distribute revision and incorporate an adaptive element. Note that in the latest version of Ofsted's pedagogical recommendations, differentiation no longer means providing learners with different resources allocated on the basis of a pre-existing assessment but adapting in real time to emerging performance. *LearnItFast* allows you to construct multimedia flashcards with the adaptive twist that each learner can use to self-assess confidence with each answer; a well-known chunk of learning can be re-learnt after a couple of days but a less well-known segment will be re-presented after 5 minutes (Figure 11.5).

USING TECHNOLOGY IN PSYCHOLOGY TEACHING

Figure 11.5 The adaptive interface of LearnItFast helps with distributed learning

11.2.7 Personalised Learning

One of the advantages of asynchronous teaching is the greater potential for personalising the learner experience. This is particularly important for learners with disabilities. I offer some thoughts on disability in the sections on accessibility (p000) and choice of learning platform (p000). It is also important to say at the outset though that the key to helping learners with any disability or bespoke need is collaboration. Don't assume any prior expertise on the part of the learner – or indeed their teaching assistant or other helper. Some learners may find the immersive environment on *Office 365*, the captions on *YouTube* and Google *Meet* or *Moodle's* dyslexia font option life-changing – or they may not. You won't know until you spend some time exploring options with them.

Now undertake Task 11.3.

Task 11.3 **Cost-benefit analysis**

Discuss with your teaching mentor the benefits and challenges of moving classes from face-to-face to online.
  You should consider

- Who are the students for whom you're designing or planning lessons?
- Where are students in their overall course of study?
- Who might they rely on to help them or facilitate their learning?
- What physical setting might they be in when engaging with your teaching?
- What devices or connectivity might they have access to?
- How digitally literate are your students?
- How adept are the students with time management, personal planning or autonomy?

Complete a literature review and look for journal articles which summarise the strengths and limitations of online teaching.

MATT JARVIS

11.3 LEGAL CONSTRAINTS ON DIGITAL EDUCATION

Working within the law when teaching psychology digitally can sometimes require a bit of knowledge and preparation. At the time of writing, three legal frameworks are of particular importance: data protection, accessibility and copyright.

11.3.1 Data Protection

As long as you are using a digital platform set up by your school or college, you as a psychology teacher should be fairly safe as regards data protection. Using external platforms however can be much more problematic. The legislation comes from the EU's General Data Protection Regulations (2018). This requires that all organisations operating within or with the European Union pay close attention to the privacy, extent and uses of the data held on individuals. Bear in mind the following:

- If you share learners' data with an external site and it is hacked, you – or at least your school or college – are liable. So make sure someone senior has approved any sites your learners sign up to and be prepared to pass the buck.
- Learner data must generally be held on servers within the European Union. American companies can still hold personal data from EU citizens but generally only on servers located in the European Union. So American companies like Google, Microsoft and Edmodo are okay, but if you are unsure about a site do check that they have European servers. A notice on a company's homepage detailing the ways in which it meets GDPR rules does *not* necessarily indicate that it meets all of them so always seek independent reviews before signing up.
- Your use of synchronous remote teaching tools like *MS Teams* and *Google Meet* will be covered by the terms of your school or college account, and data can be kept secure between users. Unless your school or college has an account, be very careful about using other tools. The moment you input a learner's name and email to invite them to an external site you risk being in breach of GDPR. There are on-going arguments as to whether some sites that claim to be GDPR-compliant really are.
- Don't sign up under-16s or knowingly allow them to sign up to external education sites. GDPR will be the least of your problems if you fall foul of international sex trafficking regulations!

11.3.2 Accessibility

Exactly what you *have* to do in law depends on what sector you work in, however there is an ethical case for all teachers to make reasonable efforts to ensure their digital content is accessible. Since 2020, the EU Accessibility Directive has required that all public sector and public-funded websites in the United Kingdom comply with the following standards:

USING TECHNOLOGY IN PSYCHOLOGY TEACHING

- Content should be perceivable to any user including those with disabilities.
- Activities should be operable by any user.
- Content should be as understandable as possible.
- Content and activities should work on any kind of device and operating system.

Schools and sixth-form colleges are exempt from the EU directive; however, FE colleges, universities and private and charitable training providers are required to adhere to them. If you are in an FE college or private training provider, you may be able to claim that implementing some requirements would be an unreasonable burden or are beyond your control as the content is provided externally. However, it is necessary to be seen to be making reasonable efforts to comply with the regulations, including having an institutional accessibility policy and undertaking accessibility audits.

A full UK government guide to conducting a basic accessibility audit can be found here: https://www.gov.uk/government/publications/doing-a-basic-accessibility-check-if-you-cant-do-a-detailed-one/doing-a-basic-accessibility-check-if-you-cant-do-a-detailed-one, but for now the following are the kind of thing you should look out for:

- Where possible, information should ideally be on a web page rather than a document, because html files are more accessible. However, there is the ability when conducting an accessibility audit to claim that hand-outs, worksheets, etc. are essential for your business.
- Text (whether on a web page or document) should have proper headings, not simply emboldened or changed in size. This allows assistive technology like screen readers to make sense of a page. Text size should be changeable without affecting the use of the page; this is important for visually impaired people.
- Pages (web and document) should have clear, descriptive titles so that a reader who cannot visually scan whole pages can decide whether to proceed and read them. Subtitles should be logically nested (e.g. H1, H2, H3, H3, H3, H2, H3, H3) so that readers using a screen-reader can navigate around a page.
- Web pages should work with styles disabled so that users who get overwhelmed by too much visual information can work with a simplified page.
- Images should have an alt text description so that a visually impaired reader can extract all the information provided on a page.
- Video and audio should have transcripts so that people who cannot or choose not to make use of video can still extract all the information from a page containing video.
- Forms and other interactives should have submit buttons clearly labelled so that anyone can use them regardless of visual acuity.
- There is a minimum contrast between text and background, depending on text size, so that mild to moderately visually impaired people are likely to be able to see the page. You can check this here: https://webaim.org/resources/contrastchecker/

This is not a comprehensive list, and no amount of preparation is a substitute for working with learners with disabilities to ensure that their particular needs are met, but it gives a flavour of the kind of things you should look at if you are based in FE or a private or charitable training provider.

11.3.3 Copyright

Probably the most common legal breaches committed by psychology teachers are in respect of copyright. Copyright law is currently in transition, with the European Union having approved a set of new rules that are set to make life quite uncomfortable for teachers in 2021. However, the United Kingdom appears not to be planning to implement the directive post-Brexit, and at the time of writing it is not clear what aspects of the directive will make their way into British law. This section is therefore necessarily brief, but I will offer some thoughts on common issues arising.

11.3.3.1 Images

You will undoubtedly use pictures in teaching materials that have been obtained online. There is some confusion around what you are allowed to use and what is off-limits. Many photo banks offer royalty-free images, but note that *royalty*-free is not the same as *copyright*-free. Royalty-free simply means that a fee is not payable per use; it can still require a flat fee. There are a smaller number of photo banks offering copyright-free images and that is what you are after. These include the following:

- Pixabay (https://www.pixabay.com)
- Unsplash (https://www.unsplash.com)
- Stocksnap (https://stocksnap.io)
- Pexels (https://pexels.com)
- Wikimedia Commons (https://commons.wikimedia.org/wiki/Main_Page)

Two other common sources of images are *Flickr* and *Google Images*. There is nothing dodgy about *Flickr*, but note that there are eight types of licence in use on the site, so ensure that if you are using it that you understand these variations in permissions.

11.3.3.2 Video

Under legacy copyright law, you are responsible for copyright breaches if you upload video files to your site but not if you link to a video-sharing site like *YouTube*. The responsibility lies with the host. However, the new EU legislation includes a 'link tax', meaning that schools and colleges will either have to obtain permission from the copyright-holder to link to a video or to be prepared to be charged. It does not appear likely that this will be implemented in UK law post-Brexit, but it's one to watch out for. Watch this space...

11.3.3.3 Text

Teachers currently have an exemption for the use of copyright material for teaching purposes. So you can post *extracts* from textbooks and articles provided you are working on a secure password-protected education platform. If you have a virtual learning environment that permits public courses, you will be much more limited in what you can share on those pages. As for video, keep a close eye out for post-Brexit changes in the law.

Now undertake Task 11.4.

Task 11.4 **Planning an online lesson**

What are you going to try this week, for whom, and why? You should consider

- What have you been told to do by your institution?
- How much time do you have?
- What digital resources do you already have available to reuse?
- Does the teaching really have to be synchronous/live?
- Do any of your students have any accessibility or literacy issues?
- How will this lesson improve student learning?
- Review and evaluation: ensure your reflection is based on feedback from students and your mentor.

11.4 DIGITAL PLATFORMS

Most readers will work at a school or college that has committed to a policy of using a particular online platform or platforms. This is not really a section therefore on how to choose your platform, more how to be aware of the potential and limitations of what you have to work with.

11.4.1 Traditional VLE Platforms

Since the 2020 lockdown and the rise of remote teaching tools, pre-existing virtual learning environments have been largely forgotten. If all you use a VLE for is to organise your hand-outs and presentations, you can indeed do this quicker and easier on *Office 365* or *Google Classroom* and perhaps you might as well mothball your *Moodle*. However, with a well-planned and constructed VLE, you can do so much more than this, *including live remote teaching*. The following are some examples of additional functions a VLE like *Moodle* can give you:

- Documentation tools like project plans, checklists and self-assessments
- Checkable peer assessment
- Interactive presentations with exportable notes and assessment questions
- Interactive video
- Interactive multimedia books
- Automated micro-learning
- Gamification
- Self-marking free prose questions
- Journals and diaries
- Audio questions and answers
- Drag and drop
- Adaptive sequencing of activities for automated differentiation
- E-portfolios
- Easy tracking of learner engagement

VLEs like *Moodle* also fully integrate with *Google Suite* and *Office 365*. At its simplest, this means that you can open a *Teams* or *Meet* live remote session from a course page. Thinking slightly more broadly these integrations mean that you and your learners have a choice of whether to 'live' in a Microsoft or Google environment and call seamlessly on more advanced functionality from your VLE or to live in the VLE and call up a live tutorial or remote lesson. Space does not permit more detail here, but suffice to say that hanging on to your VLE will carry with it a range of benefits. Note that universities, who have invested more in developing their VLE than schools or colleges, have generally *not* deprecated the importance of their VLE since taking on remote teaching. Note too that in the event of a return to conventional classroom remote teaching tools like *Teams* and *Meet* will see more limited use and the emphasis may return to asynchronous communication and independent learning – in these domains, the VLE is king.

11.4.2 MS *Teams* for Education

This is an integrated system that offers an interface designed for education and access to the complete range of Microsoft Office tools. *Teams* also offers a social interface and a well-developed meeting tool suitable for remote teaching. It's 'channels' allow structure to be imposed on a course in the form of weeks or topics.

Teams have really come into its own during lockdowns because it lends itself to remote teaching. Teachers have also tended to find the integrated *OneDrive* access a convenient repository for static resources like hand-outs and presentations. MS *Forms* provides a simple, modern interface from which to create simple quizzes. There is an assignment creation and submission tool, which probably works best when you think of it as a task generator rather than for formal assignments. In addition, Teams integrates with a modest number of free external applications including *Kahoot* and *Nearpod*.

Teams have its limitations. Its education-specific functionality is quite limited, although it can be integrated with *Moodle* for additional tools. Although there are accessibility tools like the immersive environment, (at the time of writing) the accessibility of the Teams app is quite poor, with small text and small icons around the edge of the screen coupled with slow start-up times compromising the experience for learners with visual and short-term memory problems.

11.4.3 *Google Suite* for Education

At the time of writing, Google does not provide an integrated interface like that of MS Teams. Instead as the name implies there is a suite of separate well-developed applications. Google Classroom provides a combination of social interface and assignment functionality. Meet is a meeting tool that works well for remote teaching. *Google Drive* is a rough equivalent to *OneDrive* and Google *Forms* are similar to MS *Forms*. Unlike the MS Office suite, Google also provides a good web page builder, which can give teachers and learners an additional tool for dissemination and collaboration.

Despite the differences in design philosophy the aim of Google and Microsoft is very similar; to provide storage, office, assignment and live remote teaching tools. Choice between them is very much a matter of personal preference. In my experience, learners find the Google interface more compatible with their use of technology outside formal education, while teachers tend to like the integrated experience provided by Teams. At the time of writing, *Google Classroom* provides perhaps the best designed assignment tool of any learning platform, although this can be plugged into a VLE, so you can now set Google assignments from your *Moodle*.

Now undertake Task 11.5.

Task 11.5 **How's my online lesson?**

We should all collect feedback from our students, it's a natural part of understanding what works well and finding areas to improve.

With online lessons we miss the immediate feedback from students; their faces, hands going up, comments made and energy shared. Online teaching is different, we can't quite read people's reactions or involvement in the same way.

Design and carry out an activity to collect feedback from your students about your online lessons. For example:

- Surveys and polls
- Collecting data from online teaching platforms.

MATT JARVIS

11.5 SUMMARY AND KEY POINTS

It seems likely that you will be teaching psychology in conventional, blended and remote contexts. To do this to its full potential requires access to and some mastery of a range of tools probably including but not limited to *Teams* or *Meet*. However, remember that good teaching is good teaching and technology is just a tool to help with this; it's very much a case of 'it ain't what you do, it's the way that you do it'. Some of the best digital teaching I've seen has been by teachers who do not think of themselves as 'good with computers' in a generic sense, but who have intuitively planned to use technology in ways that captures learner engagement and promotes effective learning. Certainly you don't require a particular tool or set of tools; you can probably tell that I have a preference for *Moodle*, but if you prefer to use *Nearpod* or *Edmodo* that's fine. Practice and familiarity are important as you become used to digital education – it won't show in the long run whether you were an early or late adopter. Just give it a go and find what works for you.

You should now:

- Understand the changing role of technology in teaching, and appreciate the role of asynchronous and synchronous digital education
- Apply some principles of effective learning to planning digital psychology education and use educational technology in ways that enable effective learning
- Be familiar with legal constraints around the use of educational technology, including GDPR, the EU Accessibility Directive and Copyright Law
- Know the strengths and limitations of alternative digital platforms and make informed choices/work around their constraints
- Use psychology-specific as well as generic technology and apply some generic technology to create bespoke psychology-specific tools.

Check the requirements of your initial teacher education programme to see which have been addressed in this unit.

FURTHER RESOURCES AND WEBSITES

Open University free online course: Take your teaching online https://www.open.edu/openlearn/education-development/education/take-your-teaching-online/content-section-overview?active-tab=description-tab

With the rise of subject-agnostic remote teaching technology it is easy to forget the existence of psychology-specific technology. However, from psychology dictionaries to experimental simulations there is a range of psychology tools out there (Table 11.1).

USING TECHNOLOGY IN PSYCHOLOGY TEACHING

■ Table 11.1 Psychology dictionaries

Description	Web address
American Psychological Association dictionary: Searchable, browsable & word of the day micro-learning	https://dictionary.apa.org/
Psychologydictionary.org: Searchable, browsable & word of the day + popular definitions micro-learning	https://psychologydictionary.org/
Spark notes: browsable	https://www.sparknotes.com/psychology/psych101/glossary/terms/
Psychologist world: searchable and browsable. Good focus on A-level topics	https://www.psychologistworld.com/glossary/
AQA: browsable pdf, focused on AQA specification	https://www.aqa.org.uk/resources/psychology/as-and-a-level/psychology/teach/subject-specific-vocabulary
OCR: browsable pdf, focused on OCR specification	https://ocr.org.uk/Images/358295-key-terms-guide.pdf

Repositories of Articles

If subject dictionaries provide a safety net for learners needing to focus on the basics, then repositories of articles cater for the other end of the spectrum – learners who benefit from extra stimulation. Table 11.2 shows a selection of such repositories.

■ Table 11.2 Repositories of psychology articles

Description	Web address
PsychClassics: full text classic psychology papers	https://psychclassics.yorku.ca/
The Psychologist archive: articles from *The Psychologist* magazine	https://thepsychologist.bps.org.uk/archive
Psychology Review Magazine archive: requires a subscription	https://www.hoddereducation.co.uk/subjects/psychology/products/a-level/psychology-review-online-archive
BPS *Research Digest* archive	https://digest.bps.org.uk/
Science Repository: open access journals	https://www.sciencerepository.org/journals

Research Methods Tools

You can carry out surveys, observations and experiments online. You can also carry out statistical analysis. Some of the best free tools for running experiments are shown in Tables 11.3 and 11.4.

Table 11.3 Online research methods and statistics tools

Description	Web address
Implicit associations test	https://implicit.harvard.edu/implicit/takeatest.html
Stroop test	https://faculty.washington.edu/chudler/java/timesc.html
Memory for faces	https://faculty.washington.edu/chudler/java/facemem.html
Memory for objects	https://faculty.washington.edu/chudler/pdf/memobjects.jpg
Capacity of short-term memory	https://faculty.washington.edu/chudler/stm0.html
Mental rotation test	https://www.psytoolkit.org/experiment-library/experiment_mentalrotation.html
Invisible gorilla study	https://www.simonslab.com/videos.html
Serial position effect	https://psych.hanover.edu/javatest/cle/cognition/Cognition/serialposition_instructions.html
Create simple false memories	https://psych.hanover.edu/javatest/cle/Cognition_js/exp/DRMfalseMemory2.html

Table 11.4 Descriptive and inferential statistics

Scatterplot simulation: use simulated data or upload your own from class practicals	https://shiny.rit.albany.edu/stat/corrsim/
Meta-chart: create graphs online	https://www.meta-chart.com/
From Matt: choose an inferential test and run it online or see instructions to calculate by hand (focused on A-level tests)	https://h5p.org/h5p/embed/71678
More advanced test choice tool	https://www.microsiris.com/Statistical%20Decision%20Tree/
Free online inferential stats	https://vassarstats.net/ https://www.socscistatistics.com/

For information extending what is in this chapter, we recommend you read Unit 1.4 "Using technology for professional purposes". In the core textbook for the Learning to Teach series: Capel, S., Leask, M. and Younie, S. with E. Hidson and J. Lawrence (9th edn 2022) *Learning to Teach in the Secondary School: A Companion to School Experience*. Abingdon Routledge: Taylor Francis.

FUTURE DIRECTIONS AND PROFESSIONAL DEVELOPMENT

Min Duchenski-Jassal and Jonathan Firth

INTRODUCTION

Career planning is not easy for any teacher, as it relies on numerous factors that are out of your control – what jobs will come up, for example and whether you will be successful at interviews. And it is especially hard in a niche subject like Psychology. While a great many people (students, especially!) are highly enthusiastic about the subject, schools and their headteachers do not always see the development of a large and successful psychology department as their top priority.

Despite these challenges, building a successful career as a psychology teacher is largely under your control. And the more steps you take now to plan and to account for future barriers, the more successful you will be.

This chapter helps you to think strategically about your own future development. Drawing on the psychology of identity as well as theories of motivation, we walk you through a series of techniques for planning your career and carrying out that plan. These include:

- Identifying your existing skills and considering routes for professional progression
- Developing your existing skills through practitioner action research
- Forming a long-term career plan that is both detailed and flexible

You will face barriers along the way, and undoubtedly some things crop up during your career that you were not expecting – both good and bad. Nevertheless, you can use your own psychological know-how and the techniques in this chapter to ensure that you overcome the barriers and build a highly successful career in psychology teaching.

DOI: 10.4324/9781003162223-13

MIN DUCHENSKI-JASSAL AND JONATHAN FIRTH

OBJECTIVES

At the end of this chapter, you should:

- have an outline plan/career trajectory of your own psychology teaching career.
- be aware of the role of Master's study and other qualifications and their link to management and other promoted posts.
- have started to develop the skills involved in practitioner action research.
- check which requirements of your initial teacher education programme relate to this unit.

Now complete Task 12.1.

> Task 12.1 **Audit**
>
> Check the requirements for your initial teacher education (ITE) programme to see which relate to this chapter. If there are no specific requirements around career planning, then try to find out what national frameworks and regulations will be relevant if you apply for promoted posts.

12.1 THE SCOPE OF A CAREER PLAN IN PSYCHOLOGY

The skill set of the psychology specialist.

Let us start with the positives. Although Psychology as a teaching subject is not always seen as core to the curriculum, you are a highly capable educator with a huge amount to offer. Think about what you have learned in your studies so far. You already know about (or at least have a strong foundation in) most or all of the following areas:

- Developmental psychology: how children grow, learn and change.
- Social behaviour, prejudice and discrimination.
- Working memory and intelligence, including cognitive load.
- The psychology of long-term memory.
- Research methods and educational evidence.
- Psychological differences relevant to the classroom.
- Stress and its impact on performance.

These are all things that schools are very keen for their staff to learn, and you already have the perfect background! Indeed, as a psychology teacher you will probably find that you have a head start on a great many things that are typically covered in school CPD courses (what's more, you are in a good position to critique the content of such courses!).

■ ■ ■ ■ FUTURE DIRECTIONS & PROFESSIONAL DEVELOPMENT

Psychology graduates who go into teaching tend to also be very personable, good at relating to teenagers, ethically aware and to have both strong literacy and numeracy skills. In many ways, you are already ticking a great many boxes on a future headteacher's wish list.

Psychology is also a very flexible subject, and one that combines well with numerous other subject areas. You are in a teaching area that could easily link up with the natural sciences, but which has strong connections with social science, language, sport, business, well-being and many more areas. This puts you in a good position to move into promoted posts where you are responsible for more than one department, as well as pastoral posts if that is where your interests take you.

Now undertake Task 12.2.

Task 12.2 Case study 1: An example of career progression

Having completed a bachelor degree in Social Psychology and then a PGCE Social Science (PGCE Psychology did not exist then!), I went straight into teaching A-Level Psychology at the age of 21. With students not that much younger than I was, I found this daunting but soon realised that my firm yet fair nature gained me respect from my students. I became Teacher in Charge of Psychology a year after my successful Early Career Teacher (ECT) years and managed a department of three other members of staff (who were not Psychology specialists). After a short career break to travel, I returned as a classroom teacher, teaching Psychology alongside Key Stage 3 humanities (History, Geography and RE). My relationships with students put me in a strong position to lead the Student Voice (the student council), which I did for several years. Wanting to further my career to middle management, I knew that if I stayed in the same school I would not be able to become Head of Psychology, so I applied to another school and luckily got the first head of department position that I applied for. Having moved to a school with a very different ethos, I was encouraged to enhance my professional development. I became the subject lead in the borough's school alliance (leading and bringing together heads of psychology across schools in the borough). I also completed the National Professional Qualification for Senior Leadership (NPQSL). Before I had the chance to move into senior leadership, I was encouraged by a visiting student teacher's tutor to apply for a role in higher education and was subsequently appointed subject leader for the PGCE Psychology.

Comment on case study 1:

This case study helps to demonstrate some of the strengths that a psychology teacher can bring to a school as a whole. Even a relatively new teacher may get the chance to move into a position of responsibility as the leader of their subject, and psychology-based people skills lend themselves well to management roles.

It also shows that taking time out from a career need not be a barrier over the long term. While it is very useful to have a plan or at least an aspiration in terms of the kind of promoted role you might wish to move on to, every career has its twists and turns, and there will be times when unexpected opportunities arise, as was the case with the appointment to a higher education post. At such times, you may wish to reflect on your own priorities, and consider the broader impact you could have when working with other teachers versus the more direct impact of classroom teaching.

MIN DUCHENSKI-JASSAL AND JONATHAN FIRTH

12.1.1 Broadening Your Skills

Despite all these advantages that you bring to the table, there will be areas where you could broaden your skills and qualifications in such a way that it would put you in a stronger position for the future. Consider two main strands:

- areas to strengthen that would make it easier for you to *apply* for more jobs or promoted posts.
- areas to strengthen that would make it easier to *get* those jobs and promoted posts.

Some of the other ways that you can broaden your CV and appear to be 'more than just the average psychology teacher' (if there is such a thing) include the following:

- Running a school club for example in psychology, media, games, creative writing.
- Organising school sessions focused on well-being, mental health, or study skills.
- Marking for the awarding bodies. As well as getting to know your own subject better, you will also make contacts and gain a valuable insight into how the assessment system works that could serve you well for promoted posts.
- Creating resources. Make sure your name goes on them – so that others in the teaching community start to learn who you are (and have a friend double-check your spelling and grammar, so that you don't get known for your mistakes!)
- Becoming an Early Career Teacher (ECT) mentor. After completing your own ECT years you are in the perfect position to offer advice and support based on your own experiences. Mentoring and coaching roles can enhance your pedagogical skills, as well as give you the confidence to approach and speak to other members of staff, as well as share good practice.
- Completing a Master's degree. Many Postgraduate Initial Teacher Education (ITE) courses allow you to gain Master's credits that can be transferred towards completing a full Master's degree. Furthering your professional development and subject knowledge at the same time as teaching gives head teachers a good indication of your time management and drive, as well as having many other benefits. There is more on this in Section 2.4 of this chapter.
- Publishing. A good place to start would be writing short articles for magazines such as the ATP Today journal (www.theatp.uk) or The Psychologist. Further down the line, why not think about co-authoring a textbook, or even writing one yourself.

Now undertake Task 12.3.

> ### Task 12.3 **Cost-benefit analysis**
>
> Carry out a cost-benefit analysis for the skills above. For each one, consider the time commitment that would be required alongside other costs, and consider the advantages that it might bring – not neglecting the benefits of contacts and reputation.
>
> If you are already doing quite a lot of a particular activity (for example, you already run one school club), then doing more of the same might be quite limited in its benefits – it could even undermine what you already do. So, think broadly about how you could excel in new areas.

12.1.2 Middle Management and Beyond

Exactly what kind of promoted posts might you consider for the future? The details will depend on the sector and country where you work, but some of the main options probably include:

- A head of department/head of faculty role
- A head of year/promoted pastoral role
- A 'lead' role in some other area, such as behaviour, learning technology, student voice, coaching/mentoring, special educational needs coordinator (SENCO) or research
- Deputy/Assistant headship
- Headship
- Becoming a teacher/parent governor at the same or different school
- Moving into a related education role, such as for a local authority or educational psychology service

Fundamentally, what you will be motivated to strive for depends a lot on how you see yourself as a person and a professional (Van Knippenberg, 2000). As we know from the social psychology of identity, a person's social identity is composed of a number of different strands (Hogg, 2000; Tajfel, & Turner, 1986). Clearly you see yourself as a teacher and as an educator, but do you also see yourself as a leader? As a manager? As a researcher? As someone who inspires others?

Our aspirations are often less reflective of our abilities and more on this multi-faceted social identity, and the resulting sense of whether social and professional roles are 'our kind of thing'.

We are also affected by limits on what we believe we are capable of. As psychologists we are well aware that our childhood experiences shape our thoughts and beliefs as adults, and the core beliefs that we form as children can be very powerful in shaping how we deal with new situations and experiences. Whether we grew up in a dysfunctional or very loving environment, both experiences can lead to self-limiting beliefs. Similarly, multiple features of the family environment (e.g. relationship with parents, socio-economic conditions and family values) can impact the development of self-esteem (Krauss, Orth, & Robins, 2020).

Individuals from Black, Asian and Minority Ethnic (BAME) backgrounds[1] in promoted posts are largely unrepresentative of the rest of the working population. According to Government statistics, in 2018, fewer than 3% of all headteachers and less than 5% of assistant headteachers and deputies were from a Black or Asian background, with White British making up 92.9% of all heads and 89.7% of deputy and assistant headteachers. Furthermore, of the 22,400 headteachers in 2018, over two-thirds (approx. 15,000) were women (Gov.uk, 2020). With the lack of role models in promoted positions, this can leave those from under-represented BAME backgrounds experiencing self-limiting beliefs associated with *imposter syndrome*[2] and therefore missing out on opportunities for promotion.

If you identify with a BAME background or with another social group which is under-represented, you may be wondering what you can do to overcome self-limiting thoughts and actions. Some appropriate strategies could include:

- Identifying one or more role models who can act as mentors or coaches. Find out what is available by way of coaching programmes in your school or local authority.
- Tackle imposter syndrome by critically examining your own doubts, and writing lists that objectively compare your skills with the norms for your position.
- Seek advice and guidance from others about how career opportunities and promotions can be accessed, and the steps needed to be eligible to apply. It may also help to be open about your experiences to encourage allyship amongst work colleagues.

If even after critical reflection you feel that you fall short in terms of the skills needed for a promoted role, why not add to them via further study? The following section looks at the opportunities that can be associated with studying at Master's level.

12.1.3 Master's-Level Study

There are many reasons you may choose to continue in postgraduate education after completing your teacher training. You may want to deepen your knowledge and understanding, improve your teaching and professional skills or specialise further in Psychology or another field or subject (e.g. neuroscience). ITE programmes provide a foundation for professional development in teaching and learning. The number of Master's credits awarded on ITE courses vary between training programmes. Usually, Postgraduate Certificate in Education (PGCE) programmes award up to 60 credits, while Postgraduate Diploma in

FUTURE DIRECTIONS & PROFESSIONAL DEVELOPMENT

Education (PGDE) programmes award up to 120 credits, which can contribute to the 180-credit full Master's degree. To find out more details, spending some time looking at options on the relevant university website is usually a good place to start.

Some of the benefits of a Master's degree include:

- An increase in your knowledge and understanding of teaching and learning.
- Improvement in your teaching skills or specialism in a particular field or subject.
- Contribution to career progression by opening opportunities into senior management (and can also help you earn more money)
- Carrying out your own specialised research, data analysis and writing, can improve your skills in (and help you in teaching) research methods.
- Acting as a role model for students. By engaging in learning, you can share your experiences of the learning process with your students, and better understand the challenges they are facing as they study something new.
- Teachers as life-long learners. Teachers respond to new contexts and challenges throughout their careers. Learning more about research evidence helps to ensure you do so effectively, continually improving your practice.
- Networking with other professionals, whether they are Psychology specialists or interested in the same field of work as you, gives you the opportunity to bounce ideas off (and make connections with) fellow classmates and academics.

Although people often talk of *'doing a Masters'*, there are many types of Master's degrees that you can do. Perhaps the most obvious option would be to complete a teaching-focused course such as Education Studies or Educational Neuroscience. Such qualifications will look very good on your CV when you apply for jobs or promoted posts. However, with your psychology background, you could also consider a more specialised course such as Applied Developmental Psychology, Autism Studies, or the Psychology of Education, helping to boost your credentials as an expert in your particular area of interest.

Finally, there is an increasing trend for postgraduate courses related to school management or educational leadership. Specific Master's-level training is already mandatory for headteachers in Scotland (Seith, 2020), and it may well be that such courses are required before you can apply for other promoted roles in the future. If so, this should be worked into your long-term planning (see Section 12.2).

12.1.4 Using Practitioner Action Research to Extend Your Skills

Practitioner action research is an alternative (or additional) method of engaging in professional learning, whereby teachers research a particular area of practice (as opposed to academics that carry out research from an 'outsiders' perspective). Some teachers prefer this method of engaging with research without the rigorous structure of completing a Master's degree (as well as the added cost a Master's programme may bring!).

Practitioner action research is a way for individual (or groups of) practitioners to improve the teaching and learning experience within schools. This approach exemplifies the concept of teachers as life-long learners. There are many possible areas of focus for your own practitioner research – it depends on both your students' needs and your own interests. Some priorities of general relevance include how to:

- Increase motivation among students.
- Draw on theories of long-term memory to make teaching or independent study more effective (e.g. see Putnam, Sungkhasettee, & Roediger, 2016).
- Improve students' metacognitive skills to help them self-regulate their learning (e.g. see Kornell & Bjork, 2007).
- Use social psychology principles to improve the ethos among a year group (e.g. see Reynolds et al., 2015).

Your existing research skills from psychology can come to the fore in this endeavour. Consider some of the following issues:

- What research method should you use? A field experiment might seem an obvious choice, but consider other options such as focus groups and interviews. Students' classwork also provides a form of data which you could try to analyse.
- How can you ensure that research into your own students is conducted ethically? Perhaps, for example you would use data from previous years as a baseline rather than having a control group in your research.
- What extraneous variables would you need to allow for, and how certain could you be that findings from one group of students would generalise to another group?

The benefits of carrying out practitioner action research include having your voice heard within school, which is empowering within itself. You also have the opportunity to pursue something you are passionate about and can potentially inform school policy in the process. Furthermore, you get to develop your research methods skills, which again links back to your teaching of Psychology.

There are many sources of information about action research. For instance, The Open University offers a free course on 'Learning to teach: an introduction to classroom research'. Another way to get started is to connect with others who are carrying out action research through social media platforms such as Twitter and Facebook. See also 'further reading' at the end of this chapter.

FUTURE DIRECTIONS & PROFESSIONAL DEVELOPMENT

12.2 PLANNING

12.2.1 Biases and Limitations

Progressing your career over the long term is going to involve careful and effective planning. Unfortunately, humans are not very good at planning, as psychologists know very well! We are all biased in our perception of situations, focusing overly on recent evidence and our current mood. Some example phenomena around the psychology of planning and judgements include:

- The *planning fallacy*: most people underestimate how long they will take to complete a complex task, even when they have tried it before or are given realistic examples of how long it took other people to do the same thing (Buehler *et al.*, 1994).
- The *availability heuristic*: people tend to be biased by information or examples that are recent or come easily to mind, and this can affect our judgements of probability (Tversky & Kahneman, 1974). For example, if you find it hard to think of an example of a psychology teacher who has been promoted, you may think it less likely to happen to you than it actually is.
- *Anchoring bias*: the tendency to place too much weight on information that is received early on, and finding it hard to later adjust one's thinking (Furnham & Boo, 2011). When you receive negative feedback early in your career, for example you may be biased by this later, incorrectly assuming that you are not suited to promoted posts.

While psychology graduates are not immune to such errors, we can use our experience and competence in psychology to help navigate past them on the way to building a successful career.

12.2.2 Taking Up New Roles

It is not necessary to get everything right straight away. Taking up a new leadership role is much like being a new classroom teacher – there will be a period of time where everything is very new and challenging, but before too long things will start to fall into place.

One pitfall to avoid is trying too hard to come across as a 'strong' leader – perhaps based on the stereotype of the leader as someone who wields authority through power and charisma. Social psychologists Alex Haslam, Stephen Reicher and Michael Platow (2011) note that in fact, most successful leaders are not people who stand out from the group through their unique characteristics but rather people who can represent the people that they lead in such a way that they are seen as a prototype of the group:

Overall...more prototypical leaders are not only seen as better leaders but are also more effective in getting us to do things and in making us feel good about doing those things.

As a future leader (if that is your aspiration), it is important then to ask not what makes you different from the people you wish to lead but what makes you similar and *representative* of them.

12.2.3 Flexible Planning

You want to plan for the future, but at the same time, the future is uncertain. You do not know what people are going to do, because people are inherently unpredictable. But you do need to react to it when it happens.

If this situation sounds familiar, it is because you already do exactly this – in *lesson planning*. A lesson plan is an outline of what should happen, and sets out key targets and objectives. At the same time, a good lesson plan is flexible enough to deal with problems that crop up along the way. You also plan for an entire course in a way that has to adapt and respond to events and circumstances throughout the year (e.g. Covid-19 presented a completely unprecedented situation for all schools!). Furthermore, students may be absent from lessons due to school trips, or you may find that the student rate of learning means you need to go back over material already covered. Whatever the circumstances, you need to be flexible in your planning to allow for the unexpected.

A popular time-management tool which can be applied here is the ABC technique. This involves categorising your objectives into groups. These groups are labelled as A, B and C (as the name of the technique would indicate), to signify the importance and urgency of each task. The varying activities on your to-do list are ranked using the following criteria:

A: Tasks that are most important and urgent.
B: Tasks that are important, but not as urgent.
C: Tasks that are neither important nor urgent.

Within each group, you can further rank your tasks by their relative importance. A key point to note here is that some things may appear to be urgent, but you should not be driven by this. Important tasks should take priority over less important tasks, even if they seem urgent (Covey, 2004).

Now undertake Task 12.4.

> Task 12.4 **ABC career targets**
>
> Make a list of career targets using an 'ABC' ranking – A being important and urgent, B being important but not urgent, and C being things which are nice to have, but neither urgent nor especially important.

■ ■ ■ ■ **FUTURE DIRECTIONS & PROFESSIONAL DEVELOPMENT**

12.2.4 A Five-Year Plan

Clearly, there is only so much that can be achieved in a single academic year. Careers progress slowly. The *five-year plan* is an approach used by a number of professionals, and it applies well to teaching, too. Such a plan can allow you to progress through the complex stages of your career development, even allowing for the periods of time when you may be too focused on day-to-day work to give much thought to progression.

It also makes it easier for you to set ambitious goals; a body of research has shown that goals which are more specific are less stressful, as it becomes easier to judge what is needed in order to achieve them, and success is more objective. To do this, consider breaking down large goals into a series of sub-goals, each of which can be achieved via a set of actions that are under your control (Smith, 2020).

You may well find that your plans for the later years are less concrete, and that is perfectly fine. Much of what will happen in three, four or five years depends on things that will happen before that time that are currently uncertain. The degree of flexibility should increase, then, with broader timescales, and plans which focus less on specific targets (for example, *'read the rest of this book and take notes'*) and more on general goals (for example, *'apply for a deputy head-teacher role'*) that could be achieved in multiple different ways.

Now undertake Task 12.5.

Task 12.5 **Five-year plan**

Now it is time to write your own five-year plan. There are various ways to do this, but you might want to start with a simple document or sheet of paper, structured with each year as a heading (probably academic years, but you could use calendar years if you prefer). Use the headings to brainstorm ideas of what you would like to achieve.

Once you have a lot of ideas down, you might want to transfer the information to a spreadsheet or to dedicated project management software, as these will make it easier to keep track of dependencies (one thing needing to be done before another) and requirements (such as time, or any costs associated with training).

12.2.5 Maintaining Motivation

It is easy to get excited about a plan at the beginning, but how do you maintain motivation over time, when teaching is tough, the winters are long and you have dozens of other things to think about in both your home and work life?

One simple way is to allocate a regular time to career planning. This session may be as simple as saying, 'ok, I am still on track'. But it is important to value your career planning time as much as you value the other weekly or regular tasks that you have in your schedule. So why not take some time now to block out a session, at least once a month, to review your goals and progress.

Self-determination theory, a major theory of motivation which has been applied to education and to careers, suggests that motivation is linked to three main factors (Ryan & Deci, 2017):

- Our self-efficacy – how competent do we feel in our role?
- Our connection to others – do we feel like part of a community?
- Our autonomy – to what extent do we feel in control?

Although some of these things may be out of our control, there are some things that we can do about them. If we feel overwhelmed by the difficulty of a task, we can take specific courses to upskill (see Section 2 of this chapter). And if we feel isolated, we can make a goal more meaningful and motivating by developing a sense of community; networking with others who are in the same position, for example with honest sharing of your worries and doubts.

On a more day-to-day basis, it may help to use simple, everyday strategies to motivate ourselves to work towards long-term goals (such as completion of a Master's dissertation or action research project!).

A simple 'nudge' in the form of a reminder or social cue can be more effective in motivating behaviour than a direct reward (Thaler & Sunstein, 2008). In part, this is because rewards are slow and hard to perceive, and the nudge is much more immediate. For example, if you want to motivate yourself to go to the gym, an effective nudge would be to bring your sports clothes to work so that you could go straight there at the end of the day rather than going home first. Another good nudge would be to agree to meet a friend there, leading to social pressure not to pull out. Such strategies can be used multiple times, helping you stick to and carry out long-term plans.

Now undertake Task 12.6.

> Task 12.6 **Nudge**
>
> Think of at least two 'nudges' that you could use to help you to advance a specific goal, and note these down alongside your other plans.

12.2.6 The Challenges Ahead

Let us now consider some of the challenges ahead, and how you might mentally prepare for them. Again, it is hard to know exactly what difficulties you might face, but the tools you can bring to bear when tackling them may be fairly similar across different situations.

■ ■ ■ ■ **FUTURE DIRECTIONS & PROFESSIONAL DEVELOPMENT**

Carol Dweck's (2007) research on mindset (how individuals view their abilities) has increasingly been recognised and applied in schools with regards to student motivation and achievement. Dweck argues that intelligence is not fixed and that students who have the determination to struggle with new concepts and ideas are students with a growth mindset, and through hard work they can master their difficulties in learning at any given time (Polirstok, 2017).

Such perseverance when facing challenges has been referred to as 'grit' (Duckworth et al., 2007). Those who are successful, can sustain their effort and reach their targeted goals are considered 'gritty'. How gritty do you think you are? The same lessons on resilience and motivation that we give to our own students can be applied to our own efforts at achieving goals.

Now undertake Task 12.7.

Task 12.7 **Growth mindset**

'A growth mindset isn't just about effort' (Dweck, 2015, p.20). What did Dweck mean by this? How could having a growth mindset help you achieve your career goals?

12.3 SUMMARY AND KEY POINTS

In this chapter, we have explored the many strengths that you bring as a psychology teacher, and considered some of the possible ways that you might draw upon these to advance your career. In doing so, you may choose to engage in practitioner action research, pursue Master's-level study, or both.

All the same, we recognise that career progression is daunting, particularly if you suffer from low confidence and/or identify with a group which is currently under-represented among the promoted posts in your school. We have explored a number of strategies for overcoming such challenges, from mentoring to planning. We have also looked at some of the psychological barriers to enacting a plan, and considered ways to overcome them.

There are multiple ways that you could build on your existing skills and knowledge to develop your career as a psychology teacher. We wish you luck with it, whatever you decide to prioritise.

You should now:

- have an outline five-year plan of your own psychology teaching career;
- be aware of the role of Master's study and other qualifications and their link to management and other promoted posts;
- have started to develop the skills involved in practitioner action research.

Check the requirements of your initial teacher education programme to see which have been addressed in this unit.

NOTES

1 We recognise that the reference to BAME backgrounds is contentious, as Black, Asian and Minority Ethnic individuals do not belong to a homogenous group, each having vastly different life experiences (in addition to intersectional experiences). BAME is used for the purpose of this chapter in referring to non-white individuals or people 'of colour', with regards to their marginalisation experienced within the working population.
2 Imposter syndrome (or imposter phenomenon) refers to feelings of inadequacy and perceived lack of competency, despite being capable and competent in regards to professional and academic achievements. It can be experienced by anyone and whilst initially investigated in relation to high achieving women (Clance and Imes, 1978), it has since found to be highest amongst high achievers (Dickerson, 2019), ethnic minority women (Walton and Cohen, 2007), those from the LGBTQ community (Nance-Nash, 2020) and those from underrepresented BAME backgrounds (e.g. Fazackerley, 2019; Mullangi and Jagsi, 2019).

FURTHER RESOURCES AND WEBSITES

Haslam, S. A., Reicher, S. D., & Platow, M. J. (2011). The new psychology of leadership: Identity, influence and power. Psychology Press.

Firth, J. (2019). The teacher's guide to research: Engaging with, applying and conducting research in the classroom. Routledge.

The Open University free course – Learning to teach: an introduction to classroom research can be found at: https://www.open.edu/openlearn/education-development/learning-teach-introduction-classroom-research/content-section-0?active-tab=description-tab

For information extending what is in this chapter, we recommend you read Section 8 "Your professional development" In the core textbook for the Learning to Teach series: Capel, S., Leask, M. and Younie, S. with E. Hidson and J. Lawrence (9th edn 2022) Learning to teach in the secondary school: A companion to school experience. Abingdon Routledge: Taylor Francis.

13 REFLECTIONS AND FUTURE DIRECTIONS

Deborah Gajic and Jock McGinty

INTRODUCTION

As you come to the end of your teacher training year, your initial teacher education (ITE) provided will require you to formally reflect on your experiences and plan and set targets for your early career teacher (ECT) years.

Starting out as an ECT can be daunting, but it is important to remember why you wanted to become a psychology teacher. Teaching psychology can and should be fun, it is a rewarding career. As a teacher, the learning never stops whether you have been teaching one year or 20 years. Innovation and change are what keeps the job interesting, every day is a new opportunity. Although you will learn much from more experienced colleagues, you will learn just as much from your students.

OBJECTIVES

By the end of this chapter, you should be able to:

- understand the importance of positive reflection
- self-evaluate success
- maintain vitality in your teaching
- appreciate the rewards of being a psychology teacher
- think about broadening your horizons as a psychology teacher

Check which requirements of your initial teacher education programme relate to this unit.

DEBORAH GAJIC AND JOCK McGINTY

13.1 THE IMPORTANCE OF REFLECTION

Throughout your training you reflected upon and evaluated your lessons on a regular basis. This will still be the case during your ECT (early career teacher) years and is of course invaluable to your continued professional development. However, usually we tend to focus on what did not go so well and how to improve and while this is useful, it is just as important to reflect on what went well and our own strengths as teachers. Reflection is our capacity to consciously bring to mind our awareness of teaching knowledge in action (Jarvis 2011). Some of this reflection may take place while you are teaching, reflection in action, where you are constantly modifying your practice. Other reflections take place when you are discussing your lessons with colleagues and mentors. Either way, it is important to respond cognitively to your teaching, forming your own 'craft of knowledge' (Jarvis 2011).

As psychologists, we can apply the principles of positive psychology to reflection. The term positive psychology was coined in 1954 by Abraham Maslow but is now more associated with the work of Martin Seligman (1998). Try to shift your reflective practice to what went well. Every time a lesson or an activity goes well (or even just to plan!), make a note in your planner of what went well. Think about why it was successful and how you can replicate that success with different classes and topics. It is important to realise that what works well with one class, will not necessarily work with another, class dynamics and student characteristics have a role to play. As you become a more experienced teacher you will develop the skill to swiftly adapt your plans to respond to student needs and demands.

Keeping a record of lessons that went well is also helpful for your own mental well-being. When you have those inevitable days when things are not going so well and you begin to question your own ability as a teacher, having a record of successes to refer to is a great confidence boost. As a teacher you will have annual performance reviews with your line manager, this should not be a passive process, but a positive interaction which enables you to grow and develop as a teacher. Although constructive criticism is to be expected and is helpful, retain your positive psychology focus and ask your line manager to outline your strengths and achievements over the past year too.

In Chapter 12, we discussed career development and reflection is an important tool for deciding what path you want your future career to take. For reflection to be effective, you need to be honest and realistic with yourself, but remember to be kind to yourself too. You are only human, sometimes you just need to be a 'good enough' teacher, and no one can be an outstanding teacher all the time.

13.2 INDICATORS OF SUCCESS

How do you know if you are a good teacher?

During your training you looked to your mentors and tutors for validation of your abilities and this will continue in your ECT years with validation coming

■ ■ ■ ■ REFLECTIONS AND FUTURE DIRECTIONS

from your mentor or line manager. However, none of those people are in your classroom every day, they are making snapshot evaluations based on brief observations, book trawls, student feedback etc. As discussed above the most important indicator of success can be found in your own personal reflections.

Most schools and colleges set performance management targets which include student examination success. While it is important that your students achieve to the best of their ability it is not the only indicator of successful teaching. As Yeats said, 'Education is not the filling of a pail, but the lighting of a fire'. (He was actually paraphrasing the classic scholar Plutarch.) If you have fostered a love of psychology and an enquiring mind in your students, then you have succeeded. Often it is not the students who have achieved the highest grades of whom you will be most proud, but those that have scraped a pass, against the odds.

A further indication of success is to be found in the interpersonal relationships that you form with students. This is the most rewarding aspect of teaching. However, the nature of psychology means that sometimes students will disclose information to you of a personal nature. Make sure you follow the current child protection guidance, the golden rule being never promise to keep things a secret and always report disclosures to the nominated child protection officer. This protects both you and the student.

For some, success is measured in promotions and while that can provide validation of your abilities, it is not the only route to success. If you are happy and fulfilled being a classroom teacher then that is a success too. Your own success should be defined by you, not others.

13.3 MAINTAINING VITALITY IN YOUR TEACHING

As an early career teacher you will be brimming with enthusiasm and new ideas. However, it can be a challenge to maintain those levels of enthusiasm over the years. It is only human to become a little bit jaded, especially when you are feeling tired or low at the end of term. So how do you maintain that vitality and enthusiasm in your teaching that your students deserve?

It is important to be open to new ideas and challenges. If you keep doing the same things you will always get the same results. Education is constantly evolving and so must your own practice and knowledge, if you haven't already, subscribe to the British Psychological Society (BPS) Research Digest to keep up to date with current psychological research. Additionally make sure you are on the mailing lists for the awarding body you teach so you do not miss any important updates in relation to changes to specifications and assessments. Continuing Professional Development (CPD) is vitally important and if you are in England, during your ECT years your school/college will have extra money in their budget to support you, so do not be afraid to ask if you can go on courses, conferences or webinars. Check the arrangements for the country or system you wish to work in. It might be more difficult in subsequent years, but schools/colleges still have a CPD budget and often generic whole school CPD is not relevant to psychology teachers. If you visit the Association for the Teaching of Psychology website (www.theatp.uk) you will find a list of psychology CPD providers. Not only will CPD courses update your knowledge and skills, but the networking opportunities are also equally valuable, especially as many psychology teachers are lone teachers. You might want to think about creating your own support network, if there is not already one in your area, by setting up a TeachMeet for psychology teachers. These informal gatherings can be a great source of support and provide the opportunity for standardisation of marking, sharing resources and ideas or simply to chat with like-minded individuals.

As suggested in Chapter 12, undertaking some research or further study can also revitalise your teaching. Being involved in action research helps you as a teacher be more effective at what you care most about – your teaching and the development of your students. However, whatever you choose to do, make sure it is enjoyable and sustainable for your own work/life balance.

13.4 THE REWARDS OF BEING A PSYCHOLOGY TEACHER

Being a teacher of psychology is inherently rewarding because of the interesting and inspirational nature of the subject. It lends itself to active teaching, through the recreation of research and mini practicals and students tend to find it interesting too. As most students (though some by default!) have chosen to study psychology, we have an advantage not enjoyed by teachers of core subjects like maths or science. Usually, students opt for psychology because they are curious about the subject or want to become more self-aware. Obviously, some students have unrealistic expectations of what psychology is, but even dispelling these myths can be interesting and entertaining.

Because of the nature of psychology, psychology teachers often have a unique insight into pedagogical theory, which can really inform their teaching. Many psychology teachers have an interest and expertise in SEND (see Chapter 10), and this can lead to rewarding career progression in this area. Psychology teachers can also use their expertise in PSHE (Personal, Social and Health Education) and their skills in interpersonal relationships and insights into mental health make pastoral roles a good fit. All of these qualities and skills that psychology teachers possess can lead to career progression. See Chapter 12 for further inspiration on career development.

13.5 BROADEN YOUR HORIZONS

As we write (2020/2021), two dominant themes have arisen that are impacting on education: Black Lives Matter and Decolonising the Curriculum. Much of the psychology curriculum is focused on the research of and knowledge generated by western, white male psychologists and that is a challenge. The major

REFLECTIONS AND FUTURE DIRECTIONS

awarding bodies are looking to reform their specifications to include more cultural diversity, but that on its own is not enough to address the issues. Your teaching should reflect the diversity within your classrooms and provide a balance to western, colonial history.

Students and teachers are positively enriched by exchange projects, these do not have to be physical exchanges, and virtual exchanges can be just as useful in gaining insight into other cultures. The European Federation of Psychology Teaching Associations (EFPTA) has a number of exchange and research projects that you could take part in. We have both had experience of hosting teachers from other countries and being hosted, which is a wonderfully enriching opportunity. We may have left the European Union, but we are still part of Europe!

The British Council has a Connecting Classroom Project which puts students in touch with other students from different countries. Although the Erasmus Project (student exchange) has been a casualty of Brexit, it is due to be replaced in September 2021 with the Turing Scheme, which will provide similar opportunities. For many of your students, these opportunities can be life changing and open up new horizons to them.

To broaden your own focus beyond the classroom you might wish to consider applying for Chartered Teacher status with the BPS which entitles you to use the designation CPsychol after your name. The application process is quite straightforward, you need to be a member of the BPS and write a personal statement, you will also need two referees, one can be your head teacher and the other should be someone who already holds CPsychol (this is where networking and membership of professional organisations like the ATP (www.theatp.uk) are useful). The BPS are looking for competency in the teaching of psychology covering evidence of your transferable skills, your professional attributes, your professional knowledge and professional skills.

You might also consider joining the Chartered College of Teaching. They have reduced membership rates for student teachers and ECTs. Some of the benefits include advice on:

- What to expect in your ECT years
- How to get the most out of your mentor
- How to be the best teacher in your classroom
- How to manage your workload
- How to access quality resources
- How to keep on top of your subject area
- How to manage challenging behaviour
- How to meet and engage with parents and carers.

Understandably, these suggestions might seem a bit daunting as you embark on your career as an ECT; however, it is not suggested that you do them all immediately, more that they become goals as you progress through your career.

Thank you for reading this book, we do hope you found it useful. We would like to take this opportunity to wish you every success in your career as a teacher of psychology.

13.6 SUMMARY AND KEY POINTS

You should now:

- understand the importance of positive reflection
- self-evaluate success
- maintain vitality in your teaching
- appreciate the rewards of being a psychology teacher
- think about broadening your horizons as a psychology teacher.

Check the requirements of your initial teacher education programme to see which have been addressed in this unit.

FURTHER RESOURCES AND WEBSITES

British Council Connecting classrooms project https://connecting-classrooms.british-council.org/ accessed 4/1/21

e-Twinning https://www.britishcouncil.org/sites/default/files/british_council_etwinning_erasmusplus_key_action_one_england.pdf Accessed 3/12/21

Useful Organisations to Join

The Association for the Teaching of Psychology www.theatp.uk accessed 4/1/21

The British Psychological Society www.bps.org.uk accessed 4/1/21

The Chartered College of Teaching www.chartered.college/ accessed 4/1/21

The European Federation of Psychology Teaching Associations www.efpta.org accessed 4/1/21

Possible Sources of Funding

Turing Scheme https://www.gov.uk/government/news/new-turing-scheme-to-support-thousands-of-students-to-study-and-work-abroad Accessed 4/1/21

Keeping up to date with psychological research
BPS Research Digest https://digest.bps.org.uk/ accessed 4/1/21

For information extending what is in this chapter, we recommend you read Section 3 "Classroom interactions and managing pupils" In the core textbook for the Learning to Teach series: Capel, S., Leask, M. and Younie, S. with E. Hidson and J. Lawrence (9th edn 2022) *Learning to Teach in the Secondary School: A Companion to School Experience.* Abingdon Routledge: Taylor Francis.

REFERENCES

Agarwal, P. K. (2019). Retrieval practice & bloom's taxonomy: Do students need fact knowledge before higher order learning? *Journal of Educational Psychology*, 111(2), 189-209.

Ainsworth, M. D. S., & Bell, S. M. (1970). Attachment, exploration, and separation: Illustrated by the behavior of one-year-olds in a strange situation. *Child Development*, 41, 49-67.

Allport, G. W. (1968). The historical background of modern psychology. In Lindzey, G., & Aronson, E. (eds) *Handbook of social psychology* (Vol. 1, 2nd ed.). Reading, MA: Adison-Wesley.

Amiti, F. (2020). Synchronous and asynchronous e-learning. *European Journal of Open Education and E-learning Studies*, 5(2), 60-70.

Andrew, A., Cattan, S., Dias, M. C., Farquharson, C., Kraftman, L, Krutikova, S., Phimister, A., & Sevilla, A. (2020). Inequalities in children's experiences of home learning during the COVID-19 lockdown in England. Institute for Fiscal Studies Working Paper.

Andrews, J., & Clark, R. (2011). *Peer mentoring works! how peer mentoring enhances student success in higher education*. Birmingham: Aston University.

Asch, S. E. (1951). Effect of group pressure upon the modification and distortion of judgements. In Guetzkow, H. (ed.) *Groups, leadership and men*. Pittsburg, PA: Carnegie Press.

Atkinson, R. C., & Shiffrin, R. M. (1968). Human memory: A proposed system and its control processes. In Spence, K. W., & Spence, J. T. (eds) *The psychology of learning and motivation: Advances in research and theory* (Vol. 2, pp. 89-195). New York: Academic Press.

Avramidis, E., & Norwich, B. (2002). Teachers' attitudes towards integration / inclusion: A review of the literature. *European Journal of Special Needs Education*, 17(2), 129-147.

Baddeley, A. D., & Hitch, G. (1974). Working memory. In Bower, G. H. (ed.) *The psychology of learning and motivation: Advances in research and theory* (Vol. 8, pp. 47-89). New York: Academic Press.

Ball, C. T., & Pelco, L. E. (2006). Teaching research methods to psychology undergraduate students using an active cooperative learning approach. *International Journal of Teaching and Learning in Higher Education*, 17, 147-154.

Bandura, A. (1977). *Social learning theory*. Englewood Cliffs, NJ: Prentice Hall.

Barenberg, J., Roeder, U.-R., & Dutke, S. (2018). Students' temporal distributing of learning activities in psychology courses: Factors of influence and effects on the metacognitive learning outcome. *Psychology Learning & Teaching*, 17(3), 257-271. https://doi.org/10.1177/1475725718769488.

REFERENCES

Baron-Cohen S., Jolliffe T., Mortimore C., & Robertson, M. (1997). Another advanced test of theory of mind: evidence from very high functioning adults with autism or Asperger Syndrome. *Journal of Child Psychology and Psychiatry*, 38(7), 813–822.

Baron-Cohen, S., Leslie, A. M., & Frith, U. (1985). Does the autistic child have a 'theory of mind'? *Cognition*, 21, 37–49.

Barrows, H. S., & Tamblyn, R. M. (1980). *Problem-based learning: An approach to medical education* (Vol. 1). Springer Publishing Company. New York.

Barter, C. and Renold, E., 1999. The use of vignettes in qualitative research. *Social research update*, 25(9), pp.1–6.

Barnett, S. M., & Ceci, S. J. (2002). When and where do we apply what we learn?: A taxonomy for far transfer. *Psychological Bulletin*, 128(4), 612–637. https://doi.org/10.1037/0033-2909.128.4.612

Baumert, J., Kunter, M., Blum, W., Brunner, M., Voss, T., Jordan, A., Klusmann, U., Krauss, S., Neubrand, M., & Tsai, Y.-M. (2010). Teachers' mathematical knowledge, cognitive activation in the classroom, and student progress. *American Educational Research Journal*, 47(1), 133–180. https://doi.org/10.3102/0002831209345157.

Bensley, D. A., & Spero, R. A. (2014). Improving critical thinking skills and metacognitive monitoring through direct infusion. *Thinking Skills and Creativity*, 12, 55–68.

Bernstein, D. A. (2018). Does active learning work? A good question, but not the right one. *Scholarship of Teaching and Learning in Psychology*, 4(4), 290–307.

Bernstein-Yamashiro, B., & Noam, G. G. (2013). *Teacher-student relationships: toward personalized education: New directions for youth development* (Number 137, Bernstein-Yamashiro and Gil G. Noam). John Wiley & Sons, Incorporated. Malden, MA.

Bisra, K., Liu, Q., Nesbit, J., Salimi, F., & Winne, P. (2018). Inducing self-explanation: A meta-analysis. *Educational Psychology Review*, 30(3), pp.703–725.

Bjork, E. L., & Bjork, R. A. (2011). Making things hard on yourself, but in a good way: Creating desirable difficulties to enhance learning. In Gernsbacher, M. A., Pew, R. W., Hough, L. M., Pomerantz, J. R., & FABBS Foundation (eds) *Psychology and the real world: Essays illustrating fundamental contributions to society* (pp. 56–64). Worth Publishers.

Black, P., Harrison, C., Lee, C., Marshall, B., & Wiliam, D. (2004). Working inside the black box: Assessment for learning in the classroom. *Phi Delta Kappan*, 86(1), 9–21.

Black, P., & Wiliam, D. (2003). In praise of educational research: Formative assessment. *British Educational Research Journal*, 29(5), 623–637.

Black, P. J., Harrison, C., Lee, C., Marshall, B., & Wiliam, D. (2003). *Assessment for learning: Putting it into practice*. Berkshire, England: Open University Press.

Black, P. J., & Wiliam, D. (1998a). Assessment and classroom learning: Assessment in Education. *Principles, Policy and Practice*, 5(1), 7–73.

Black, P. J., & Wiliam, D. (1998b). *Inside the black box: Raising standards through classroom assessment*. London: King's College London School of Education.

Bloom, B. S., Engelhart, M. D., Furst, E. J., Hill, W. H., & Krathwohl, D. R. (1956). *Taxonomy of educational objectives: The classification of educational goals. Handbook I: Cognitive domain*. New York: David McKay Company.

Boaler, J., Wiliam, D., & Brown, M. (2000). Student's experiences of ability grouping – disaffection, polarisation and the construct of failure. *British Educational Research Journal*, 35(5), 630–648.

Boneau, C. A. (1990). Psychological literacy: A first approximation. *American Psychologist*, 45, 891–900 (available at https://web.archive.org/web/20150227074717/http://people.auc.ca/brodbeck/4007/article12.pdf)

Bowlby, J. (1946). *Forty-four Juvenile Thieves*. London: Bailliere, Tindall & Cox.

Bramming, P., Hansen, B. G., Bojesen, A., & Olesen, K. G. (2012). (Im) perfect pictures: Snaplogs in performativity research. *Qualitative Research in Organizations and Management: An International Journal*.

REFERENCES

Bransford, J. D., Brown, A. L., & Cocking, R. R. (2000). *How people learn: Brain, mind, experience and school.* Washington, DC: National Academy Press.

British Psychological Society. (2018). *Code of ethics and conduct.* Leicester: BPS.

British Psychological Society. (BPS) (n. d). *Careers: Your journey into psychology.* https://careers.bps.org.uk/

Bruner, J. (1960). *The process of education.* Cambridge MA: Harvard.

Capel, S., Leask, M., and Younie, S. with Hidson, E., & Lawrence. J. (9th edn 2022) *Learning to Teach in the Secondary School: A Companion to School Experience.* Abingdon Routledge: Taylor Francis.

Chappuis, J. (2015). *Seven strategies of assessment for learning* (2nd ed.). New York: Pearson Education.

Clark, I. (2012). Formative assessment: Assessment is for self-regulated learning. *Educational Psychology Review*, 24(2), 205-249.

Clark, R., & Andrews, J. (2012). Peer mentoring in Higher Education: a reciprocal route to student success. In Andrews, J., & Clark, R. (eds) *Compendium of effective practice in higher education retention and success* (pp. 71-75). Aston University.

Clutterbuck, D. (1991). *Everyone needs a mentor.* London: IPM.

Coetzee, S., & Van der Merwe. (2010). Industrial psychology students' attitudes towards statistics *SA Journal of Industrial Psychology*, 36, 1-8.

Coolican, H. (2018). *Research methods and statistics in psychology.* London: Routledge.

Cottrell, S. (2017). *Critical thinking skills: Effective analysis, argument and reflection.* Macmillan International Higher Education.

Craik, F. I., & Lockhart, R. S. (1972). Levels of processing: A framework for memory research. *Journal of Verbal Learning and Verbal Behavior*, 11(6), 671-684.

Craik, F. I. M., & Watkins, M. J. (1973). The role of rehearsal in short term memory. *Journal of Verbal Learning and Verbal Behavior*, 12, 599-607.

Creemers, B. P. M., & Kyriakides, L. (2008). *The dynamics of educational effectiveness: a contribution to policy, practice and theory in contemporary schools.* London: Routledge.

Curtiss, S. (1977). *Genie: A psycholinguistic study of a modern-day "wild child".* New York: Academic Press.

Davidesco, I., & Milne, C. (2019). Implementing cognitive science and discipline-based education research in the undergraduate science classroom. *CBE Life Sciences Education*, 18(3), es4. https://doi.org/10.1187/cbe.18-12-0240.

Department for Education. (2011). *Teachers' standards.* London: DfE.

Department for Education. (2014). *Assessment principles.* London: DfE. https://www.gov.uk/government/publications/assessment-principles-school-curriculum.

Department for Education. (2015). *Special educational needs and disability code of practice: 0 to 25 year.* London: DfE.

Dewey, J. (1916). *Democracy and education. An introduction to the philosophy of education. With a Critical Introduction by Patricia H. Hinchey (2018)* (Timely Classics in Education). Gorham, ME: Myers Education Press.

Dewey, J. (1938). *Experience and education.* New York: Kappa Delta Pi. http://ruby.fgcu.edu/courses/ndemers/colloquium/experienceducationdewey.pdf [Accessed 31.10.2020].

Dolmans, D. H., Snellen-Balendong, H., Wolfhagen, I., & van der Vleuten, C. (1997). Seven principles of effective case design for a problem-based curriculum. *Medical Teacher*, 19(3), 185-189. https://doi.org/10.3109/01421599709019379

Dunlosky, J. (2013). Strengthening the student toolbox: study strategies to boost learning. *American Educator*, 37(3), 12-21 (available at https://www.aft.org/sites/default/files/periodicals/dunlosky.pdf).

Dunlosky, J., Rawson, K. A., Marsh, E. J., Nathan, M. J., & Willingham, D. T. (2013). Improving students' learning with effective learning techniques: promising directions from cognitive and educational psychology. *Psychological Science in the Public Interest*, 14(1), 4-58.

REFERENCES

Dunn, D. S., Halonen, J. S., & Smith, R. A. (eds) (2008). *Teaching critical thinking in psychology a handbook of best practices*. Blackwell Publishing Ltd.

Dweck, C. S. (1986). Motivational processes affecting learning. *American Psychologist* (Psychological Science and Education), 41(10), 1040-1048. https://doi.org/10.1037/0003-066X.41.10.1040

Dweck, C. S. (2006). *Mindset: The new psychology of success*. New York: Random House.

Ecclestone, K., & Brown, A. (2002). Improving post-16 learning: the challenges for the Teaching and Learning Research Programme from a version of papers given to the Department for Education and Skills Research Conference and to the Learning and Skills Development Agency Research Conference at the University of Warwick, 11-13th December, 2002.

Edwards, D., & Mercer, N. (1987). Common knowledge. The development of understanding in the classroom. London: Methuen.

Education Endowment Foundation. (2018). *Teaching and learning toolkit: Feedback*. London: Education Endowment Foundation. https://educationendowmentfoundation.org.uk/pdf/generate/?u=https://educationendowmentfoundation.org.uk/pdf/toolkit/?id=131&t=Teaching%20and%20Learning%20Toolkit&e=131&s=.

Education inspection framework: overview of research January 2019, https://www.gov.uk/government/publications/education-inspection-framework-overview-of-research

Elliott, V., Baird, J., Hopfenbeck, T. N., Ingram, J., Thompson, I., Usher, N., Zantout, M., Richardson, J., & Coleman, R. (2016). *A marked improvement? A review of the evidence on written marking*. London: Education Endowment Foundation. https://educationendowmentfoundation.org.uk/public/files/Presentations/Publications/EEF_Marking_Review_April_2016.pdf.

Freire, P. (1996). *The pedagogy of the oppressed*. New revised ed. London: Penguin.

Geiselman, R., & Fisher, R. (1989). Field test of the cognitive interview: enhancing the recollection of actual victims and witnesses of crime. *Journal of Applied Psychology*, 74(5), 722-727.

Halpern, D. F. (1998). Teaching critical thinking for transfer across domains: Disposition, skills, structure training, and metacognitive monitoring. *American Psychologist*, 53(4), 449-455.

Halpern, D. F. (2017). Whither psychology. *Perspectives on Psychological Science*, 12(4), 665-668. https://doi.org/10.1177/1745691616677097.

Haney, C., Banks, W. C., & Zimbardo, P. G. (1973). A study of prisoners and guards in a simulated prison. *Naval Research Review*, 30, 4-17.

Harlow, H. F., & Zimmermann, R. R. (1958). The development of affective responsiveness in infant monkeys. *Proceedings of the American Philosophical Society*, 102, 501-509.

Hattie, J. (2009). *Visible learning: A synthesis of over 800 meta-analyses relating to achievement*. London: Routledge.

Hattie, J., & Timperley, H. (2007). The power of feedback. *Review of Educational Research*, 77(1), 81-112.

Hatziapostolou, T., & Paraskakis, I. (2010). Enhancing the impact of formative feedback on student learning through an online feedback system. *Electronic Journal of e-Learning*, 8(2), 111-122.

Hawe, E., & Parr, J. (2014). Assessment for Learning in the writing classroom: an incomplete realisation. *The Curriculum Journal*, 25(2), 210-237.

Hodge, S. (2019). Transformative learning for knowledge: From meaning perspectives to threshold concepts. *Journal of Transformative Education*, 17(2), 133-153.

Hooks, B. (1994). *Teaching to transgress: Education as the practice of freedom*. New York: Routledge.

Hulme, J. (2014). Psychological literacy: From classroom to real world. *The Psychologist*, 27(12), 932-935.

REFERENCES

Independent Teacher Workload Review Group. (2016). *Eliminating unnecessary workload around marking*. London: Independent Report. https://assets.publishing.service.gov.uk/government/uploads/system/uploads/attachment_data/file/511256/Eliminating-unnecessary-workload-around-marking.pdf.

Jacobsen, A. M., & Diseth, Å. (2020). Why choose psychology? An investigation of Norwegian high school students. *Psychology Learning & Teaching*, 19(2), 128-142. https://doi.org/10.1177/1475725719872134.

Jarvis, M. (2011). *Teaching psychology 14-19: Issues and techniques* (1st ed.). London: Routledge. https://doi.org/10.4324/9780203810170.

Jeffries, C., & Maeder, D. W. (2005). Using vignettes to build and assess teacher understanding of instructional strategies. *Professional Educator*, 27, 17-28.

Karpicke, J. D., Lehman, M., & Aue, W. R. (2014). Retrieval-based learning: An episodic context account. In B. H. Ross (Ed.) *Psychology of learning and motivation* (Vol. 61, pp. 237-284). Academic Press.

Kasprowicz, R. E., Marsden, E., & Sephton, N. (2019). Investigating distribution of practice effects for the learning of foreign language verb morphology in the young learner classroom. *The Modern Language Journal*, 103(3), 580-606.

Kelley, T. L. (1927). *Interpretation of educational measurements*. New York: Macmillan.

Kerr Lawrence, N., Serdikoff, S., Zinn, T. E., & Baker, S. C., (2008). Have we demystified critical thinking? In Dunn, D. S., Halonen, J. S., & Smith, R. A. (eds) *Teaching critical thinking in psychology a handbook of best practices*. Blackwell Publishing Ltd.

Kessler, R. C., Berglund, P., Demler, O., Jin, R., Merikangas, K. R., & Walter, S. E. E. (2005). Lifetime prevalence and age-of-onset distributions of DSM-IV disorders in the national comorbidity survey replication. *Archives of General Psychiatry*, 62(6), 593-602. https://doi.org/10.1001/archpsyc.62.6.593.

Kim, L. E., & Asbury, K. (2020). 'Like a rug had been pulled from under you': The impact of COVID-19 on teachers in England during the first six weeks of the UK lockdown. *British Journal of Educational Psychology*, 90(4), 1062-1083.

King, A. (1993). Sage on the stage to guide on the side. *College Teaching*, 41(1), 30-35.

Kirschner, P. A., Sweller, J., &and Clark, R. E. (2006). Why minimal guidance during instruction does not work: an analysis of the failure of constructivist, discovery, problem-based, experiential, and inquiry-based teaching. *Educational Psychologist*, 41(2), 75-86.

Kohlberg, L. (1963). The development of children's orientations toward a moral order. *Human Development*, 6(1-2), 11-33.

Küpper-Tetzel, C. E., Kapler, I. V., & Wiseheart, M. (2014). Contracting, equal, and expanding learning schedules: The optimal distribution of learning sessions depends on retention interval. *Memory & Cognition*, 42(5), 729-741. https://doi.org/10.3758/s13421-014-0394-1.

Livari, N., Sharma, S., & Ventä-Olkkonen, L. (2020). Digital transformation of everyday life-How COVID-19 pandemic transformed the basic education of the young generation and why information management research should care? *International Journal of Information Management*, 55, 102183.

Loftus, E. F., & Palmer, J. C. (1974). Reconstruction of auto-mobile destruction: An example of the interaction between language and memory. *Journal of Verbal Learning and Verbal behavior*, 13, 585-589.

Major, A., & Calandrino, T. (2018). Beyond chunking: Micro-learning secrets for effective online design. *FDLA Journal*, 3(1), 13.

Maslow, A. H. (1954). *Motivation and personality*. New York: Harper and Row.

Mayer, R. E. (2009). *Multimedia learning* (2nd ed.). Cambridge University Press.

McGovern, T. V., Corey, L., Cranney, J., Dixon, W., Holmes, J. D., & Kuebli et al. (2010). Psychologically literate citizens. In Halpern, D. F. (ed.) *Undergraduate education in*

REFERENCES

psychology: A blueprint for the future of the discipline (pp. 9-27). Washington, DC: American Psychological Association.

McLaughlin, M. (2020, Saturday January 25). *Pupils put at risk in 'Lord of the Flies' experiments*. The Times. https://www.thetimes.co.uk/article/pupils-put-at-risk-in-lord-of-the-flies-experiments-ls2fjpjtf.

Mercer, N. (1995). *The guided construction of knowledge: Talk amongst teachers and learners*. Clevedon: Multilingual Matters.

Mercer, N. (2000). *Words and minds: How we use language to think together*. London: Routledge.

Meyer, J. H. F., & Land, R. (2003). Threshold concepts and troublesome knowledge: linkages to ways of thinking and practicing. In Rust, C. (ed.) *Improving student learning – theory and practice ten years on* (pp. 412-424). Oxford: Oxford Centre for Staff and Learning Development (OCSLD).

Milgram, S. (1963). Behavioural study of obedience. *Journal of Abnormal and Social Psychology*, 67, 391-398.

Miller, G. (1956). The magical number seven, plus or minus two: Some limits of our capacity for processing information. *Psychological Review*, 63, 81-97.

Munroe-Chandler, K., Hall, C., & Fishburne, G., (2008). Playing with confidence: The relationship between imagery use and self-confidence and self-efficacy in youth soccer players. *Journal of Sports Sciences*, 26(14), 1539-1546. https://doi.org/10.1080/02640410802315419.

Nickerson, R. S. (2020). Technology in education in 2020: Thinking about the not-distant future. In *Technology in education: Looking toward* (pp. 1-9). London: Routledge. Edited By Raymond S. Nickerson, Philip P. Zodhiates.

Novak, G., Patterson, E., Gavrin, A., & Christian W. (1999). *Just-in-time teaching: Blending active learning with web technology*. Englewood NJ: Prentice Hall.

Paivio, A. (1971). *Imagery and verbal processes*. New York: Holt Rinehart & Winston.

Paivio, A. (2006). Dual coding theory and education. In Neuman, S. (ed.) *Pathways to literacy achievement for high poverty children*. The University of Michigan School of Education.

Paivio, A., & Csapo, K. (1973). Picture superiority in free recall: Imagery or dual coding? *Cognitive Psychology*, 5(2), 176-206. https://doi.org/10.1016/0010-0285(73)90032-7.

Panadero, E., & Romero, M. (2014). To rubric or not to rubric? The effects of self-assessment on self-regulation, performance and self-efficacy. *Assessment in Education: Principles, Policy & Practice*, 21(2), 133-148.

Pawl, A., Barrantes, A., Pritchard, D. E., & Mitchell, R. (2012). What do seniors remember from freshman physics? *Physical Review Special Topics—Physics Education Research*, 8, 020118.

Paxton, P. (2006). Dollars and sense: Convincing students that they can learn and want to learn statistics. *Teaching Sociology*, 34(1), 65-70.

Perkins, D. N., & Salomon, G. (1992). Transfer of learning. *International Encyclopedia of Education*, 2, 6452-6457.

Peterson, L. R., & Peterson, M. J. (1959). Short-term retention of individual verbal items. *Journal of Experimental Psychology*, 58, 193-198.

Petocz, P., & Reid, A. (2007). *Learning and assessment in statistics*. IASE /ISI Satellite.

Piaget, J., & Inhelde, B. (1969). The Psychology of the Child London: Routledge & Kegan Paul.

Pitchforth, J., Fahy, K., Ford, T., Wolpert, M., Viner, R. M., & Hargreaves, D. S. (2019). Mental health and well-being trends among children and young people in the UK, 1995-2014: Analysis of repeated cross-sectional national health surveys. *Psychology Medicine*, 49(8), 1275-1285. https://doi.org/10.1017/S0033291718001757. Epub 2018 Sep 11. PMID: 30201061; PMCID: PMC6518382.

REFERENCES

Pollard, A. (1990). Towards a sociology of learning in primary schools. *British Journal of Sociology of Education*, 11(3), 241-256.

Pollard, A. (ed.) (1987). *Children and their Primary Schools: a new perspective*. Lewes, East Sussex: Falmer Press.

Porter, A., Cartwright, T., & Snelgar, R. (2006). *Teaching statistics and research methods to heterogeneous groups: The Westminster experience ICOTS-7*.

Rawson, K. A., & Dunlosky, J. (2011). Optimizing schedules of retrieval practice for durable and efficient learning: How much is enough? *Journal of Experimental Psychology: General*, 140(3), 283-302. https://doi.org/10.1037/a0023956.

Rawson, K. A., Vaughn, K. E., Walsh, M., & Dunlosky, J. (2018). Investigating and explaining the effects of successive relearning on long-term retention (advance online publication). *Journal of Experimental Psychology: Applied*, 24(1), 57-71.

Remmers, H.H., Shock, N.W. and Kelly, E.L., 1927. An empirical study of the validity of the Spearman-Brown formula as applied to the Purdue rating scale. *Journal of Educational Psychology*, 18(3), p.187.

Renkl, A., & Atkinson, R. K. (2003). Structuring the transition from example study to problem solving in cognitive skill acquisition: A cognitive load perspective. *Educational Psychologist*, 38, 15-22.

Research Update. http://www.soc.surrey.ac..uk/sru/SRU25.html. [Accessed 31.10.2020].

Richards, A., Rivers, I., & Ackhurst, J. (2008). A positive psychology approach to tackling bullying in secondary schools: A comparative evaluation. *Educational & Child Psychology*, 25(2), 72-90.

Richmond, A. S., & Kindelberger Hagan, L. (2011). Promoting higher level thinking in psychology: Is active learning the answer? *Teaching of Psychology*, 38(2), 102-105.

Rodriguez, V. (2012). The teaching brain and the end of the empty vessel. *Mind, Brain and Education*, 6(4), 177-185.

Roediger, H. L., & Karpicke, J. D. (2011). Intricacies of spaced retrieval: A resolution. In Benjamin, A. S. (ed.) *Successful remembering and successful forgetting: A festschrift in honor of Robert A. Bjork* (pp. 23-47). Psychology Press.

Rogers, C. R. (1969). *Freedom to learn*. Columbus, OH: Merrill Publishing Company.

Rohrer, D., Dedrick, R. F., & Hartwig, M. K. (2020). The scarcity of interleaved practice in mathematics textbooks. *Educational Psychology Review*, 32(3), 873-883.

Rosenshine, B. (2012). Principles of instruction: Research-based strategies that all teachers should know. *American Educator*, 36(1), 12-19, 39. (available at https://www.aft.org/sites/default/files/periodicals/Rosenshine.pdf)

Rosenthal, R. (1994). Science and ethics in conducting, analyzing, and reporting psychological research. *Psychological Science*, 5(3), 127-134.

Rosenthal, R., & Jacobson, L. (1968). *Pygmalion in the classroom*. New York: Rinehart and Winston.

Rutter, M., and the English and Romanian Adoptees Study Team (1998). Developmental catch-up and deficit following adoption after severe early global privation. *Journal of Child Psychology and Psychiatry*, 39, 465-476.

Savin-Baden, M. (2007). *A practical guide to problem-based learning online*. London, UK: Routledge.

Savin-Baden, M., & Major, C. H. (2004). *Foundations of problem-based learning* New York: Open University Press - McGraw Hill Education.

Schön, D. A. (1983). *The reflective practitioner: how professionals think in action*. New York: Basic books.

SchoolsWeek. (2019). *A level results 2019: Psychology*. London: SchoolsWeek.co.uk. https://schoolsweek.co.uk/a-level-results-2019-psychology/.

Scoville, W. B., & Milner, B. J. (1957). Loss of recent memory after bilateral hippocampal lesions. *Journal of Neurology, Neurosurgery and Psychiatry*, 20, 11-21.

REFERENCES

Seligman, M. E. P. (1998). The president's address (annual report). *American Psychologist*, 54, 559-562.

Sieber, J. E., & Stanley, B. (1988). Ethical and professional dimensions of socially sensitive research. *American Psychologist*, 43(1), 49-55.

Silva, A. B. D., Bispo, A. C. K. D. A., Rodriguez, D. G., & Vasquez, F. I. F. (2018), Problem-based learning: A proposal for structuring PBL and its implications for learning among students in an undergraduate management degree program. *Revista de Gestão*, 25(2), 160-177.

Smith, M., & Firth, J. (2018). *Psychology in the classroom: A teacher's guide to what works*. London: Routledge.

Sperry, R. W. (1968). Hemisphere deconnection and unity in conscious awareness. *American Psychologist*, 23(10), 723.

Stavnezer, A. J., & Lom, B. (2019). Student-led recaps and retrieval practice: A simple classroom activity emphasizing effective learning strategies. *Journal of Undergraduate Neuroscience Education*, 18(1), A1-A14.

Stephen, S. A. K., & McCormick-Pritchard, M. (2021). Students' perceptions of emergency remote instruction during the COVID-19 pandemic. *Journal of Higher Education Theory and Practice*, 21(11), 63-72.

Stobart, G., & Gipps, C. (1997). *Assessment: A teacher's guide to the issues*. London: Hodder and Stoughton.

Stroop, J. R. (1935). Studies of interference in serial verbal reactions. *Journal of Experimental Psychology*, 18(6), 643-662.

Swaffield, S. (2011). Getting to the heart of authentic assessment for learning. *Assessment in Education: Principles, Policy and Practice*, 18(4), 433-449.

Sweller, J. (1988). Cognitive load during problem solving: Effects on learning. *Cognitive Science*, 12, 257-285.

Sweller, J. (2011). Cognitive load theory. In *Psychology of learning and motivation* (Vol. 55, pp. 37-76). Academic Press.

Sweller, J., Ayres, P., & Kalyuga, S. (2011). *Cognitive load theory*. New York: Springer.

Taala, W., Franco Jr., F. B., & Teresa, P. H. S. (2019). Library literacy program: Library as battleground for fighting fake news. *Open Access Library*, 6, e5296.

Tatalovic, M. (2009). Science comics as tools for science education and communication: a brief, exploratory study. *Journal of Science Communication*, 8(4).

Tomlinson, S. (1982). *A sociology of special education*. London: Routledge & Kegan Paul.

Topping, K. J., (2005). Trends in peer learning. *Educational Psychology*, 25(6), 631-645.

Tunstall, P., & Gipps, C. (1996). Teacher feedback to young children in formative assessment: A typology. *British Educational Research Journal*, 22(4), 389-404.

Van Der Post, A. et al. (2009). *Children and teenagers with Asperger's: The journey of parenting from birth to teens*. Brentwood: Chipmunk Publishing.

Van Gelder, T. (2005). Teaching critical thinking: Some lessons from cognitive science. *College Teaching*, 53(1), 41-48.

Van Ijzendoorn, M. H., & Kroonenberg, P. M. (1988). Cross-cultural patterns of attachment: A meta-analysis of the strange situation. *Child Development*, 59(1), 147-156

Von Glaserfeld, E. (1995). *Radical constructivism: A way of knowing and learning (Studies in mathematics education)* New York: Routledge Falmer.

Vygotsky, L. S. (1978). *Mind in society: The development of higher psychological processes*. Cambridge, MA: Harvard University Press.

Walkerdine, V. (1993). Beyond Developmentalism? *Theory & Psychology*, 3(4), 451-469. https://doi.org/10.1177/0959354393034004

Watkins, C. (2005). *Classrooms as learning communities: What's in it for Schools?* London: Falmer Routledge. https://doi.org/10.4324/9780203390719.

REFERENCES

Weinstein, Y., Gilmore, A. W., Szpunar, K. K., & McDermott, K. B. (2014). The role of test expectancy in the build-up of proactive interference in long-term memory. *Journal of Experimental Psychology: Learning, Memory, and Cognition*, 40(4), 1039-1048. https://doi.org/10.1037/a0036164.

Weinstein, Y., Madan, C. R., & Sumeracki, M. A. (2018). Teaching the science of learning. *Cognitive Research*, 3, 2. https://doi.org/10.1186/s41235-017-0087-y.

Weinstein, Y., Nunes, L. D., & Karpicke, J. D. (2016). On the placement of practice questions during study. *Journal of Experimental Psychology: Applied*, 22(1), 72-84.

Wicks, D. A. (2021). Minimising Zoom fatigue and other strategies for a successful synchronous class experience. Tackling Online Education: Implications of Responses to COVID-19 in Higher Education Globally, 1.

Wiggins, S., Hammar Chiriac, E., Larsson Abbad, G., Pauli, R., & Worell, M. (2016). Ask not only 'what can problem-based learning do for psychology?' but 'what can psychology do for problem-based learning?' a review of the relevance of problem-based learning for psychology teaching and research. *Psychology Learning & Teaching*, 15(2), 136-154. http://doi.org/10.1177/1475725716643270 [Accessed 2.11.20].

Wiliam, D. (2011). What is assessment for learning? *Studies in Educational Evaluation*, 37(1), 3-14.

Wiliam, D. (2017). *Embedded formative assessment: (strategies for classroom assessment that drives student engagement and learning)*. IN: Solution Tree. Bloomington, IN.

Willingham, D. (2004). *Ask the cognitive scientist: The privileged status of story*. American Federation of Teachers. https://www.aft.org/periodical/american-educator/summer-2004/ask-cognitive-scientist.

Willingham, D. (2019). *How to teach critical thinking*. Education Future Frontiers.

Wing, L. (1988). The continuum of autistic characteristics. In Schopler, E., & Mesibov, G. B. (eds) *Diagnosis and Assessment in Autism. Current Issues in Autism*. Boston, MA: Springer. https://doi.org/10.1007/978-1-4899-0792-9_7

Wissman, K. T., & Rawson, K. A. (2016). How do students implement collaborative testing in real-world contexts? *Memory*, 24(2), 223-239. https://doi.org/10.1080/09658211.2014.999792.

Wray and Lewis (undated) https://warwick.ac.uk/fac/soc/ces/research/teachingandlearning/publications/framesrai.pdf

Yorke, M., & Knight, P. (2006). *Embedding employability into the curriculum* (Learning and employability series 1). York: Higher Education Academy.

Zimmerman, B. J., & Schunk, D. H. (2001). *Self-regulated learning and academic achievement: Theoretical perspectives* (2nd ed.). Mahwah, NJ: Lawrence Erlbaum Associates.

INDEX

Note: Bold page numbers refer to tables; *italic* page numbers refer to figures.

ABC career targets 168
active learning 143–145, *144*
affective assessment systems 109
AfL *see* assessment for learning (AfL)
Ainsworth, M.D.S. 99
Amiti, F. 141
anchoring bias 167
Andrews, J. 101
Asbury, K. 141
ASC/D *see* Autism Spectrum Conditions/Disorders (ASC/D)
assessment for learning (AfL) 112–116
Association for the Teaching of Psychology (ATP) 2, 10–11; application 60–62
asynchronous technology 142
Atkinson, R.C. 97
Atkinson-Shiffrin 'modal model' 65
ATP *see* Association for the Teaching of Psychology (ATP)
attention deficit (hyperactivity) disorder (ADD/ADHD) 134
Autism Spectrum Conditions/Disorders (ASC/D) 131
availability heuristic 167

Baddeley, A.D. 28
Baird, J. 120
BAME *see* Black, Asian and Minority Ethnic (BAME)
Bandura, A. 16, 98
Barnett, S. M. 66
Baron-Cohen, S. 131
Barrows, H.S. 83
Baumert, J. 13
Bensley, D.A. 76

biological area 38–39
Bjork, E.L. 20
Bjork, R.A. 20
Black, Asian and Minority Ethnic (BAME) 164
Black, P. 36, 37, 110, 111
Bloom's taxonomy 21, 136, 137, *137*
Boneau, C.A. 94, 95
Bowlby, J. 35
BPS *see* British Psychological Society (BPS)
brain jelly moulds 38
British Council 177
British Higher Education system 101
British Psychological Society (BPS) 2, 11, 175; ethical guidelines 57–60; in schools and colleges 60–62
Bruner, J. 112

career plan 159; biases and limitations 167; broadening your skills 162; challenges 170–171; five-year plan 169; flexible planning 168; maintaining motivation 169–170; master's-level study 164–165; middle management and beyond 163–164; practitioner action research 165–166; roles 167–168; scope 160–161
Ceci, S. J. 66
Clark, R. 101
classroom 4–5; flipped 45; practical research 43–44
CLT *see* Cognitive Load Theory (CLT)
Clutterbuck, D. 100
cognition 131
cognitive area 27–30

INDEX

cognitive load theory (CLT) 16-18, 27, 145, *146*
comic books 23
communication tools 141
comorbidity 135
Continuing Professional Development (CPD) 175-176
copyright 152-153
core study mapping 39
coronavirus pandemic 140, 141
correlational research 49-51
correlation coefficients 49-50
cost-benefit analysis 149, 163
CPD *see* Continuing Professional Development (CPD)
Craik, F.I.M. 97, 143
create teaching resources 18
Crime Scene Investigation (CSI) 9
critical thinker 70-71
critical thinking 69; barriers 72-75; characteristics 80; create framework for 76-77; creating opportunities for 77; evaluative thought 71; skills required for 75-76; writing activities 79
cultural diversity 35

data protection 150
Davidesco, I. 20
Department for Education teacher standards 3-4
descriptive statistics 51
developmental area 33-36
Dewey, J. 83, 112
digital education: accessibility 150-152; copyright 152-153; data protection 150; Google Suite 155; MS teams 154-155; platforms 153; traditional VLE platforms 153-154
digital learning 143
distributed learning 18-19, 148
dual coding theory 23-24
Dweck, C. 171
dyscalculia 132
dyslexia 132
dyspraxia 132

early career teacher (ECT) 1, 162, 173
Edinburgh Zoo 46
Education and Health Care Plan (EHCP) 129
Education Endowment Foundation 102, 116
Edwards, D. 112

effective classroom management techniques 29
effective feedback 116-118
EFPTA *see* European Federation of Psychology Teaching Associations (EFPTA)
EHCP *see* Education and Health Care Plan (EHCP)
elaboration 22-23
electronic resources 7
Elliott, V. 120
Embedded Formative Assessment 103
employability skills 105-106
English Department for Education 109
ethics 55, 56-57, 138; Association for the Teaching of Psychology application 60-62; BPS guidelines 57-60; practice 56-57; teaching activities 62-67
European Federation of Psychology Teaching Associations (EFPTA) 177
evaluation: assessment objectives for 77-78; create framework for 76-77; tasks 78-79
exam questions 115
exit/entrance cards 115
experimental methods 42; classroom practicals 43-44; sampling techniques 44-45; writing hypotheses 43, **43**
expertise reversal effect 18, 146
extraneous cognitive load 16, 18, 28-29
'eyeball test' 51

family structures, and life choices 36
feedback: effective 116-118; student responses to 118-119
five-year plan 169
flexible environment 46
flexible planning 168
flipped classroom 45
flipped learning technique 47
floating facilitator model 88
formative assessment 110-111
four corners 115

GCSE 9-10, *136*
germane cognitive load 16, 29
Google Classroom 20, 142
Google Meet 141, 142
Google Suite 155

Halpern, D.F. 78, 80
hand signals 115

INDEX

Harrison, C. 111
Haslam, A. 167
Hattie, J. 116
Hatziapostolou, T. 116
Hawe, E. 112
Her Majesty's Chief Inspector (HMCI) 29
Hitch, G. 28
HMCI see Her Majesty's Chief Inspector (HMCI)
Hodge, S. 15
Hopfenbeck, T.N. 120

images 152
inclusion 125–126; environment 127–129; psychology accessible *136*, 136–137, *137*; supporting SEND 129–135, *130*
independent learning 47
individual differences area 36–37
inferential statistics 51; critical value tables 52; non-parametric tests 53; parametric tests 53; probability testing 52; test of difference 53, *54*; values calculation 52
initial teacher education (ITE) 1, 2, 173
'Inside the Black Box' 111
Intentional Content 46
interactive learning 146–147
interleaved practice 20
intrinsic cognitive load 16, 28
ITE see initial teacher education (ITE)

Jarvis, M. 8, 9, 10
Jeffries, C. 84
just in-time teaching technique (JiTT) 50–51

Kahoot 103
Kelly, E. L. 97
Kim, L.E. 141
Knight, P. 105
Knowledge of Maslow's hierarchy 4
Kohlberg, L. 65
Kroonenberg, P.M. 35

Land, R. 14
Learning Culture 46
learning stick 64
LearnItFast 148, *149*
Lee, C. 111
lesson plan 168
Lockhart, R.S. 143
Lom, B. 23

Maeder, D.W. 84
Major, C.H. 83
master's level 1, 4, 30, 32, 46, 50, 66, 78, 85, 116, 118, 136, 137, 141, 142, 156, 160, 162, 164–166, 170, 171
Mayer, R.E. 65
McGovern, T.V. 93
MCQs see multiple choice questions (MCQs)
memorable learning 147–148, *149*
mental health 133
Mercer, N. 112
Meyer, J.H.F. 14
micro-learning 145, *146*
Microsoft Teams 141, 142
Milgram, S. 30, 31, 32, 58, 65, 67
Miller's Magic 7 28
Milne, C. 20
model examination answers 31–32
'more knowledgeable other' (MKO) 113
multiple choice questions (MCQs) 46, 102

naturalistic observation 45–47
neurodevelopmental disorders 134
non-experimental methods: correlational research 49–51, *50*; naturalistic observation 45–47; self-report studies 48–49
non-parametric tests 53
nudges 170

Office365 142
online lesson planning 153
online study tools 103
online teaching challenges 143

Paivio, A. 39
PALS 8
parametric tests 53
Paraskakis, I. 116
Parr, J. 112
PBL see problem-based learning (PBL)
PEEL technique 33
peer-assisted learning (PAL) 101
peer instruction 121
peer mentoring 101–102
personalised learning 149
Peterson, L.R. 98
Peterson, M.J. 98
'the picture superiority effect' 23, 24
planning fallacy 167
Platow, M. 167
Playdoh 38

INDEX

PMLD *see* Profound and Multiple Learning Difficulties (PMLD)
Pollard, A. 112
Pose-Pause-Pounce-Bounce 37
Postgraduate Certificate in Education (PGCE) programmes 164
Postgraduate Diploma in Education (PGDE) programmes 164-165
PowerPoint 46
practice testing 148
practitioner action research 165-166
'Principles of Instruction' 98
problem-based learning (PBL) 83-84, 88-90
Professional Educator 46
Profound and Multiple Learning Difficulties (PMLD) 131
psychological literacy: definition 93; employability develop skills 105-106; important 94-95; innovative assessment 102-105; peer mentoring and peer-assisted learning 100-102; science practitioners 96-100; work volunteering 107
'psychologically privileged' information 65
psychology: benefits of study 8; characteristics and requirements of 5-6; core curriculum 8-9; definition 14; GCSE assessment objectives 10; reasons for popularity 8; role, in schools 6-7; sources of support 10-11
'Psychology's Top 100' concepts 95, **95-96**
psychology teachers: characteristics and skills of 3-5; content knowledge 13; pedagogical content knowledge 13; pedagogical knowledge 13; 'required level of knowledge' 13
psychometric tests 36

Quizlet 103
quizzes 115

RAG (red/amber/green) assessment 42
recap and retrieval practice (R&RP) 23
reflection: importance 174; indicators of success 174-175; vitality 175-176
reflection time 115
Reicher, S. 167
research methods 41; classroom practicals 43-44; experiments 42-43; inferential statistics 51-54, **54**; non-experimental methods 45-51; sampling techniques 44-45; skills and knowledge audit 42; writing hypotheses 43, **44**
response cards 115
retrieval practice 20-22
rewards 176
Richards, A. 15
rigour hypothesis 8
Rivers, I. 15
Rosenshine, B. 30, 102
royalty-free 152
R&RP *see* recap and retrieval practice (R&RP)
Rutter, M. 34

salient learning 147, *147*
sampling techniques 44-45
Savin-Baden, M. 83
Schön, D.A. 89
school research studies 60-61
science practitioners 96-97; knowledge, understanding and application 97-100; teaching science content 97
select-organise-integrate (SOI) model 65, 66
self-determination theory 170
self-evaluation, of prior knowledge 4
self-regulated learners (SRL) 119-120, **120**; good-quality questions 122; peer- and self-assessment 121
self-report studies 48-49
Seligman, M. 174
SEMHD *see* social, emotional and mental health difficulties (SEMHD)
SEND *see* Special Educational Needs and Disabilities (SEND)
sexy subject hypothesis 8
Shiffrin, R.M. 97
short-term working memory 16
Sieber, J.E. 34
social area 30-33
social diversity 35
social, emotional and mental health difficulties (SEMHD) 133
socially sensitive research 34
spaced learning 148
spaced practice 18-19
spacing effect 64, 65
Special Educational Needs and Disabilities (SEND) 125; Assess, Plan, Do, Review Cycle 130, *130*; Code of Practice for England 129; communication and interaction difficulties 130-131

INDEX

specification to teach 10
Specific Learning Difficulties (SpLD) 131
speech, language and communication needs (SLCN) 130
Spero, R.A. 76
Sperry, R.W. 38
SpLD *see* Specific Learning Difficulties (SpLD)
SRL *see* self-regulated learners (SRL)
Stanley, B. 34
Stavnezer, A.J. 23
storyboards 23, 24
Stroop effect 27
'Study Buddies' 101
successive re-learning 148
summative assessment 110
Sweller, J. 17, 18, 145
synchronous technology 141–142

Tamblyn, R.M. 83
TBVs *see* text-based vignettes (TBVs)
teaching areas 26; biological area 38–39; cognitive area 27–30; developmental area 33–36; individual differences area 36–37; social area 30–33
technology: effective learning and teaching 143–149, *144, 146, 147, 149*; synchronous and asynchronous delivery 141–142; wider social context 142
test-potentiated learning 148
text-based vignettes (TBVs) 84–85; constructing 85–86, *87*; for PBL 88–90
therapy hypothesis 8
think-pair-share **43**, 115
threshold concepts 14–15, 32

time-management tool 168
time pressure 140
Times Educational Supplement (TES) 48
timing of practice 64–66
Timperley, H. 116
transfer, of learning context 66

validity 97
Van Der Post, A. 126
Van Gelder, T. 70
Van Ijzendoorn, M.H. 35
variability, of practice 67
video 46, 152–153
virtual learning environment (VLE) 145
vitality 175–176
Von Glaserfeld, E. 45
Vygotsky, L.S. 32, 100, 112, 113

Walkerdine, V. 112
Watkins, M.J. 97
webcams 46
whole-class feedback 103–105
Wiggins, S. 84
Wiliam, D. 36, 37, 103, 110, 111
Willingham, D. 71, 76
Wing, L. 131
working memory model 28, *29*, 132–133
writing frames 33

Yorke, M. 105
Youth Employment UK Employability Review 105

zone of proximal development (ZPD) 32, 100, *100*, 113
Zoom 141, 142

Taylor & Francis Group
an **informa** business

Taylor & Francis eBooks

www.taylorfrancis.com

A single destination for eBooks from Taylor & Francis with increased functionality and an improved user experience to meet the needs of our customers.

90,000+ eBooks of award-winning academic content in Humanities, Social Science, Science, Technology, Engineering, and Medical written by a global network of editors and authors.

TAYLOR & FRANCIS EBOOKS OFFERS:

- A streamlined experience for our library customers
- A single point of discovery for all of our eBook content
- Improved search and discovery of content at both book and chapter level

REQUEST A FREE TRIAL

support@taylorfrancis.com

Routledge
Taylor & Francis Group

CRC Press
Taylor & Francis Group

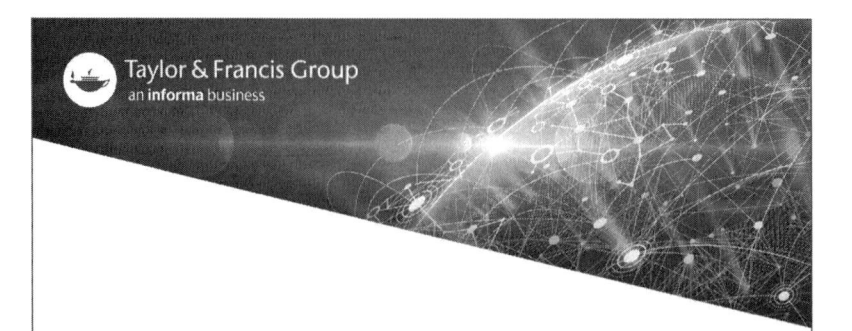

Printed in Great Britain
by Amazon